Language and Culture

LANGUAGES FOR INTERCULTURAL COMMUNICATION AND EDUCATION
Editors: Michael Byram, *University of Durham, UK*
Alison Phipps, *University of Glasgow, UK*

The overall aim of this series is to publish books which will ultimately inform learning and teaching, but whose primary focus is on the analysis of intercultural relationships, whether in textual form or in people's experience. There will also be books which deal directly with pedagogy, with the relationships between language learning and cultural learning, between processes inside the classroom and beyond. They will all have in common a concern with the relationship between language and culture, and the development of intercultural communicative competence.

Other Books in the Series
Developing Intercultural Competence in Practice
    Michael Byram, Adam Nichols and David Stevens (eds)
Intercultural Experience and Education
    Geof Alred, Michael Byram and Mike Fleming (eds)
Critical Citizens for an Intercultural World: Foreign Language Education as Cultural Politics
    Manuela Guilherme
How Different Are We? Spoken Discourse in Intercultural Communication
    Helen Fitzgerald
Audible Difference: ESL and Social Identity in Schools
    Jennifer Miller
Context and Culture in Language Teaching and Learning
    Michael Byram and Peter Grundy (eds)
An Intercultural Approach to English language Teaching
    John Corbett
Critical Pedagogy: Political Approaches to Language and Intercultural Communication
    Alison Phipps and Manuela Guilherme (eds)
Vernacular Palaver: Imaginations of the Local and Non-native Languages in West Africa
    Moradewun Adejunmobi
Foreign Language Teachers and Intercultural Competence: An International Investigation
    Lies Sercu with Ewa Bandura, Paloma Castro, Leah Davcheva, Chryssa Laskaridou, Ulla Lundgren, María del Carmen Méndez García and Phyllis Ryan

Other Books of Interest
Age, Accent and Experience in Second Language Acquisition
    Alene Moyer
The Good Language Learner
    N. Naiman, M. Fröhlich, H.H. Stern and A. Todesco
Language Learners as Ethnographers
    Celia Roberts, Michael Byram, Ana Barro, Shirley Jordan and Brian Street
Language Teachers, Politics and Cultures
    Michael Byram and Karen Risager

For more details of these or any other of our publications, please contact:
Multilingual Matters, Frankfurt Lodge, Clevedon Hall,
Victoria Road, Clevedon, BS21 7HH, England
http://www.multilingual-matters.com

**LANGUAGES FOR INTERCULTURAL
COMMUNICATION AND EDUCATION 11**
Series Editors: Michael Byram and Alison Phipps

Language and Culture
Global Flows and Local Complexity

Karen Risager

MULTILINGUAL MATTERS LTD
Clevedon • Buffalo • Toronto

Library of Congress Cataloging in Publication Data
Risager, Karen
Language and Culture: Global Flows and Local Complexity/Karen Risager.
Languages for Intercultural Communication and Education: 11
Includes bibliographical references.
1. Language and culture. I. Title. II. Series.
P35.R57 2006
306.44–dc22   2005021287

British Library Cataloguing in Publication Data
A catalogue entry for this book is available from the British Library.

ISBN 1-85359-859-3/EAN 978-1-85359-859-3 (hbk)
ISBN 1-85359-858-5/EAN 978-1-85359-858-6 (pbk)

Multilingual Matters Ltd
UK: Frankfurt Lodge, Clevedon Hall, Victoria Road, Clevedon BS21 7HH.
USA: UTP, 2250 Military Road, Tonawanda, NY 14150, USA.
Canada: UTP, 5201 Dufferin Street, North York, Ontario M3H 5T8, Canada.

Typeset by Saxon Graphics, Derby.
Printed and bound in Great Britain by the Cromwell Press Ltd.

Contents

Foreword   x

Michael Byram

Acknowledgements   xiii

1 Language and Culture in a Global Perspective   1

Introduction: Inseparability of Language and Culture?   1

Language and Culture: Generic and Differential   2

An Analytical Distinction between Language and Culture   5

Foreign- and Second-language Teaching: An Illustrative
    Vantage Point   6

The Concept of Foreign Language and Transnational Mobility   7

First Language and 'First-language Culture'   9

The Whorfian Hypothesis: First Language vs. Foreign/
    Second Language   11

Culture in Relation to Language vs. Language in Relation
    to Culture   12

Overview of This Book   16

**2 *Tour de France* in German Language Teaching:
   A Preliminary Analysis**   19

Introduction   19

Tour de France in German Language Teaching   19

Linguistic Practice   20

Cultural and Linguistic Context   21

Cultural and Linguistic Content   22

Tour de France: A Multidimensional Relationship
    between Language and Culture   23

Tour de France: An Element of the Spread of Language
    and Culture in the World   24

The Nationalisation of Language Studies   26

The Internationalisation of Language Studies:
    Denationalisation?   28

Conclusion   30

3   The Concept of Culture: An Introduction   **32**

Introduction   32
The Concept of Culture: Hierarchical, Differential
    and Generic   32
The Concept of Culture in European Cultural History:
    An Ancient Metaphor   34
Intersections between the Two Sets of Culture Concepts   37
The Concept of Language in European Cultural History   38
Concepts of Culture in Anthropology   39
Practice-oriented Concepts of Culture and Cultural Studies   48
Conclusion   51

4   Language, Nation and Culture: The German Tradition   **54**

Introduction   54
The Concept of Nation With or Without a Linguistic
    Criterion   54
The Concept of Nation With a Linguistic Criterion:
    Central and Eastern Europe   55
Johann Gottfried von Herder   56
Wilhelm von Humboldt   58
Herder, Humboldt and National Romanticism   60
Conclusion   61

5   Cultural Complexity   **64**

Introduction   64
Ulf Hannerz: The Two Loci of Culture and the
    Cultural Process   64
American and European Sources of Inspiration   66
The Global Ecumene   67
Four Frameworks of Cultural Flow   68
Hannerz vs. Friedman   69
Conclusion   72

6   A Sociolinguistic View of Language   **74**
Introduction   74
Linguistic Practice   74
Linguistic Resources   79
The Linguistic System as a Discursive Construction   81
The Loci of Language: 2 + 1   84
Conclusion   85

7   Linguistic Flows and Linguistic Complexity   88

Introduction   88
Linguistic Flows in Social Networks   88
'Linguistic Flows' or 'Language Spread'?   90
First Language / Early Second Language vs. Foreign Language /
    Late Second Language   92
Flows of First Language or Early Second Language   93
Flows of Foreign Language or Late Second Language   94
Textual Flows   96
Lexical Flows   96
Global Flows and Local Complexity: Danish and Denmark   97
Linguistic Complexity and Homogeneity in Language
    Teaching   100
Conclusion   107

8   Languacultural Dimensions   110

Introduction   110
Michael Agar: Languaculture   110
Paul Friedrich: Linguaculture   114
Languaculture: Three Cultural Dimensions of Language   114
The Loci of Languaculture: 2 + 1   119
Languaculture in Linguistic Practice   119
Languaculture in Linguistic Resources   124
Languaculture in 'The Linguistic System'   128
The Whorfian Hypothesis and the Concept of
    Languaculture   131
The Term 'Languaculture'   133
Conclusion   134

9   Discourse and Double Intertextuality   137

Introduction   137
A Concept of Discourse that is Content-oriented,
    Yet Still Linguistic   137
A Non-differential Concept of Language   139
Double Intertextuality   140
Translation of Discourse from Language to Language   142
Discursive Resources   144
Order of Discourse   145
Conclusion   146

10   Cultural Contexts   **149**

Introduction   149
The Linguistic Concept of Context   149
Cultural Context Seen As a Complex Historical
    Macro-context   152
First-language Context, Foreign-language Context and
    Second-language Context   154
Cultural Contexts in Language Teaching   155
Life Context   156
Does 'Language' Have a Cultural Context?   157
Conclusion   159

11   Cultural Contents   **161**

Introduction   161
Cultural References and Representations: Internal
    and External   161
Cultural References and Cultural Words   163
Internal Cultural References: Are Language and Culture
    Inseparable?   166
Cultural Representations   167
Internal Cultural Representations: Are Language
    and Culture Inseparable?   168
Cultural References and Representations in Language
    Teaching   169
Does 'Language' Have a Cultural Content?   170
Conclusion   171

12   Linguistic, Discursive and Cultural Flows   **173**

Introduction   173
Linguistic Flows   174
Discursive Flows   176
Cultural Flows   179
Tour de France: A Local Integration Process   180
Conclusion   183

13   The Language-Culture Nexus   **185**

Introduction   185
The Communicative Event   185
The Language-Culture Nexus: A Local Integration   186
The Language-Culture Nexus: Convergent or Divergent?   187

Objective and Subjective Dimensions of the
  Language-Culture Nexus   189
Language-Culture Nexuses at Higher Levels   189
The Core of the Language-Culture Nexus: Reference
  to Reality   191
Conclusion   192

14   Language and Culture: A Multidimensional Relationship   194
Language and Culture: Separability and Inseparability   194
Implications for Language and Culture Pedagogy   196
Further Perspectives   198

References   **201**

Foreword

I have known Karen Risager for many years. I contacted her after seeing some of her writings in the 1980s, when so little of substance was written about what at the time I called 'cultural studies in foreign-language education'. We have worked together on a comparative investigation of teachers' views of language and culture teaching in Denmark and England, and the analysis of these in the policy and political context in which teachers work. I have also had the pleasure of teaching with her at Roskilde University. It was therefore with great pleasure that I received some time ago a copy of her book *Det nationale dilemma i sprog – og kultur-pædagogikken. Et studie i forholdet mellem sprog og kultur* (The National Dilemma in Language and Culture Pedagogy. A Study of the Relationship between Language and Culture), published in Danish in 2003 by Akademisk Forlag, Copenhagen. This is a milestone in research on language and culture and in the analysis of language teaching as it has evolved since the late 19th century. It makes a major contribution to the history of language teaching as well as being a new perspective on the way in which the relationship between language and culture should be understood in the contemporary world.

The ways in which those who work in universities carry out research and scholarship are heavily influenced by their material conditions and the opportunities they have to combine research with teaching and administration. The notion of the researcher concentrating on nothing else but research is a thing of the past, if it ever existed, but from time to time someone like Karen Risager focuses all their energy on their research and makes a major contribution to a field. For this she was awarded the degree of DrPhil, a higher doctorate which is the recognition of a major contribution by the researcher to the development of a field of study. It is unfortunate that it may disappear from the Danish and other European university systems, because this will reduce the opportunities for this kind of scholarly work.

It was evident to me immediately that the contents of *Det nationale dilemma i sprog- og kulturpædagogikken. Et studie i forholdet mellem sprog og kultur* had to be made available to the wider world, and I am very happy that two books derived from the Danish original – not simply a translation but a reworking of the original for a new audience – are to be published in the LICE series. This first book addresses the question of the relationship between language and culture. It is therefore not only addressed to those concerned with language and culture pedagogy but finds its starting point in language teaching, since this is a locus of action where the relationship between language and culture can be seen in sharp focus. The author ensures that we understand the issues from the beginning by describing a teaching event in an ordinary German class in Denmark, and constantly refers us back to this event as the analysis of language and culture unfolds throughout the following chapters. She is concerned, however, with the theoretical issues involved in the relationship, which are significant for all research on language and culture, and it is in this wider context that the book has its significance.

Karen Risager's main purpose is to demonstrate that there is no necessary link between language and culture. This is done by careful analysis of different levels in language and by the stage-by-stage argument that we need to look at language from several perspectives and see the relationship between language, as revealed from each of these perspectives, and the cultural phenomena other than language that are part of our world of communication and interaction.

The argument is put very succinctly from the beginning that 'languages spread across cultures, and cultures spread across languages'. In order to demonstrate what she means by this, the author introduces the metaphor of 'flow' and argues that languages flow through our societies not least but not only as a consequence of the high mobility, real and virtual, in which we live. In doing so, languages are sociologically separate from other cultural phenomena, even though they may be psychologically related to a particular culture and cultural experience for individuals in their own selves. This analysis reveals some of the loose thinking that has been part of discussions of the relationship of language and culture in debates in pedagogy – including my own. Yet it is important to remember that the main focus of the book is to analyse the issues as they impinge on any discipline dealing with language. For example, the author criticises the tendency of linguistics to focus on the analysis of languages as first languages, when there is evidence of the widespread presence of languages as second and foreign languages, in contexts that are different from the first- (often national) language context. This is surely right and also extremely important if linguistics and other language-focused disciplines are to have a role in enabling a greater understanding of people and societies in the current century.

The book begins and ends, however, with language and culture pedagogy. In the final chapter, the author develops the implications of her analysis for teaching. These are radical and a challenge to the habitual assumptions of many language teachers in schools and universities. The focus, she says, is not the geographical language area where a language is spoken, either as first, second or foreign language, but the worldwide networks in which languages are to be found and through which they flow. We should be studying texts produced by all kinds of language users, for all kinds of purposes. Language teachers need to become aware of the impact of language flows on their professional purposes, on the object they study and teach, and on their learners. It is for this reason that this book is a fitting and significant addition to our series called Languages, Intercultural Communication and Education, and provides the foundation for the second book, which will concentrate on the shift in pedagogy from a national to a transnational paradigm.

Michael Byram
March 2005

Acknowledgements

This book has been developed from my Danish-language book entitled *Det nationale dilemma i sprog- og kulturpædagogikken: Et studie i forholdet mellem sprog og kultur* [The National Dilemma in Language and Culture Pedagogy: A Study of the Relationship between Language and Culture]. This was published by Akademisk Forlag, Copenhagen, in 2003.

The present volume, *Language and Culture: Global Flows and Local Complexity,* is based on Parts I and III of that volume, revised by myself, and translated into English by Dr John Irons, to whom I am most grateful.

The rest of the original text (Parts II and IV) is due to be translated by Dr Irons shortly, and will be published by Multilingual Matters Ltd as *Language and Culture Pedagogy: From a National to a Transnational Paradigm.*

I want to thank the Danish Research Council for the Humanities for supporting me throughout my work. They offered me research leave in the years 1998–2000, they supported the publication of the Danish book at Akademisk Forlag, and they financed the translation into English. I also want to thank the Department of Language and Culture, Roskilde University, for their backing and inspiration.

During the elaboration of the original text I received constructive criticism, encouragement and suggestions from many colleagues, friends and family members, not least Ulrich Ammon, Flemming Gorm Andersen, Michael Byram, Inger M. Clausen, Anette Danbæk, Uwe Geist, Annette S. Gregersen, Frans Gregersen, Hartmut Haberland, Jesper Hermann, Anne Holmen, Christian Horst, Karen Sonne Jakobsen, Bent Johansen, Susanne Kjærbeck, Ebbe Klitgaard, Claire Kramsch, Karen Lund, Arne Thing Mortensen, Michael Svendsen Pedersen, Kirsten Holst Petersen, Robert Phillipson, Bent Preisler, Kasper Risager, Elsebeth Rise, Klaus Schulte, Lotte M. Vandel and Johannes Wagner. I am most grateful to them all.

Karen Risager

Chapter 1

Language and Culture in a Global Perspective

Introduction: Inseparability of Language and Culture?

Since the 1990s, large sections of linguistics – including anthropological linguistics, sociolinguistics and research into intercultural (language) communication, translation, language acquisition and language teaching – have to an increasing extent highlighted the relationship between language and culture. This has led to intensified research into how cultural differences express themselves and are created via various forms of linguistic practice and discourse, how culturally different conceptual systems and world views are contained in the semantic and pragmatic systems of the various languages, and how language development and socialisation contribute to the development of cultural identities and cultural models of the world.[1]

This integrative view of language is one I share. The investigation of the interface between language and culture is necessary both for the theoretical understanding of language and linguistic practice as parts of larger wholes and for the development of the various areas of practice where language plays a central role. The increased focus on the relationship of language not only to the societal, structural context but also to the cultural meaning-conveying context is, in many ways, a promising sign.

There is, however, an aspect of this development that is problematic. There is often a too unambiguous focusing on the close relationship between language and culture, one that has a tendency to imply a simple identification of language and culture. The enthusiasm for working on uncovering the culturality of language quite often finds expression in such mottoes as: 'language and culture are inseparable'; 'language and culture are intimately linked'; 'language is culture and culture is language'. Such assertions are, for example, extremely frequent within the subject area that forms my point of departure here, i.e. language and culture pedagogy (represented by such people as Byram, 1989; Byram, Morgan and colleagues, 1994; Roberts *et al.*, 2001). In recent years there have been researchers who more or less explicitly have turned against the simplified identification of language and culture and emphasised the complexity of the relationship between them, e.g. Byram (1997), Freadman (2001) and Kramsch (2002a, 2004). However, there still lacks a comprehensive analysis of the structure of this complexity, a lack that this book seeks to redress.

It was the widespread assertion of the inseparability between language and culture in culture pedagogy that originally provoked me to write this book. I wished to demonstrate that language and culture *can* in certain respects be separated. This does not mean that it is my intention to deny that in many respects there are clear links between language and culture. Nor is it my intention to oppose the practical efforts being made to integrate the linguistic and cultural sides of language teaching more successfully with each other throughout the entire educational programme. But I feel it is necessary for the further development of linguistics, including language and culture pedagogy, to examine and criticise the assertion concerning the inseparability of language and culture.

What I mean more concretely by the thesis that language and culture can be separated in certain respects will gradually emerge from the discussion as the book proceeds. This theoretical discussion consists mainly of a number of conceptual analyses. A discussion of the relationship between language and culture is synonymous with a particular construction of the concepts of language and culture and with the use of certain particular analytical angles of approach to the relation between these two constructions. Central concepts in the theoretical construction are 'languaculture', 'discourse' and 'language-culture nexus'. Even at this early stage, I can say that the analysis will involve a deconstruction of the concepts of language and culture.

My guiding principle in the following is, to put it briefly, the idea that languages spread across cultures, and cultures spread across languages. Linguistic and cultural practices change and spread through social networks along partially different routes, principally on the basis of transnational patterns of migration and markets. I am, then, adopting a view of language and culture that stresses transnational dynamics in a global perspective.

Language and Culture: Generic and Differential

In this book, the linguistic concept of language is the central focus, not the metaphorical uses of the language concept that one meets in other cultural and societal studies, not least those with a semiotic or formal orientation, and in everyday language (cf. concepts such as the language of bees, of film, of dance, of architecture, of advertising, of logic, of psychoanalysis, of power, of love, etc.). The Cultural Studies movement typically operates with an extended concept of language, as, for example, described by Stuart Hall:

> How does language construct meanings? How does it sustain the dialogue between participants which enables them to build up a culture of shared understanding and so interpret the world in roughly the same ways? Language is able to do this because it operates as a *representational system*. In language, we use signs and symbols – whether they are sounds, written words, electronically produced images, musical notes, even objects – to stand for or represent to other people our concepts, ideas and feelings. (Hall, 1997: 1, italics in the original)

The metaphorical uses of the concept of language, which have been characteristic manifestations of modern and modernist developments since the turn of the 20th century, have been and are highly productive – and a stance has per se to be taken regarding them if one is interested in the relationship between language and culture from the point of view of Cultural Studies. In this book, however, I am adopting a perspective that derives from linguistics, not Cultural Studies, which is why I intend to restrict myself to dealing with human verbal language. When talking about language in the following, it is to this sense of the word that I am referring.

As mentioned, I am basing my theory on an integrative conception of language, which means my basic premise is that language is to be conceived as an integral part of culture and society and of the psyche, and that the study of language should have this understanding as its point of departure. I am of the opinion, for example, that linguistic practice is always cultural, in the sense that it is in itself a form of cultural (meaningful) practice, and because it is imbedded in a larger cultural (meaningful) context on which it leaves its own mark. It is, however, very important when examining the relationship between language and culture to distinguish between language and culture in the generic sense, on the one hand, and language and culture in the differential sense, on the other.[2]

In the generic sense, we are dealing with language and culture as phenomena shared by all humanity (often referred to as *langage* (Fr.) and 'culture-in-general' respectively). The generic sense comes in two forms: a psychological/cognitive one and a social one – one can view language and culture as psychological/cognitive phenomena which, to some extent or other, have certain species-specific (neuro-)physiological prerequisites, or one can view language and culture as social phenomena that have developed as part of the social life of the human species. At the generic level, it makes no sense to say that language and culture can be separated. Human culture always includes language, and human language cannot be conceived without culture. Linguistic practice is always embedded in some cultural context or another.

In the differential sense, we are dealing with various languages and various cultural phenomena. We are dealing with specific forms of linguistic practice, such as 'whole' languages, language varieties, registers and loan words, as well as with specific forms of cultural practice: various meanings and meaningful forms (in relation to such sign systems as images, fashion, food, music, dance), various norms and values, symbols, ideas and ideologies. The question of language and culture spread belongs to the differential level, as does the question of language teaching (teaching of specific languages and specific cultural phenomena). Theoretical concepts such as foreign language/second language, child language/children's culture and written language/literate culture belong to the differential level. It is the differential level that takes centre stage in this book.

At the differential level, one has to distinguish between a general and a specific level; the theoretical concepts of foreign language, child language and written language belong to the general level. It is only when we, for example, look at German as a foreign language, Norwegian child language and French written language that we move onto the specific ('descriptive') level. General theoretical issues of language spread as a phenomenon belong to the general level, while issues such as the spread of the English language belong to the specific level. It is the general level that is central in this book, although I illustrate the analyses with examples from teaching in specific languages. The recurring example has been taken from German teaching.

It should, of course, be emphasised that the differences between the languages are relative. In every language (every form of linguistic practice) there are items that are specific to precisely this language, other items that it shares with certain other languages, and some that must assumed to be universal and which the language in question shares with all other known languages. All languages are thus, to varying degrees, bearers of both the linguistically particular and the linguistically universal. Something similar applies to the cultural forms and relations: some are specific, some are more or less widespread, and some must be assumed to be universal and familiar to all known societies.

There is a logical difference between talking about 'language' in the generic sense and about 'all known languages' in the universal (and differential) sense. There is a difference between claiming that a particular linguistic phenomenon is a necessary ingredient in the very concept of 'language', and in making it seem plausible that a linguistic phenomenon exists in some form or other in the languages we have examined empirically to date. This is a central issue in the discussion between universal grammar and empirical language typology. A quite similar question naturally arises regarding other cultural phenomena than language. But that discussion will not be raised here.

I believe that the confusion concerning the relationship between language and culture is basically that one fails to distinguish clearly between the generic and the differential level. Very few people have seen this distinction clearly. Among those I have encountered is Lévi-Strauss, who in connection with a conference for anthropologists and linguists in Indiana in 1952 wrote:

> ... it has seemed to me on many occasions that we have unconsciously, in the course of the same discussion, slipped from one level to another ... Initially, the interest has been with the relationship between *one* language and *one* well-defined culture ... ... We have also discussed at another level where the question asked is no longer that of the relationship between *one* language and *one* culture but rather between language and culture in general. (Lévi-Strauss, 1958: 77, italics in the original)[3]

An Analytical Distinction between Language and Culture

To be able to implement a discussion of the main theme of this book it is necessary to establish an analytical distinction between 'language' and 'culture'. Later on, I will place the concepts 'languaculture' and 'discourse' in the interface between 'language' and 'culture' – see Chapters 8 and 9.

Distinguishing between language and culture is for me synonymous with distinguishing between (on the one hand) linguistically formed culture and (on the other hand) non-linguistically formed culture. The former calls for the presence of verbal-language text, spoken and/or written – I am here referring to the broad linguistic concept of text that is used in critical discourse analysis and systemic functional linguistics. It would, however, be far too long-winded to insist on using the expressions 'linguistically formed culture' and 'non-linguistically formed culture' throughout the book. For that reason, I will from now on use the terms 'language' and 'culture' with the following meaning:

- 'language' = linguistically formed culture;
- 'culture' = non-linguistically formed culture.

This analytic distinction affects in principle both the generic and the differential level, but it is the differential level that is of more central importance here. At the generic level, 'language' in general and 'culture' in general are, as mentioned, inseparable and interwoven in some way or other. But at the differential (and specific) level, one can, for example, ask: what specific forms of culture are associated with the Danish language? And what specific forms of culture are associated with the English language? And these are questions that can only be decided empirically. This issue – placed within a deconstructionist framework – I will return to in Chapter 6.

Foreign- and Second-language Teaching: An Illustrative Vantage Point

The aim of this book is to contribute to the scientific understanding of the relationship between language and culture. The analytical approach draws on a particular field of practice: foreign- and second-language teaching. This vantage point is, I believe, especially productive when seeking to understand the relationship between language and culture, for the following reasons:

Firstly, foreign- and second-language teaching is a highly complex linguistic and cultural reality in the sense that there is always more than one language involved, and that it is always a question of a number of cultural perspectives that relate to differences in national, ethnic and social history, etc. In this multilingual and multicultural reality it is not difficult to find examples of language and culture not always being inseparable – depending on how one defines language and culture, which is something that I will return to later. In Chapter 2 I introduce this complexity with the aid of a teaching vignette that will be the recurring example in the analyses presented in the book.

Secondly, for decades culture pedagogy has dealt with cultural subjects in connection with language and language development. Culture pedagogy is a meeting place for both language people and people who study culture and literature (Brøgger, 1992; Byram, 1997; Kramer, 1997; Kramsch, 1993; Zarate, 1993[4]). So culture pedagogy is in a privileged position when trying to create a better understanding of the relationship between language and culture, one where not only the concept of language but also that of culture is taken up for consideration. This is an important point: one cannot arrive at a satisfactory understanding of the relationship between language and culture without working in an inter-disciplinary way with both the concept of language and that of culture. For this reason, I have added certain chapters that introduce various relevant aspects of the concept of culture (Chapters 3–5), and which I will refer to in the subsequent chapters.

The Concept of Foreign Language and Transnational Mobility

It is important to distinguish between the societal role of a language and its role in the language learning of the individual. The concept of a foreign language in particular is sometimes used in the one sense and at other times in the other – and this can give rise to misunderstandings.

When one speaks of a language in its societal role, one is thinking of it as belonging to a special category of languages. This, for example, can be the category of national language, official language, majority language, minority language or heritage language. In this sense, a foreign language traditionally refers to 'a language that is spoken abroad'. I do not myself make use of the foreign-language concept in this sense. Furthermore, I also feel it is unfortunate because it is territorially based and implies a foreignness and exclusion that are unjustified from a transnational point of view.[5]

When one speaks of a language in its role in the language learning of the individual, one is thinking of whether it functions as a first language, second language or foreign language. It is this individual-orientated sense that I wish to make use of in the following. The relevant differences here are at what point in life one has learned/acquired[6] the language, and for what purpose.

A first language[7] is typically learned in the family in early childhood as part of one's fundamental social, emotional and intellectual development. A second language may have been learned early on in life or later, not primarily as part of close family socialisation but 'outside' it: in the playground, at school, during education, at work, etc. The second language is existentially important for the person in question, who needs it in order to be able to live life as a participating citizen in society, with all that that entails. A foreign language is a language one has not learned as a small child but later on, as a young person or adult, and where the aim may be more specific, e.g. to be able to read specialised literature or fiction in the original language or to be able to use the language during brief stays in one of the target-language countries.[8]

This means that any language at all can figure as a first language, second language or foreign language according to the societal circumstances. A minority/heritage language such as Maori will, for example, be a first language for the person learning it as a small child in the family; it will be a second language for the person learning the language outside the family, possibly later in life, to such an extent that (s)he can function in many contexts within the Maori-speaking linguistic community; and it will be a foreign language for the person who learns the language only in order to become familiar with, for example, its history or grammatical structure. With regard to the discussion of the relationship between language and culture – for instance, concerning the individual – it is the time when learning takes place that is the crucial factor. The most relevant categories are thus, on the one hand, the first language and the second language learned early on, and, on the other hand, the foreign language and the second language learned later on. (See also Chapter 7.)

In connection with globalisation and intensified transnational mobility there are many cases in which it is possible to note a glide from language functioning as a foreign language towards it functioning as a second language (cf. Holmen & Risager, 2003).

When, for example, a Danish woman marries a Turkish man from the Turkish-speaking minority in Denmark and learns Turkish, does she learn the language as a foreign language or a second language? I would say that Turkish functions as a second language for her to the extent that she speaks the language daily in the Turkish-speaking community. Another example: a Dane is an upper-secondary-level teacher of Russian – and one can probably say that the language is a foreign language to him. But one can also claim that the language in certain respects is a second language to him, for he is unable to function in his professional environment – the Danish and the transnational Russian-teacher environment – unless he speaks the language pretty well and has a wide linguistic repertoire. Here I would describe his Russian as a blend of foreign language and second-language competence.

A third example: as it becomes increasingly normal to stay abroad for considerable lengths of time, e.g. in connection with studies or work, what originated as foreign-language competence in connection with foreign-language teaching turns into something that is reminiscent of second-language competence. Take, for example, a course of French teaching in Denmark which includes one or more school students studying alongside French students in a French school. In the French context, French almost functions as a hybrid between a foreign language and a second language for these Danish students (but teaching is typically in the form of first-language teaching). A fourth example: when foreign university students come to Denmark in order to study for a few months and learn Danish, here too there is a hybrid between Danish as a foreign language and Danish as a second language. A fifth example: when one studies Arabic in Denmark with the dual purpose of mediating contact between Denmark and the Arabic-speaking countries and of mediating contact between the Danish-speaking majority and the Arabic-speaking community in Denmark, Arabic does not only function as a foreign language in the traditional sense.

So one can say that the concept of a foreign language is potentially dissolving in connection with intensified transnational mobility. In principle, this applies to all languages, but it is perhaps most pronounced for those languages that dominate international communication – at present, English first and foremost. As English becomes increasingly widespread as the language of international communication, one can envisage it completely ceasing to function as a foreign language and becoming a second language for larger and larger parts of the world – a language that everyone needs in their everyday lives as world citizens at both local and global levels. (It is, however, possible that English will, around 2050, have to share this role with a number of other languages: Mandarin, Hindi/Urdu, Spanish and Arabic, cf. Graddol, 1997 and Maurais, 2003.)

First Language and 'First-language Culture'

Within language and culture pedagogy, not least since the 1980s, an assumption has often been expressed that there is a close connection between language and culture. This is used as an argument for saying that language teaching must inevitably be accompanied by teaching about cultural phenomena in the countries where the target language is spoken ('the target-language countries'). Byram, for example, talks of 'language-and-culture' (Byram, Morgan and colleagues 1994)[9] and Galisson (1994) talks of *langue-culture*. One could say that culture pedagogy is characterised by the idea of culture-bound language, a concept that is, for example, found in the following quotation, taken from an article by the German culture pedagogue P. Doyé:

> The very nature of language forbids the separation of language from culture. If language is considered as a system of signs, and signs are characterized by the fact that they are units of form and meaning, it is impossible to learn a language by simply acquiring the forms without their content. And as the content of a language is always culture-bound, any reasonable foreign-language teaching cannot but include the study of a culture from which the language stems. (Doyé, 1996: 105)

The idea of culture-bound language can be linked to the first-language bias within linguistics in a broad sense (also called native-speaker bias or monolingual bias). Large sections of linguistics are strongly influenced by this bias, which means that one studies language without fully realising that one is only studying it in its capacity as first language.[10] This means that one does not generally think of the fact that the idea of a close relationship (or inseparability) between language and culture in practice deals only with language in its capacity as first language. The National-Romantic idea of an inner connection between the national language and the national culture has in practice to do with those who from their childhood have grown up with the first language and 'the first-language culture' (*die muttersprachliche Kultur*, as it is called in German).

This is a very important point in relation to language and culture pedagogy and its conception of the relationship between language and culture. For the above-mentioned culture-pedagogical expressions 'language-and-culture', *langue-culture*, etc. relate implicitly to this understanding. Language and culture pedagogy is in the paradoxical situation that it builds on the above-mentioned first-language bias while dealing precisely with language as foreign- and second-language. This has to do with the fact that one traditionally imagines that the ideal for foreign- and second-language teaching is to attain as near first-language competence as possible. For the person who, for example, is learning Japanese, the alleged relationship between the Japanese language and Japanese culture does not exist as a reality but as a norm – and as a norm that is difficult to attain. The idea of a close relationship (or inseparability) between language and culture in a descriptive sense does not give any immediate meaning when the language functions as a foreign language or a late second language (see Chapter 7).

It has been the first-language speaker who constituted the only acceptable model for language learning – despite the fact that the teacher, who is perhaps the only real model, normally speaks the language as a foreign language (in foreign-language teaching). This, though, is now coming under scrutiny (cf. Davies, 2004; Kramsch, 1998b), so I envisage the possibility of a broader view of language opening up within language and culture pedagogy, one that also includes the target language used as a second language and a foreign language. When, for example, Danish students are on exchange visits to British universities, they meet English spoken as first language, second language and foreign language – and such conditions make topical the question as to what models English teaching should be aiming at, both in the receptive sense: what types of English the learners come into contact with; and in the productive sense: what types of English they themselves learn to speak and write.

The Whorfian Hypothesis: First Language vs. Foreign/Second Language

When talking about the relationship between language and culture, the first association for linguists and anthropologists will probably be the Whorfian hypothesis (or the Sapir/Whorf hypothesis) concerning the relationship between language (culture) and cognition. This book, however, is not directly to do with the Whorfian hypothesis, for two reasons: firstly, because the Whorfian hypothesis adopts a cognitive approach, while I adopt one based on cultural and social theory; and secondly, because the Whorfian discussion is traditionally dominated by the first-language bias.

In the linguistic and anthropological context the Whorfian hypothesis figures as a mainly cognitively orientated issue which focuses on the relationship between language and thought, especially as far as the classic structuralist formulation of the issue is concerned which has prevailed since the American anthropologist B.L. Whorf's work on North American languages in the 1930s. In this research tradition, the culture category has lain on the horizon as a, for the most part, unanalysed entity, as exemplified in, for example, J. Fishman's article from 1960: *A Systematization of the Whorfian Hypothesis*, in which he refers to culture only on one single occasion: 'Psychologists have not been noticeably concerned with the unique "Englishness" of English and how it affects cognition – in the individual and in the culture – differently than the "Navahoness" of Navaho' (Fishman, 1960: 323).

As the shift has taken place from a structuralist to a more functional and pragmatic interest in linguistics since the 1970s, the discussion about linguistic relativity has also changed character and has to an increasing extent included considerations about the relationship between language use/discourse and cultural context (Cooper & Spolski, 1991; Fishman *et al.*, 1985; Gumperz & Levinson, 1996; Hymes, 1974; Kramsch, 2004; Niemeier & Dirven, 2000; Ochs, 1988; Scherzer, 1987). Today, most of non-autonomous linguistics has a relativist or Whorfian tinge.

The discussion about linguistic relativity has all the time been characterised by the first language bias: It has had – and still has – to do with how native-language users are influenced cognitively by the language they speak, and how their language use interacts with the immediate context and the broader cultural context, which implicitly means the cultural context in which the language has mainly developed historically speaking, or the first-language context (e.g. Berman & Slobin, 1994). In one of the major examinations of linguistic relativity, Gumperz and Levinson (1996), Gumperz takes the first step towards problematising this basis:

The simple association of one tribe, one culture, one language, which was implicit in the older Humboldtian and Sapir/Whorf traditions, . . breaks down. We can have speakers of the same language fractionated by interpretive subsystems associated with distinct social networks in complex societies, and conversely, we can have social networks that transcend cultural and grammatical systems to create shared interpretive systems beneath linguistic diversity. (Gumperz & Levinson, 1996: 361)

But Gumperz does not take the next step: he does not comment on the absolutely fundamental point of departure for research into linguistic relativity – he deals only with first language and first-language culture, and presupposes a close relationship between these two.

It has not been until very recently that research has emerged that touches on the issue of linguistic relativity in relation to the bilingual/multilingual subject (Kramsch, forthcoming; Pavlenko, 1999). That research will be able to shed light on the question: what is the relationship between language and culture, not only when the language in question is a first language but also when it is a foreign or second language?

Culture in Relation to Language vs. Language in Relation to Culture

In this book I am dealing mainly with culture seen in relation to language and not the converse. This means that I consider language and look at the relations culture may have to language. In fact, it is much more common for the converse relation to be described, i.e. for culture to be considered and to look at the relations language may have to culture. The latter has been characteristic of the Whorfian tradition, and individual sociolinguists/anthropological linguists, such as Fishman and Kramsch, have discussed more systematically the relation of language to culture. At this juncture, I would like to mention briefly Fishman's and Kramsch's approaches.

Fishman: Language in relation to culture

J.A. Fishman is probably the sociolinguist who has dealt most and for the longest time with the relationship between language and culture, especially in connection with the struggle for linguistic diversity as part of ethnic and ethnocultural diversity (Fishman, 1960, 1982, 1991, 1996; Fishman *et al.*, 1985). On several occasions (1985, 1991 and 1996) he has distinguished three 'links' between language and culture:

- language as a part of culture;
- language as an index of culture;
- language as symbolic of culture.

Concerning the first point, Fishman (e.g. 1996: 452, which is an article in an encyclopedia of social science) describes language as 'an inevitable part', 'a major and crucial part' of culture, and 'all those who seek fully to enter into and understand a given culture must, accordingly, master its language'. Fishman also says that 'language shift, or loss of a culture's intimately associated language, is indicative of extensive culture change'. All these quotations argue that it is important for social researchers not to neglect language when dealing with 'a given culture'. In Fishman (1991) (which is more detailed and probably written after Fishman (1996), which is a 'second edition'), he draws attention to the fact that this relationship is reciprocal: language is a part of its 'associated' culture, but culture is also a part of its 'associated' language.

The second point: 'language as an index of culture', Fishman describes as follows: 'The role of language as an index of culture is a byproduct (at a more abstract level) of its role as part of culture. Languages reveal the ways of thinking or of organizing experience that are common in the associated cultures' – a little further down, he talks about 'culture-bound languages'. Here, Fishman is indirectly referring to the discussion of the Whorfian hypothesis, which has greatly preoccupied him (e.g. Fishman, 1960, 1982).

The third point: 'language as symbolic of culture', Fishman explains as follows: 'Language movements and language conflicts utilize languages as symbols to mobilize populations to defend (or attack) and to foster (or reject) the cultures associated with them.' In Fishman (1991), he emphasises that the relationship is reciprocal, that language and culture symbolise each other (in the consciousness of both 'insiders' and 'outsiders').

As can be seen, Fishman is talking here about culture-bound language and about the fact that language and culture are 'intimately associated' with each other. Naturally, one cannot know with any certainty to what extent and in what way Fishman is of the opinion that language is culture-bound – it ought, for example, to be stressed that Fishman does not support the strong but the weak version of the Whorfian hypothesis.[11]

Kramsch: Language in relation to culture

Claire Kramsch, as one of the most important more recent researchers within the field of language, culture and learning, says in her book *Language and Culture* (1998a: 3) that:

- language expresses cultural reality;
- language embodies cultural reality;
- language symbolises cultural reality.

Kramsch's presentation moves the view of the relationship between language and culture in a post-structuralist direction, even though she herself does not use this term in her 1998 book.[12] She is a discourse theorist who talks about 'meaning as action'. Her book is broadly based on recent socially- and culturally-orientated linguistic thinking, especially Gumperz, Le Page, Tabouret-Keller, etc. The first point: 'language expresses cultural reality' Kramsch explains in the following way:

> The words people utter refer to common experience. They express facts, ideas or events that are communicable because they refer to a stock of knowledge about the world that other people share. Words also reflect their author's attitudes and beliefs, their point of view, that are also those of others. In both cases, language expresses cultural reality. (Kramsch, 1998a: 3)

This description, which focuses on vocabulary, is fairly close to Fishman's no. 2: 'language is an index of culture', even though Fishman is probably thinking more of the grammatical categories of language, as did Whorf. But Kramsch does not use the holistic and essentialist concept of culture that Fishman does – she uses a more general expression, 'cultural reality', which she admittedly does not discuss explicitly, but which stands for something common: 'common experience, shared knowledge', etc. The second point: 'language embodies cultural reality' she explains as follows:

> But members of a community or social group … also create experience through language. They give meaning to it through the medium they choose to communicate with one another, for example, speaking in the telephone or face to face, writing a letter or sending an e-mail message, reading the newspaper or interpreting a graph or a chart. The way in which people use the spoken, written, or visual medium itself creates meanings that are understandable to the group they belong to, for example, through a speaker's tone of voice, accent, conversational style, gestures and facial expressions. Through all its verbal and non-verbal aspects, language embodies cultural reality. (Kramsch, 1998a: 3)

Here we have the idea that the way in which linguistic practice is implemented helps create and shape meaning. The third point: 'language symbolises cultural reality' is described as follows:

... language is a system of *signs* that is seen as having itself a cultural value. Speakers identify themselves and others through their use of language. (Kramsch, 1998a: 3, italics in the original).

This is approximately the same as Fishman's no. 3: 'language symbolises culture', but, while Fishman is particularly interested in the macrosociolinguistic and political aspects, Kramsch is thinking more of the linguistic interaction at the micro-level, in roughly the same way as Le Page and Tabouret-Keller (see Chapter 6).

Kramsch: Language and culture in an ecological perspective

In a lecture given in 2002 (Kramsch, 2002a), Kramsch discusses the concept of culture within applied linguistics from a post-structuralist and ecological perspective, underlining the complexity of language acquisition and socialisation, during which the individual and the social, the linguistic and the cultural become intertwined in discourse in many ways, along many different time lines and intersecting various levels of cause and effect. This holistic approach is also seen in her introduction to an anthology on language acquisition and socialisation that she has edited (Kramsch, 2002b).

I share Kramsch's post-structuralist and dynamic view of language and culture in an ecological and historical perspective. But while Kramsch wishes first and foremost to demonstrate the varied interconnectedness of language and culture in discursive practice, I wish to subject the *borders* of this interconnectedness to a critical examination via a theoretical analysis that throws light on *both* deconnections and reconnections. The theoretical landscape between the sciences of language and culture is complex and apparently infinitely intricate. So there is very much a need for an analytical tool that can create a certain degree of clarity – and the following is my suggestion for such an analytical tool.

Culture in relation to language

Both Fishman (1996) and Kramsch (1998a) focus on the relationship of language to culture. But I think it is theoretically more interesting to make the opposite link and focus on the relationship of culture to language. In such a way one is able, so to speak, to extend language theory in various directions, to link the concept of culture to various aspects of the concept of language. At the same time, it is important to adopt a theoretical stance towards the concept of culture itself, so that one does not fall into the trap of treating 'culture' as an unreflected-on border concept.[13]

In the coming chapters, I intend to analyse culture as a macro-context for linguistic practice (e.g. Japanese in Tokyo vs. Japanese in Melbourne), and as a thematic content for linguistic practice, particularly concentrating on cultural representations (a text in Japanese about Tokyo vs. a text in Japanese about Melbourne), and as meaning dimensions in linguistic practice itself (Japanese languacultures in all their diversity).

Overview of This Book

Chapter 2 contains a provisional analysis of the multidimensional relationship between language and culture, using the teaching vignette *Tour de France* as its point of departure.

Chapter 3 is an introduction to the concept of culture, especially in the cultural-anthropological tradition.

Chapter 4 is an introduction to the tradition concerning the relationship between language, nation and culture from the time of Herder and Humboldt.

Chapter 5 is an introduction to Ulf Hannerz's theory of cultural complexity and cultural flows in the global ecumene.

Chapter 6 starts the analysis of the relationship between language and culture by beginning with a sociolinguistic view of language. Here I argue in favour of distinguishing between three 'loci' of language: linguistic practice, linguistic resources and the discursively constructed idea of a linguistic system.

Chapter 7 focuses on language spread, or rather language flows, in the world, both when the language functions as a first language/early second language and when it functions as a foreign language/late second language. I emphasise the importance of adopting a dynamic view of languages from a global perspective.

Chapter 8 marks the first stage of the analysis of the relationship between language and culture. Here I introduce the concept of languaculture. I distinguish between languaculture in linguistic practice, languaculture in linguistic resources, and languaculture in the linguistic system. In addition, I distinguish between languaculture in the first language/early second language and languaculture in the foreign language/late second language.

Chapter 9 marks the second stage of the analysis of the relationship between language and culture. Here I introduce a discourse concept taken from critical discourse analysis and argue that linguistic and discursive flows do not necessarily move along the same paths in the world. This has an effect on, among other things, the understanding of the concept of intertextuality.

Chapter 10 is one half of the third stage of the analysis. Here I discuss the relationship between on the one hand linguistic/discursive practice and on the other 'the cultural context'. The cultural context is viewed both at the micro-level and – especially – at the macro-level, and I distinguish between first-language, foreign-language and second-language contexts.

Chapter 11 is the second half of the third stage of the analysis. Here I discuss the relationship between on the one hand linguistic/discursive practice and on the other 'the cultural content'. The cultural content is viewed as thematic content, and I analyse thematic content on two levels: cultural references and cultural representations. Among the cultural references, I distinguish between internal and external cultural references, and I also discuss the concept of 'cultural word'. Among the cultural representations, I distinguish between internal and external cultural representations.

Chapter 12 is a chapter that concretises the thesis I have mentioned earlier: that languages spread across cultures, and cultures spread across languages. The chapter gives a picture of linguistic, discursive and other cultural flows in the world and of how language teaching forms these in its own special way.

Chapter 13 contains a description of the concept of 'language-culture nexus'. I distinguish here between convergent and divergent language-culture nexi, and discuss certain questions that have to do with empirical exploration of experienced vs. imagined communities.

Chapter 14 is the conclusion of the analyses. It provides an overview of how one can understand the relationship between language and culture as a multidimensional one, and formulates some implications for language and culture pedagogy and for linguistics in general.

Notes

1. Among the many publications to be found within the field of 'language and culture' during the last couple of decades, one could mention: Gumperz (1982), Friedrich (1986), Snell-Hornby (1988), Byram (1989), Kramsch (1993), Scollon & Scollon (1995), Palmer (1996), Gumperz and Levinson (1996), Gee (1996), van Dijk (1997), Duranti (1997), Wierzbicka (1997), Foley (1997), Kramsch (1998a) and Hinkel (1999), Niemeier & Dirven (2000) and Risager (2003).
2. The concepts of 'generic' and 'differential' are used by Bauman, 1999 (1973) (cf. Chapter 3).
3. '... il m'est apparu qu'à maintes reprises, nous avons inconsciemment, au cours de la même discussion, glissé d'un niveau à un autre ... En premier lieu, on s'est occupé du rapport entre *une* langue et *une* culture déterminée ... ... Nous avons aussi discuté à un autre niveau, où la question posée n'est plus celle du rapport entre *une* langue et *une* culture, mais plutôt du rapport entre *langage* et *culture* en général.' (Translation by JI.)

4. In Risager (2003) I have undertaken a relatively comprehensive historical analysis of international culture pedagogy since the 1960s, concentrating in particular on its discourse on language, culture and nation.

5. Attempts have also been made to replace the term foreign language by 'modern languages', 'other languages', 'community languages', or (within the European Union) 'partner languages' – all with differing politico-ideological implications.

6. In the following I distinguish between language / culture learning in a formal school context, and language / culture acquisition in an informal context. This is not, then, based on a Krashen-type distinction between learning and acquisition (Krashen & Terrell, 1983), but is more a pragmatic distinction between various contexts.

7. There are several facets of the concepts 'first language' and 'mother tongue' that I do not intend to deal with here. Apart from being the language one has learned first, there can also be other criteria for saying that a language is a first language or mother tongue: which language one identifies oneself with, which language one is most proficient at, and which language one uses most (see Skutnabb-Kangas, 2000).

8. Some people also operate with a special third language problematics, e.g. English as a 'third language' for people who have Turkish as their first language and Danish as their second language in Denmark (cf. Cenoz & Jessner, 2000). I do not intend to discuss that issue here.

9. Also in the plural: 'language-and-cultures'.

10. This tendency can also be found within anthropology, cf. this definition of culture: 'Culture may be seen as the world view of the natives …' (Friedrich, 1989: 299).

11. There is also a French structural anthropologist (Houis, 1968) who has written about the relationship between language and culture – a 38-page-long article in which a distinction is made between three relations: language as a part of culture, language as a product of culture, and language as a prerequisite (condition) of culture. His presentation is, however, usually unclear in the sense that he at times writes *langage* (the generic level), and at other times *langue* (the differential level).

12. Kramsch does not refer to Fishman's conception of the relationship between language and culture.

13. The Estonian sociolinguist E. Oksaar outlined in Oksaar (1988) a 'cultureme theory' which operates on the transition between language and culture. A 'cultureme' is an abstract entity in culture, e.g. 'to greet', 'to remain silent', 'to say thank you', 'to pay a compliment', i.e. culturemes have similarities with language acts but are thought of at a more general level, as they can be expressed wholly or partially via other means than verbal language in the narrow sense. The theory is, however, only described quite summarily, and is not linked to any culture-theoretical discussion.

Chapter 2

Tour de France *in German Language Teaching: A Preliminary Analysis*

Introduction

My point of departure for the following is a vignette inspired by a realised teaching sequence (Svensson, 1998) – one which I have extended and adapted for my own purposes. The idea is that the vignette can serve as an example that recurs throughout the book. The analysis in this chapter is thus only provisional, and has been placed here so that the reader can gain as early as possible an impression of some of the main ingredients in the coming analysis of the relationship between language and culture. It is important to emphasise that the analysis of languaculture does not come until later (Chapter 8).

Tour de France in German Language Teaching

The imagined sequence can be described as follows:

> In German lessons in Class 10 (the optional class for 16–17 year-olds) in the Danish Folkeskole, the topic *Tour de France* has been chosen, based on a number of articles taken from German magazines. There are both male and female students, most of them are Danish, and there is also a boy with an Iranian background and a girl with a Dutch background in the class. The teacher is a Danish woman. The teaching takes place in autumn 1996, after the summer in which the Danish rider Bjarne Riis won the race (he rode for the German *Telekom* team). The magazines have an overall German perspective, but there are also interviews with some of the riders, both German and other nationalities. The class works with text extracts and discusses them, mainly in German, and also sometimes in Danish. Some of the students prepare and perform certain role-play activities in German taken from the riders' (imagined) lives. Others write individual fictive extracts from 'a rider's diary'. A group is given the task of trying to make a German version of the Danish song 'Ten small cyclists'. The class also talks (in Danish) about differences in the use of the German and Danish past

and present perfect tenses and how the forms are used in the students' texts of 'a rider's diary'.

The main point of this account is that language teaching, here German language teaching, can in practice move considerably around the traditional view of the core of the subject – here, German language and culture. On the basis of differing qualifications and experiences, students use (mainly) German, to work with European and regional French subject areas from a German and Danish angle, and this takes place in an educational context in Denmark, a neighbouring country to Germany. That reflects a relatively high degree of complexity regarding both linguistic and cultural dimensions.

Linguistic Practice

If we take linguistic practice as our point of departure in the teaching sequence, considering the sequence as being exclusively 'German teaching' and solely concentrating on the students' and teacher's use of 'German' would mean considerably reducing its complexity. One must adopt a sociolinguistic perspective that makes the linguistic diversity apparent. In fact we are dealing with a multilingual situation, characterised by a code-switching based on the participants' different linguistic experiences and competencies in German and other languages as well as the demands regarding comprehension that the various subtopics make, e.g. the grammatical explanations that are given in Danish. Various types of Danish are used since the students have different social, regional and linguistic backgrounds and are of both sexes. Various types of German are used: firstly, there is the German written language in the magazines; secondly, the pupils' individual interlanguages (the Danes' interlanguages also differ from those of the Iranian and Dutch pupils); thirdly, there is the teacher's individual use of the German language. Moreover, a certain amount of French occurs, since there are French words and expressions represented in the illustrations in the German magazines and also topic-related loan words in Danish and German, e.g. étape, champion, classement, soigneur. There may even be some Farsi and Dutch – in the pupils' inner speech at least. In addition, there will presumably be some English in the form of loan words in the languages involved (e.g. sport, sprint, team, fan, power) as well as in the form of interferences, since English is the first[1] foreign language of most of the pupils. Finally, in connection with the verbal communication one can observe various gestures and other body movements that reflect the different socialisation contexts of those taking part.

But all those involved know very well that what really means something is that the students are developing their oral and written proficiencies in a relatively well-defined German linguistic norm. The idea of a
target-language norm forms and governs the linguistic practice and the
concrete choice of language. The target language German naturally has
pride of place and, unlike the other languages, linguistic practice in
German is characterised by two different ways of using the language: as a
communication language (language of instruction), when the focus is not
mainly on the language but on the content or the task, and as a practice
language, when the main focus is on developing (inter)language via exer-
cises of various types (reading aloud, translation, tasks, etc.)

In Chapter 8, I will give a more detailed theoretical account by means of
an analysis of the various dimensions of the concept of languaculture (the
semantic-pragmatic dimension, the poetic dimension and the identity
dimension).

Cultural and Linguistic Context

The relationship between language and culture can, among other things,
be seen as one between linguistic practice and the cultural and linguistic
context in which it occurs. The *Tour de France* sequence takes place in a
learning context in the Danish state education system, where the subject
German has a particular official status and is surrounded by a wide range
of different attitudes to German and German teaching, to Germany and
Germans. Attitudes have to do with the fact that Germany is a large neighbouring country to the small country of Denmark, which has been at war
with Germany on several occasions, and with a certain dependency relationship to Germany both economically and politically.

The texts used mainly come from magazines published in Germany, a
'first-language context'.[2] In addition, we are dealing with a reference
context linked to the theme *Tour de France* in France, in Europe, in the
world ('the world's greatest cycle race').

The context contains other languages that are otherwise used in the
language community. When German is taught in Denmark, this takes
place in a language-sociological landscape that is characterised by local
linguistic hierarchies between languages, typically with English at the top
and German probably ranking sometimes above, sometimes beneath
French and Spanish, but anyway ranking above the so-called immigrant
languages: Arabic, Turkish, Urdu, Somali, etc. In certain cases, this can
influence what takes place in German teaching, e.g. with regard to the
linguistic attitudes that are communicated concerning when and why

switches are made between German and Danish, and regarding how references are possibly made to English (English near-equivalents, English loans into German, etc.).[3]

Cultural and Linguistic Content

The relationship between language and culture can also be conceived as that between linguistic practice and the thematic content it bears and forms. In this context, it is most interesting to look at cultural representations of various parts of the world.

The *Tour de France* theme contains many different cultural representations and perspectives that complement each other, or are at odds with each other. One can talk about its being held as a major sports event in France (part of the race also took place in the Netherlands, Belgium and Italy) and as an international media event including coverage in the German public forum. The special German connection was partly the German *Telekom* team in general, partly Jan Ullrich, who that year was Riis' second-in-command.

The theme is open to many different approaches. These include approaches that concentrate on the economic aspects – the various company teams, the main sponsors (Coca Cola, Fiat etc.), the TV rights, the caravan – and ones that concentrate on the more sport-related aspects over and above the *Tour* itself: other events such as the *Tour de France* for women and the *Tour de France* for tourist cyclists. The theme can also give rise to a race-related (?) question: why is it almost exclusively white people who are involved in top-level cycling? And the theme can also give rise to an issue related to world history: why is top-level cycling traditionally dominated by Europeans?

The teaching takes place in Denmark, a country where the cycle is an important means of transportation, where cycle races also command a great interest and where cycling is a part of the national sense of identity. There is obviously a Danish angle to the theme apart from the nationality of the person Bjarne Riis. But all the cultural experiences of the participants are more or less different. This applies to the theme – and it applies to the countries involved.

In relation to the theme, the background knowledge and attitudes of the participants towards the *Tour de France* are involved to a certain extent. Many of the participants have followed the coverage of the *Tour de France* on television and read about it in the newspapers. They have gained some media-communicated images of what the *Tour de France* is all about at the symbolic level – as well as images of various types of countryside, etc.

Their differing experiences of Danish cycling culture are included, experiences that are linked to the various lifestyles of their families and their lives as girls and boys respectively. The experiences of the Dutch girl and the Iranian boy are also included. The Danish slant is further strengthened by work on the song 'Ten small cyclists'.

In relation to France, Germany and Denmark there are a number of national stereotypes that are widespread in Denmark, although in reality there are many nuances, and the experiences of the students and the teacher of the three countries may be very different. In addition, there are of course the personal experiences of the Dutch girl and knowledge of Dutch stereotypes – and a corresponding situation with the Iranian student.

The content of the teaching sequence is highly complex and points outwards to various external forms of subject-relatedness. The theme of the *Tour de France* gives rise to both everyday-cultural and symbolic approaches as well as to more specifically sport-related ones. The German sequence could therefore, in theory, be implemented in some form of cooperation or other with physical education. The *Tour de France* was launched by the teacher as a German teaching topic (a 'sports topic'), but it can of course also be understood as a topic to do with France.[4] The potential of the theme for French lessons could have become evident from a possible cross-curricular cooperation between German and French.[5] Finally, the grammatical aspect must be mentioned: the conversations in Danish about the use of the German tense system, an element of the teaching that in certain respects can be enhanced via cross-curricular cooperation with other language subjects, including Danish as a first language.

Tour de France: A Multidimensional Relationship between Language and Culture

A provisional conclusion can be as follows: firstly, there is a multidimensional relationship between language and culture in this teaching sequence (in what sense is there any truth in the statement: 'German language and German culture are inseparable'?). Secondly, the sequence is characterised by national categories: Denmark, Germany, France, yet at the same time by a considerable individual variation in linguistic and cultural experiences. Thirdly, there are European and global dimensions in the sequence, both as regards the composition of the participants (they are of various nationalities) and as regards the theme itself.

The *Tour de France* in the German teaching example is untraditional but not unrealistic. It is of course easy to come up with examples of teaching sequences that focus to a greater extent on the target language as well as on cultural and social phenomena in the target countries. A sequence in English teaching in a Danish upper secondary school, for example, where both the teacher and the students have Danish as their first language, where English is spoken exclusively, where the work has to do with comprehending and discussing a short story about English conditions written by an Englishman who speaks English as his first language. Or, even more focused, a sequence in Danish as a second language that takes place in Denmark; the teacher has Danish as his/her first language, the students come from various linguistic backgrounds but speak Danish exclusively, and the work is on a newspaper article from a Danish newspaper, written by a journalist with Danish as his/her first language on a topic that can be said to be specifically Danish, e.g. the large pigmeat production in Denmark. But in foreign- and second-language teaching a multidimensional linguistic and cultural contact will, under all circumstances, be involved, one in which sex, social class, life experiences and mastery of language will be able to play a role. To date, however, we lack completely ethnographically oriented classroom research that takes both interaction in the class and the thematic content being dealt with into account.[6]

It must be emphasised that the reason for including this vignette is to demonstrate the nature of the complexity I am interested in. When planning an actual empirical investigation, one naturally has to select which aspects of this whole one wishes to focus on. But it is important that the selection takes place on the basis of an analytical understanding of the multidimensional whole.

Tour de France: An Element of the Spread of Language and Culture in the World

This more descriptive but naturally theory-laden presentation of the imagined teaching sequence in German will now be followed by a brief further theoretical interpretation that will serve as a guideline for the discussion in the rest of the book – an interpretation that places the German teaching sequence in a globalisation-theoretical framework:

Language teaching in the classroom and in schools must not be treated as an isolated field of practice. It must be considered in an overall global perspective, as part of language spread and culture spread. Language teaching is a particular institutionally-shaped learning space where cultural, discursive and linguistic flows merge, are transformed under the given pedagogical, social and material conditions and are sent on in the – in the final resort – global flow of meaning.

Each of those participating in the learning process (including the teacher) has a unique life history when it comes to linguistic and cultural resources. They have all learned their first language and other languages in particular social and cultural contexts, and their linguistic and cultural resources are an important part of their identity. Each of them contributes with an individual perspective and horizon of understanding to the shared work on language, culture and society as a more or less conscious aspect of work on developing language skills. The media-communicated accounts of the *Tour de France* that they may happen to know constitute a horizon of understanding for what takes place in the teaching – and thus teaching is linked to the other kinds of cultural flows in society.

The language teacher is an important agent in the orchestration of this interaction between various life histories and horizons of understanding: (s)he, along with the students, influences what types of linguistic, discursive and cultural flow gain access to the learning space, and how they are dealt with there. The teacher oversees pedagogically determined linguistic and cultural norms: the German language norm, norms of behaviour in certain social environments in German-speaking countries, etc., and may handle this role in various ways. (S)he also has more or less direct influence on how linguistic, discursive and cultural flows are spread outside the learning space, via dissemination in the family and the local area, via the use of media, via use in work contexts, on trips, etc.

Language teaching, then, plays a part in the cultural and linguistic globalisation process. Seen from this overall perspective, language teaching socialises the learners involved to assume a number of roles or 'figures' that are typical in the globalisation perspective, such as 'the tourist', 'the vagabond', and 'the cosmopolitan' (Bauman, 1998; Hannerz, 1992a). Foreign-language and second-language teaching contribute in their separate ways to this socialisation: foreign-language teaching lets students 'out' into the world outside the country's borders, while second-language teaching lets students 'in' to a life as a citizen in the country.

This is intended to be a dynamic, holistic image of language teaching as a social and cultural practice, an image that one does not otherwise see in language and culture pedagogy. The metaphor of flow goes against the usually static image of 'the context' and emphasises the lines of connection between language teaching and the outside world. It is an image that shows that language teaching is a kind of language policy and cultural policy, and that the teacher is an important agent in this context (cf. Byram & Risager, 1999). Whereas in the above I took as my point of departure an ethnographically inspired description of the teaching sequence in question, here I place the sequence in a global context inspired by the sociology of knowledge, the main reference being to Hannerz (1992a): *Cultural Complexity. Studies in the Social Organization of Meaning*. The main ideas of this book will be introduced in Chapter 5.

The Nationalisation of Language Studies

The *Tour de France* example problematises the traditional national paradigm of language subjects – one that can appear in a political and ethnic variant: the political variant, which is the more common, identifies language with one or more national states, e.g. German in Germany and Danish in Denmark. The ethnic variant would rather identify language with a community in which linguistic identity is linked to ethnic identity, e.g. Korean in Australia.

Modern language subjects acquired their (politically) national form in connection with the nation-building period in Europe and the rest of the world from the 18th century – a project that was one of the most important elements of the general modernisation process. The nationalisation of language subjects was intensified in the period from the latter half of the 19th century well into the 20th century in connection with the capitalist and colonialist rivalry between the European great powers. Since the second half of the 19th century, language subjects have mainly conveyed a unified picture of the various national states, of 'the language', 'the country', 'the people', 'the literature'. They have had – and still have to a certain extent – an identity as national philologies whose task is to study and mediate the history of the national language, literature and other texts as a central factor in the development and self-understanding of the nation. Much has changed within this area in the 1990s, and the subject of English, especially as a foreign language outside the English-speaking countries, is probably the language that has moved farthest from the traditional national identity.

The national shaping of language subjects becomes clearly evident when one examines how their mediating role was conceived in the preceding period. Before the national idea (and to a varying extent nationalism) affected the language subjects, they were more universal and encyclopedic in their orientation. The philosopher and educationalist J.A. Comenius (1592–1670), for example, provided his primer *Janua lingvarum reserata* (1649) with an encyclopedic content divided into 100 chapters, about the elements, the earth, the body, the economy, grammar, music, geography, history and angels. It was extremely popular, was translated into several languages, and also appeared in multilingual editions with reading passages divided into, for example, a Latin, Greek and French column. Another example of this exceptionally broad thematic approach is the Danish reader by Peter Hjort: *Den Danske Børneven. En Læsebog for Borger- og Almue-Skoler [The Danish Children's Friend. A Reader for Primary and Board Schools]* (sixth edition, 1852). It contains many reading passages of a slightly more practical nature, although still broad and encyclopedic, about the globe and its surface, trees, Africa, Peter the Great, law and order and the human soul.[7]

But from the latter half of the 19th century onwards, language subjects became nationalised[8] and included in the general educating of the population to a view of the world that was nationally structured – and this is something I do not intend to examine in detail here. In brief, a geographical division of labour developed between language subjects, a narrowing and a focusing: the subject English turned towards England, the English and the English language; the subject French towards France, the French and the French language, etc. Later arrivals, such as Spanish, Chinese, Japanese, etc., came to focus on the target language countries and their national cultures.

The process of nationalisation is part of the more comprehensive and long-lasting process of globalisation, as emphasised by the cultural sociologist R. Robertson· The process of globalisation is a process that involves both globalisation and localisation, and Robertson sometimes uses the word 'glocalisation' to underline this dual aspect.[9] The world is becoming to an ever greater extent a structural unity, at the technological, the economic, the political and the cultural as well as the linguistic level, and this applies both to more objective societal developments and to subjective developments, since it is possible to observe an ever greater awareness of belonging to one humanity, of living in one global society, in one common location, etc.

During the selfsame process, the world is also separating out to a greater extent into localities, each with its own specially cultivated distinctive nature (its 'culture'). The localities can be 'spaces' of many different kinds and are not necessarily defined by territory. A locality may be a residential precinct, a town, a region, a nation or a continent, but it may also be an ethnic minority, a diaspora, a transnational company, a transnational social movement, or a transnational professional network. An important point is that the local carries within it the global, e.g. a transnational company will display a number of features that are signs or results of globalisation – and that a residential precinct, for example, may also do.[10]

The emergence and development of nation states in the period since the 18th century is an example of a localisation process that is part of the long-lasting process of globalisation which had its beginnings in 15th-century Europe. Globalisation and nationalisation are two sides of the same coin. The European process of integration, together with opposition towards it, is also part of the process of globalisation and localisation. The nationalisation of language subjects should thus be seen as part of the linguistic and cultural process of globalisation and localisation.

In the above, I have used 'nationalisation' as a verbal noun without an agent. But there are agents (single individuals, groups and institutions) that create this development – directly or indirectly, intentionally or unintentionally – and in the earlier *Tour de France* example I paid attention to the teacher as agent. The teacher helps shape the development in the classroom and the school, including the development in a national direction or other directions. The nationalisation of the school takes place, among other things, via language and culture policy 'from below'.

The Internationalisation of Language Studies: Denationalisation?

Seeing that language subjects have experienced nationalisation since the latter half of the 19th century, does internationalisation then mean *de*nationalisation? In my opinion, it mostly does not.

When, within organisation theory, one speaks of the internationalisation of companies and institutions, one is often referring to the development of a greater, enhanced contact with other countries – with all that may imply in the way of international activities: travel activity, use of e-mail and telephone conferences, etc. So here we are mainly dealing with breaking with a one-sided domestic orientation, and this does not of itself question the actual conception of the world being composed of national states.

That is not the problem in foreign-language teaching, where one mainly operates per definition with other countries: one or more target-language countries. Therefore there are those who believe that foreign languages are international in themselves, that under all circumstances they contain a built-in international dimension. Here too, though, this does not necessarily mean going beyond the national paradigm.

Much present-day foreign-language teaching is characterised by a bilateral scheme, i.e. one deals with the target-language country in question and the learners' own country in a more or less explicitly comparative approach, or one that focuses on mutual relations. The scheme does not, however, have to be bilateral – it can also be multilateral and yet be characterised by the national paradigm: if an e-mail network is established in English teaching in Denmark between the Danish class and schools in

Russia and China, and all use English as their language of communication, this will mean a diversification of international relations. There are contacts with other countries than those that lie immediately within the horizon of the language subject, and this resembles in a certain sense the type of internationalisation that was mentioned to begin with: the break with a domestic orientation.

Study trips and exchanges abroad are, however, an important driving force in a development that can involve denationalisation, i.e. a weakening and relativisation of the national paradigm. When one travels, one always ends up in a particular locality, and this locality can be seen as being representative of the target country (the national paradigm) or as being one that has a particular identity in itself (going beyond the national paradigm, i.e. denationalisation). If this experience also causes learners to perceive the distinctive in the locality where their own school lies in their home country, a transnational link is thereby created between two localities in the respective countries. Here, internationalisation is synonymous with a subnational localisation, i.e. one focuses on specific localities that lie 'below' the national level.

Here is an example taken from Byram and Risager (1999), which deals with language teachers' discourse concerning internationalisation. It is a French teacher in the Danish Folkeskole who is expressing an opinion (in 1993):

> The district we visit, the school we have contact with, is situated in a suburban area outside Strasbourg where there are many blocks of flats. I mean, we have contact with a school that has many foreign workers or many people of foreign origins as they say, and it's a very good thing for us to experience. And I must say that our school doesn't have as many. And that means we experience something that widens our horizon, I think. Also some negative things, they widen the horizon in another direction as well ... And there are some social differences, because we can see that pupils live with different types of families. And some live with Moslems, where you eat in a special way. We have been there during the period called Ramadan, where we experience that they are not allowed to eat during the daytime and in spite of that they offer the Danish guest lots of things. And we have experienced that sometimes they move out of the bedroom, and they don't have room enough, you see, their living conditions are different. And that's one of the things we talk about. Maybe that's something you might just experience by exchanging with a class in Taastrup (a town in Denmark). But now it is France by chance, so that's why it comes up like this" (639, f, 40, Fr[11]). (Byram & Risager, 1999: 131)

We are far here from the traditional national framework of reference: 'French language and French culture'. The example makes clear the necessity of adopting a pedagogical attitude to not only cultural but also linguistic variation in the target-language countries, i.e. in the precinct on the outskirts of Strasbourg talked about here.

The teacher's comment about perhaps being able to experience the same thing in Taastrup west of Copenhagen overlooks an important pedagogical point: the students are well aware that there are various groups of immigrants and refugees in their own country – maybe they even know some of them personally. But their picture of France will normally be much more vague and stereotypical, on the basis of representations of France and the French in the media, adverts and commercials, etc. To strengthen the image of France in French teaching is not least to give the students the opportunity of experiencing life in a particular locality in France as something that is just as differentiated as life in the localities in Denmark they happen to know personally.

For language teaching, internationalisation is particularly interesting to the extent that it contributes to subnational localisations and to an awareness of transnational connections: an awareness that various environments have been connected, awareness of the specificity of the environments involved – their particular history and identity, their particular form of linguistic and cultural complexity, their particular form of 'organisation of diversity' (Hannerz, 1992a). *Tour de France* is a teaching sequence that has potential for going beyond the national perspective in such a way. It should be noted that this does not mean that it cannot also be legitimate and important to deal with national structures and national identities in language teaching and in language studies in general.

Conclusion

This chapter has attempted to concretise the idea of the multidimensional relationship between language and culture in a fictive teaching sequence. Many other examples could have been used. One of the aims of the chapter has been to emphasise that, when one is dealing with language and language teaching, one must be interested not only in language and language teaching and its variation in relation to the context but also in the thematic content that is being developed (produced and received) by virtue of linguistic practice. Another way of putting it is that there is a need not only for a pragmatic/sociolinguistic perspective, but also for a culture-analytical/hermeneutic perspective that concerns itself with meanings, discourses, cultural representations and identities. At the same time, it is also important to view language teaching not as an activity in an isolated classroom but as one that places the participants in contact with comprehensive flows of languages, discourses and other cultural phenomena in the world.

Notes

1. This is an ambiguous term: It can mean 'first learned', or 'most used'.
2. At the same time, Germany is a second language context. E.g. the magazines are naturally also read by people in Germany who speak German as a second language.
3. Cf. Berns (1990) regarding language teaching in various (macro)contexts.
4. In the French sense of identity the concept of the *Tour de France* has considerable national-symbolic importance. A schoolbook with the name *Le Tour de la France par Deux Enfants* (published in 1891 and written by G. Bruno – a pseudonym) was a best-seller from the 1870s well into the 20th century in first-language teaching in France. It deals with two orphan brothers who are seven and fourteen. They undertake a journey alone on foot (and by water) around France and also get to know a great deal about the geography and history of France. Their home region is Lorraine, the north-eastern part of which was taken over by Germany after the war of 1871. Their experiences are narrated in a highly patriotic spirit.
5. In one of his 'Mythologies', R. Barthes has interpreted the *Tour de France* as an Odyssean epic with heroes and labours, i.e. emphasised the more universal nature of the race (Barthes, 1970 (1957)).
6. All one can point to in this connection are investigations of teaching of bilingual students (e.g. Willett (1995), van Lier (1996), Platt & Troudi (1997), Norton (2000), but they cut across subjects and do not deal with the relation of language to the subject-related content of the teaching.
7. One can sense a common narrative structure in the two books, from the down-to-earth to the heavenly.
8. As the non-classical subjects became upgraded and partially nationalised: national geography, national history, etc.
9. E.g. Robertson, 1992: 173. The word is probably a loan translation from Japanese marketing terminology
10. This idea of the global in the local makes the sociological study of globalisation empirically possible, as Ulrich Beck points out (2000: 49).
11. Means: respondent/interviewperson no. 639, (f for feminine) woman in her forties, teaches French.

The Concept of Culture: An Introduction

Introduction

When analysing the relationship between language and culture, it is necessary to deal with both the concept of language and that of culture. The three following chapters therefore focus on certain dimensions of the concept of culture which provide a basis for understanding the later analyses. Chapter 3 gives a brief outline of the development of the concept of culture in European cultural history and North American cultural anthropology. Cultural anthropology is the branch of anthropology that has taken the keenest interest in the actual concept of culture and its relationship to the concept of language, and, as known, it is American cultural anthropology that forms the framework of the Whorfian tradition. It is also cultural anthropology that is the most important source of inspiration for Ulf Hannerz's theory of cultural complexity, which I will deal with in Chapter 5.

The Concept of Culture: Hierarchical, Differential and Generic

In the following I intend to begin by giving a short presentation of the three dimensions of the concept of culture described by the Polish-British sociologist Zygmunt Bauman in his book *Culture as Praxis* from 1973 (reprinted with a new introduction in 1999):

- The hierarchical concept of culture.
- The differential concept of culture.
- The generic concept of culture.

The hierarchical concept of culture is the well-known one in which a culture is something that the individual human being or individual society either 'has' or 'does not have', or 'has' at a higher or lower level. This concept cannot exist in the plural and it is always value-laden. The criteria for what 'culture' is – and thus the 'ideally human' – are something for which a struggle takes place in a society. To attain culture is actually to attain an ideal nature:

There is an ideal nature of the human being, and the culture means the conscious, strenuous and prolonged effort to attain this ideal, to bring the actual life-process into line with the highest potential of the human vocation. (Bauman, 1999: 7)

The differential concept of culture has to do with culture as something that marks off groups of people from each other. This concept can be used in the plural. Typically, a culture is a cohesive unit that various anthropologists have described with the aid of such terms as ethos, genius, pattern, configuration, style and the like. A culture has the nature of a system that is self-contained and resists mixing; it mainly alters as the result of encounters with other cultures ('cultural clashes'). Cultures viewed in such a way can be compared, and the comparisons can result in cultural universals being collected and categorised. Cultures can be seen both 'from the outside' and 'from the inside'[1]; the former involves observing behaviour on the basis of a general or universal conceptual apparatus, while the latter involves listening to and trying to understand what categories are relevant for the indigenous people themselves – consciously or unconsciously. Bauman notes that it is easier to distinguish an individual language from other languages than to distinguish one 'culture' from other 'cultures':

Contrary to the case of language, the differential concept of culture is not (or, in any case, not as much as the term 'languages') implied by the immediately given reality independently of researchers' activities. It is implied rather by the empirical strategy chosen by students of culture. (Baumann, 1999: 25)

The generic concept of culture has to do with what is common to humanity, that which distinguishes humanity from nature and all other living creatures. One could say that the more one emphasises the diversity of cultures and their mutual incompatibility, the more one needs, despite everything, to have a concept that applies to all humanity. The generic concept of culture can give rise to the view that there is only one culture, i.e. human culture everywhere and at all times. Bauman discusses what can be said to be characteristic of human generic culture and arrives at the following conclusion:

The continuous and unending structuring activity constitutes the core of human praxis, the human mode of being-in-the-world. To carry on this active existence man is supplied with two essential instruments – … tools and language. (Bauman, 1999: 43)

The concept of language, which Bauman broaches on several occasions but does not deal with systematically, can also be described using these three dimensions: the hierarchical concept of language refers to linguistic quality, to norms and ideologies about language and language use, including linguistic creativity and linguistic works of art. The differential and generic concepts of language correspond to the distinction made in linguistics between structurally different codes (*langues*) versus the human language as such (*langage*) – a distinction I have already touched on in Chapter 1.

In the following, I wish to give a brief overview of the semantic development of the concept of culture within the cultural history of Europe and, where relevant, use Bauman's three dimensions to further illustrate this development.

The Concept of Culture in European Cultural History: An Ancient Metaphor

The semantic development of the concept of culture[2] in European and recent North American cultural history has been described by R. Williams in his encyclopedia article on '*Culture*' in *Keywords* (1988 (1976)), by Fink (1988) and by Márkus (1993). The word 'culture' (first known as the classical Latin *cultura*, the semantic field of which in particular had to do with the cultivation of land and care of flora and fauna) spread after its history in classical and medieval Latin to most European national languages as an academic term that did not enter everyday language until the course of the 19th century – initially in Germany (Márkus, 1993). The word has been subject to a number of semantic transformations engendered by the general cultural and social history of Europe. En route, the concept has undergone differing semantic changes in the various linguistic communities (especially England/France on the one hand and the German-speaking area on the other). These developments have to do with the meaning of the concept of culture in relation to the neighbouring concepts of 'civilisation' (in an English, French and German version) and the German concept of *Bildung*.

This is not the place to engage in a detailed historical, semantic analysis of the concept of culture. On the other hand, it is important to know something of the culture-historical basis of the present-day concept of culture, which Fink (1988) refers to as hypercomplex. So in the following I will simply summarise the most important paths of development. To do so, I intend – like such people as Williams (1988) and Fink (1988) – to distinguish between three concepts of culture that have come into being at different times but all of which can be refound in present-day understandings of the concept:

- The individual concept of culture.
- The collective concept of culture.
- The aesthetic concept of culture.

Firstly, however, what could be called the technological concept of culture should be mentioned, which is the earliest meaning we know (classical Latin *cultura*, derived from the root *col-* = to cultivate).[3] It has to do with the process of cultivating / caring for the earth, flora and fauna. This meaning, which was the primary one until the 16th century, can still be found in such terms as the culture of bacteria or pearls, agriculture, etc. I do not intend to deal any further with this meaning as such, but it is important to have it at the back of one's mind during the entire following presentation. We are dealing with an old but still living metaphor, which means that it can be difficult to completely ignore a concept of culture that has to do with the earth, with roots, growth, etc.

The individual concept of culture

We know of the individual concept of culture from at least the time of Cicero, who uses the metaphorical expression *cultura animi*, i.e. cultivation of the soul / mind, and this has to do with the individual's mental cultivation,[4] either via self-development or later, from the time of Augustine c. 400 AD, via God's cultivation of the soul (as a ploughman: God's word opens man's heart and sows its seed within). For the first 16 centuries *cultura animi* (or, from the 16th century, *cultura* without a logical object) designates a process of mental cultivation, a pedagogical process. Not until the 17th century can the concept also signify the result of this process, i.e. the mental (intellectual, spiritual, aesthetic) level the person involved has attained. One begins to speak of 'the cultivated person'. The individual concept of culture is generally speaking characterised by a hierarchical understanding of culture (the hierarchical concept of culture), since one imagines a process of development from an uncultivated, or less cultivated, stage to a cultivated,or more cultivated, one.

With the emergence of the European national written languages, the word was loaned into these, first as *couture* in Old French, later the Latinised version of *culture* in Middle French, and this version passed on into the English *culture*, the German *Cultur*, later spelt *Kultur*, cf. *cultuur* in Dutch, *kul'tura* in Russian, *kultur* in Danish and Swedish, and *kulttuuri* in Finnish.[5]

The collective concept of culture

From the end of the 17th century, a collective[6] concept of culture developed alongside the individual one. The collective concept of culture has to be divided into a hierarchical and a non-hierarchical variant. The hierarchical variant is the earlier, and it deals with either the societal conditions for the individual process of cultivation, or with what 'cultivated people' have in common. The hierarchical element is that one perceives certain groups in society, or certain peoples, as being cultivated (the Europeans) and others as being uncultivated (i.e. 'savage'). This hierarchical concept of culture was challenged in the 1770s and 1780s by J.G. von Herder, who historicised and 'dehierarchised' the concept of culture by emphasising that all the peoples of the world participate in a gradual, historical process of cultivation, and that every people possesses culture. Herder believed, then, that on the one hand culture is something common to humanity which distinguishes humans from animals (the generic concept of culture), and on the other hand that each people has its particular share of this culture – the beginnings of the differential concept of culture (see also Chapter 4).

In general, one can say that by virtue of the interplay between the individual and the collective meaning the concept of culture is an epochal concept which to a particular extent characterises modern society. It thematises the possibility for individuals to be able to cultivate themselves and to become members of the cultivated classes no matter what their origins, without innate privileges. Márkus, for example, says about the turning point at the end of the 18th century and the early 19th century: 'The enormous success of the concept of "culture" from this time on is evidently interconnected with the social change that replaced the feudal distinction of estates with a new principle of social stratification legitimated in terms of individual achievement to be reached – in one way at least – through the channels of education and "self-improvement"'. (Márkus, 1993: 9).

The concept of culture has had its competitors in the concepts of 'civilisation' and *Bildung* since the 17th century. Even though 'culture' and 'civilisation' can be used as synonyms in English and French, they can also be contrasted, and then 'culture' is normally used for the individual (intellectual, moral) process of development, while 'civilisation' is used for the collective (political, possibly technological) process of development. In the German area, there have been three concepts since around 1780: *Kultur*, *Bildung* and *Zivilisation*.[7] They can be used as synonyms, but if a difference is made, then *Bildung* is mostly used for individual mental development and *Kultur* for collective but also mental, moral development – unlike *Zivilisation*, which is mainly used for something external, artificial, maybe even decadent (Fink, 1988: 17).[8] In the German context, this semantic field is strongly affected by the contemporaneous development of the German national movement, partly in its rejection of the French-influenced princely courts in the German states, which were typified by *Zivilisation*, and partly in its cultivation of unity in (the German) language, people and spirit (the genuine, distinctive, original *Kultur*), resulting from the constant question: 'Was ist eigentlich unsere Eigenart?' (What is in actual fact our distinguishing characteristic?) (Elias, 1969 (1939): 4).[9]

The aesthetic concept of culture

In the course of the 19th century, a number of special spheres crystallise in connection with modern development, including 'art' with its subsections: literature, the visual arts, music, etc. These become a reference for the aesthetic concept of culture which develops during the same period, alongside other concepts of culture, and which adopts a narrowing, individual and hierarchising direction that focuses in particular on artistic products as supreme achievements of symbolic-aesthetic creativeness. It is this concept of culture that appears to be the most widespread in everyday language today, partly in its more exclusive, highbrow meaning, and partly expanded in various popular-cultural directions as a result of the Cultural Studies movement since the 1960s: popular culture, youth culture, sport, rock music, tattooing, etc. It is also this use of the concept of culture that we find in everyday language when we talk about a particular cultural sector within the ministry of culture. Some people here talk about 'culture as a sector concept', and in this connection culture can be thought of, as is known, in a relatively 'narrow' or relatively 'broad' way (in the latter case possibly including sport: body culture).

Intersections between the Two Sets of Culture Concepts

The three concepts of culture – the individual, the collective and the aesthetic – are of a different nature from those Bauman operates with: the hierarchical, the differential and the generic. The last-named have more the nature of aspects. The two types of categorisation can be used partially independently of each other.

The individual, the collective and the aesthetic can all be thought of as being hierarchical or non-hierarchical, as has been explained above. They can also be thought of in a differential perspective, where special emphasis is placed on differences: individual and social differences; differences in aesthetic tradition. And all three can also be thought of at the generic level, where the emphasis is on what is common to people's mental and social constitution, or to human creative activity and imagination – so they stress a fundamental anthropological humanism.

The Concept of Language in European Cultural History

The description of the cultural history of the concept of culture in Fink and Williams does not explicitly include the concept of language, probably because it is conceived as being self-evident that language is a part of culture. Williams does not include 'language' in *Keywords. A Vocabulary of Culture and Society*. But he writes about the cultural history of the concept of language in Williams (1977), where he points to parallels in the development of the concepts of language and culture, especially since the 18th century. It is not generally difficult to demonstrate that language has individual, collective and aesthetic dimensions just as culture has.

But it is important to distinguish between the history of concepts and that of lexis and semantics. There possibly exists a common European concept of language the history of which can be explored, such as the important philosophical relationship between 'language' and 'reality'. But the concept of language has a much more varied lexical-semantic history than the concept of culture. The concept of language is borne by a considerable number of words of various origins, both 'native' words and loan words, in Europe, e.g. *glossa, lingua, langue, langage, language, Sprache, sprog, språk, speech, parole, mål, tale, taal, jazyk, kieli* etc., which complicates matters a good deal.

The word 'culture' is a common European loan word created in Roman antiquity, and in European history it has been used for a relatively abstract and academic concept. Unlike this, the various words for the concept of language, which are also much older, probably have more practically oriented meanings. Some of them have perhaps had an individual meaning (to do with the language of a particular person), while others have perhaps had a collective (hierarchical) meaning in the direction of the common language that characterises 'us' as opposed to 'the others' (cf. the ancient Greek idea of 'barbarians' = people who speak unintelligible languages). There is also a completely different metaphorics, which in many cases has the tongue as its starting point. But to pursue such considerations would far exceed the scope of this book.

Concepts of Culture in Anthropology

In the course of the 19th and 20th centuries an academic division of labour has developed, with the individual concept of culture being elaborated by, in particular, pedagogy and psychology, the collective concept of culture by, in particular, anthropology, ethnology, linguistics and history, and the aesthetic concept of culture by, in particular, the aesthetic disciplines, including comparative literary history.

Anthropology is particularly pertinent to the analysis of the relationship between language and culture in a foreign-/second-language perspective, for three reasons: firstly, its gaze is turned on 'the unfamiliar', on unfamiliar cultures and societies, as is language and culture pedagogy. At the same time, anthropology has a comparative epistemological interest and an interest in understanding the relationship between the ethnographer and the people with whom (s)he is in dialogue. This corresponds to the preoccupation of culture pedagogy in the comparison between the target-language countries and the students' own country, and its interest in giving the students the opportunity of establishing personal contacts with people in the target-language countries.

Secondly, anthropology has turned to an increasing extent since the 1980s from a primary empirical focus on small and socially less complex societies to including studies of modern complex ones, e.g. large multicultural cities, and anthropologists have drawn on Cultural Studies and postmodern thinking in order to expand the understanding of the oppositions and developmental dynamics of a modern multicultural society. This partial 'crossover' has made anthropology an increasingly relevant element of culture pedagogy since its main focus is on cultural and societal relations in modern societies.

Thirdly, anthropology is, as mentioned, a discipline that has been aware of the linguistic dimension of culture (in the differential sense), at any rate when it comes to cultural anthropology. Both American cultural anthropology and French structuralist (cultural) anthropology have drawn inspiration from various forms of linguistics, and American linguistic anthropology has in addition had the Whorfian discussion concerning the relationship between language/culture and thought.

In the following, I therefore intend to focus on the concept of culture in cultural anthropology. It is important to draw attention to the fact that what now follows is by no means a brief overview of 'the history of anthropology'. Many important sections are ignored or merely mentioned: all of British social anthropology, which only to a limited extent has dealt with issues that approach language (the most important exceptions are Malinowski (1923), Ardener and Leach[10]), materialist and ecological trends within cultural anthropology and the Marxist-inspired trends of the 1970s and early 1980s. It should also be pointed out that I do not intend here to deal with linguistic anthropology. This branch has precisely concentrated on language (in culture) and has not worked on culture and concepts of culture as such. The Whorfian discussion, which as mentioned does not have to do with culture but with the relationship between language/culture and thought, will be dealt with in Chapter 8.

Classic evolutionism

The classic[11] theory of evolution that developed from the 1860s onwards supported the view that all societies in the world are moving towards the same evolutionary goal, but at different speeds. Primitive societies around the world are kinds of 'living fossil' that have not advanced as far as European societies. They are variously described as less civilised/cultivated or as uncivilised/uncultivated. Evolutionism, then, represented a clearly hierarchical conception of culture, one in which culture and civilisation were almost synonymous, e.g. in this definition of E.B. Tylor, who is reckoned as being the first to describe the particularly anthropological subject area[12]:

> Culture or Civilization, taken in its wide ethnographic sense, is that complex whole which includes knowledge, belief, art, morale, law, custom, and any other capabilities and habits acquired by man as a member of society. (Tylor, 1903 [1865]: 1)

Tylor describes his project as, among other things, to investigate 'the civilization of the lower tribes as related to the civilization of the higher nations' (Taylor, 1903 [1865]: 1). Tylor does not, by the way, use the word 'culture' in the plural (Stocking, 1966).

Diffusionism and holism

The European – especially German – concept of culture in the 19th century was taken across the Atlantic by the German-born Franz Boas (educated in physics and geography) in the years around 1900 in connection with his involvement in ethnographic studies of American Indian cultures and languages. He was the man who organised anthropology in the USA as a cohesive and independent discipline that was to give a professional academic education (Darnell, 1969). It was his vision of anthropology that came to characterise the subject in the inter-war years. In that vision, the concepts of both culture and language enjoyed a prominent position. The subject came to comprise four elements: cultural anthropology, linguistic anthropology, archaeological anthropology and biological/physical anthropology. The concept of culture was the central overall concept, in contrast to the situation in Europe (especially Great Britain and France), where it was the concept of society, because of the important influence of Durkheim's sociology.[13]

From c.1910 Boas and his followers gave the concept of culture the culture-relativist (anti-hierarchical) character it has had ever since in most of American anthropology (Stocking, 1966: 871). Boas was highly critical of evolutionism and its innate ethnocentrism and racism. He was, on the other hand, positively interested in diffusionism, which was a trend in the first couple of decades of the 20th century that had as its aim to explain similarities between various cultures by means of diffusion, i.e. migration, cultural contacts and borrowing, as an alternative or supplement to explaining them as inventions that had taken place independently of each other. Boas' position here was a double one: on the one hand he felt that cultural traits divide and spread in culture areas[14] and interact with other cultural traits, and on the other he also felt that cultural traits integrate with each other and form a coherent pattern. The latter can be considered to be a holistic conception of culture, one where emphasis is placed on culture as an integrated whole (and the whole also comprises the material and social relationships).[15] At the same time, he, like the (rest of the) German tradition, had a collective psychological approach to culture, which caused him to show an interest in 'the genius of the people'.

This double view of culture resulted in two main schools in subsequent American cultural anthropology: one that concentrated on gathering large amounts of ethnographic material (housing interiors, family patterns, food and drink, taboos, etc.) and the organisation of thematically based databanks for comparative purposes, and one that was interested in the psychological approach to culture, the so-called 'culture-and-personality' school. Typical of the latter was its holistic view of the individual culture as a configuration or a pattern[16], cf. R. Benedict, *Patterns of Culture* 1946 (1934), and one of the key concepts was 'ethos': the characteristic moral, aesthetic and emotional tone of the culture concerned. This conception of culture was particularly popular from the 1930s to the 1950s[17], and had a number of different variants, from clearly whole-oriented, gestalt-inspired variants to those inspired by behaviourism, which focused on cultural patterns of behaviour.

The holistic concept of culture is to be found among such American cultural anthropologists as A. L. Kroeber and C. Kluckhohn, as a result of a thorough historical-semantic analysis of the concept in the book *Culture – A Critical Review of Concepts and Definitions*:

> Culture consists of patterns, explicit and implicit, of and for behavior acquired and transmitted by symbols, constituting the distinctive achievement of human groups, including their embodiments in artifacts; the essential core of culture consists of traditional (i.e. historically derived and selected) ideas and especially their attached values; culture systems may, on the one hand, be considered as products of action, on the other as conditioning elements of further action. (Kroeber & Kluckhohn, 1952: 357)

This definition is considered to be one of the last attempts to lay down a comprehensive definition of (the anthropological) concept of culture, i.e. one that would apply in all contexts. Since then, there has been more or less of a consensus that it was not possible to lay down any 'authorised' definition of culture.

The concept of cultural relativism (excursion)

Cultural relativism, as formulated by Boas and his followers, has been an important force, particularly in American cultural anthropology, and has also spread far beyond it. This is not the place to trace its history; in this excursion I simply want to draw attention to the fact that one can distinguish between three types of cultural relativism (as per Whitaker 1996: a conventional anthropological, an ethical and an epistemological.

Conventional anthropological cultural relativism has the fundamental belief that many differences exist in behaviour and mentality around the world, and that these differences are not based on racial, biological differences but are to be understood as the result of culture-historical development.

Ethical cultural relativism claims that moral and ethical values are a product of the unique development through history of each individual culture. Some people would reply to this that in that case one must insist on tolerance towards all values, no matter their content – and then one is a cultural relativist in this sense. Others (myself included) feel that it is possible to accept the existence of different values and understand their historical background and yet at the same time criticise them in the light of one's own ethical principles.

Epistemological cultural relativism claims that each culture has its own world view which cannot be mediated to others. If one emphasises this conception of closure or incommunicability, one is a cultural relativist in this sense. A common counter-argument against this form of cultural relativism is that people from different cultural contexts can in practice communicate with each other despite certain comprehension difficulties. But, as it can be difficult or impossible to ascertain the extent of a possible miscommunication, this argument is in principle untenable. Epistemological cultural relativism can therefore not be disproved empirically. But one can place more or less emphasis on it in one's basic epistemological attitude. Personally, I prefer not to place too much emphasis on it.

A note in passing: linguistic relativism (à la Whorf) is a special instance of epistemological cultural relativism. Linguistic relativism claims that a specific part of culture, namely language, plays a special role for knowledge – either by determining which categories one can use to gain knowledge of the world (the strong hypothesis), or by influencing habitual thought (the weak hypothesis).

Sapir on language and culture

Sapir, who was active in the middle of the contrasting views of diffusionism and holism, has in his book *Language* from 1921 a chapter with the title *'Language, Race and Culture'*, which contains a presentation that is excellent in many respects of the relationship between language and culture. The main message is: 'Language, race and culture are not necessarily correlated' (Sapir, 1921: 215).[18]

He begins with a statement that 'language does not exist apart from culture' (Sapir, 1921: 207), where he deals with language and culture in the generic sense, cf. Chapter 1. Apart from that, however, he operates on the basis of the holistic and differential concept of culture of the time, understood in a diffusionist framework in the sense that he focuses on culture as something that spreads out over an area. Sapir emphasises that language can spread across cultural areas:

> Languages may spread far beyond their original home, invading the territory of new races and of new culture spheres. A language may even die out in its primary area and live on among peoples violently hostile to the persons of its original speakers. Further, the accidents of history are constantly rearranging the borders of culture areas without necessarily effacing the existing linguistic cleavages. (Sapir, 1921: 208)

Sapir draws attention to the disruptive influence of the national language norm on 'natural distribution':

Particularly in more primitive levels, where the secondarily unifying power of the 'national' ideal does not arise to disturb the flow of what we might call natural distributions, is it easy to show that language and culture are not intrinsically associated. Totally unrelated languages share in one culture, closely related languages – even a single language – belong to distinct culture spheres. (Sapir, 1921: 213)

On the other hand, he underlines that the 'content' of language is closely linked to culture but he supplements this with a strong warning not to identify language with its vocabulary, i.e. to have a too narrow view of language:

It goes without saying that the mere content of language is intimately related to culture... In the sense that the vocabulary of a language more or less faithfully reflects the culture whose purposes it serves it is perfectly true that the history of language and the history of culture move along parallel lines. But this superficial and extraneous kind of parallelism is of no real interest to the linguist except in so far as growth or borrowing of new words incidentally throws new light on the formal trends of the language. The linguistic student should never make the mistake of identifying a language with its dictionary. (Sapir, 1921: 219)

Sapir is naturally right in saying that language is more than its vocabulary, and in my discussion of languaculture (Chapter 8) and cultural words (Chapter 11) I will look more closely at how one can describe part of the language/culture relationship from a broader semantic-pragmatic perspective.

A meaning-oriented concept of culture

In the 1950s and 1960s, dissatisfaction gradually grew with the amorphous holistic concept of culture, and people tried to limit and clarify it in various ways. One can distinguish here between two tendencies: on the one hand, those who preferred to consider cultures as adaptation systems in relation to natural surroundings and who therefore emphasised the material, technological, economic and social aspects of people's lives (e.g. L. White, M. Sahlins, M. Harris), and on the other hand, those who preferred to consider cultures as ideational systems (systems of meanings) that had a more or less independent status in the societal whole. In the latter tendency the concept of culture came to have similarities with the concept of language or text.

With these imitations and clarifications of the concept of culture there was an opportunity to discuss the relationship between 'the cultural' and 'the social', i.e. that between the system of meaning and the social structure, and to have a better dialogue between on the one side culture-orientated American (and German) anthropology and on the other side society-orientated British (and partially French) anthropology.

Among the anthropologists who chose to focus on the meaning-oriented dimension one can distinguish, up to the 1970s, between three main tendencies (as does Keesing, 1974): cognitive anthropology, structuralist anthropology and symbolic anthropology. The three tendencies have in their separate ways transferred theories and methods to do with language and texts to the realm of cultural analysis.

A cognitive concept of culture

W. Goodenough is the main representative of the first phase of cognitive anthropology, which was inspired by the American structural linguistics of the 1950s: taxonomic linguistics, componential analysis, etc. The tendency is also called ethnosemantics, 'ethnoscience' or new ethnography. Goodenough saw culture as being analogous to language, and therefore he transferred linguistic methods to an analysis of culture. It is also this tendency that has used the concept 'cultural grammar' for the cultural rules and systems that were uncovered. Apart from the tendency being inspired as regards method by contemporary linguistics, it was also produced by precisely the rejection by this type of linguistics of semantic studies. The entire semantic field of research was thus open to anthropology.

Cognitive anthropology mainly understands culture as knowledge: the locus of culture is in human consciousness. In 1964 (1957) Goodenough gave this definition of the cognitive concept of culture:

> A society's culture consists of whatever it is one has to know or believe in order to operate in a manner acceptable to its members and do so in any role that they accept for any one of themselves. Culture, being what people have to learn as distinct from their biological heritage, must consist of the end product of learning: knowledge, in a most general, if relative, sense of the term. By this definition, we should note that culture is not a material phenomenon; it does not consist of things, people, behavior, or emotions. It is rather an organization of these things that people have in mind, their models for perceiving, relating and otherwise interpreting them. (Goodenough, 1964: 36)

As far as method is concerned, a cognitive ethnographical analysis of culture has to do with studying the content in and the structures of this knowledge, e.g. by an analysis of the conceptual system of the informants within a particular area: kinship system, plant life (ethnobotany), diseases and their treatment (ethnomedicine), etc. This analysis can, for example, comprise componential analysis of the semantic elements that are part of the system. This form of cognitive anthropology was especially popular in the 1960s.

In 1974, R.M. Keesing proposed that one should rather build on the thoughts of generative linguistics concerning 'competence' and deep and surface structure, and apart from that make use of Labov's thoughts concerning social variation within 'competence'. Keesing pointed out that cultural knowledge is shared at deeper levels and varies on the surface, and that we are dealing with a knowledge of what rules and systems *others* make use of:

> Culture, conceived as a system of competence shared in its broad design and deeper principles, and varying between individuals in its specifications, is then not all of what an individual knows and thinks and feels about his world. It is his *theory of what his fellows know, believe, and mean*, his theory of the code being followed, the game being played, in the society into which he was born. (Keesing, 1974: 89, italics in the original)

Keesing (as to a certain extent Goodenough) emphasises then that the cultural system (on the surface) is distributed variously throughout the population, and therefore his concept of culture can also be described as distributional.

Keesing's definition has been quite widespread right up to the present day, e.g. within the field of intercultural communication, cf. Gudykunst (1998).[19] Today, one could interpret it as a definition of cultural competence (not intercultural competence, for the definition does not refer to any plurality of cultural identities, only to 'the society into which he was born').

A structuralist concept of culture

The French anthropologist C. Lévi-Strauss is the main exponent of this tendency. He was inspired by Boas, but also by linguistic structuralism and cybernetics. An acquaintance with the Prague School's phoneme theory, via R. Jakobson, caused him to attempt to transfer the idea of unconscious thought structures to the broader area of culture, and he formulated a theory of how social phenomena could be analysed as an expression of cumulative processes of consciousness shared by all humanity. An acquaintance with cybernetics caused him to emphasise the binary logic of the processes of consciousness. Regarding method, a structuralist analysis of culture thus typically deals with arriving at an understanding of symbolic pairs of opposites in culture, such as nature/culture, female/male, cold/hot, human/animal, bad/good, e.g. via a study of kinship systems or myths.

Lévi-Strauss has been inspired by the Boas tradition, but except for that he belongs to the tradition of European social anthropology which, as mentioned, has had 'society' as an overall concept. Lévi-Strauss specifically uses the concept of culture for symbolic, communicative systems:

> All culture can be thought of as a whole made up of symbolic systems, the highest-ranking of which are language, matrimonial rules, economic relations, art, science, and religion. All these systems aim to express certain aspects of physical reality and social reality and, furthermore, the relations that these two types of reality maintain between each other and that the symbolic systems themselves maintain between themselves. (Lévi-Strauss, 1966: XIX)[20]

Lévi-Strauss is particularly interested in viewing the symbolic systems on the one hand as substantially different and on the other hand as realisations of formally uniform patterns that cut across different societies, e.g. within major areas of culture. So he has both a generic and a differential approach to the analysis of culture (he himself uses the terms 'universal' and 'particular'). This places structuralist anthropology in the opposite camp to cognitive anthropology, which has a more unambiguously differential (particular) conception of culture. Structuralist anthropology was particularly prevalent from the 1960s to the early 1980s.

An interpretive concept of culture

It is in particular the American anthropologist Clifford Geertz who has been the driving force in developing interpretive anthropology, which is the best known of the tendency that Keesing refer to as symbolic anthropology.[21] Geertz's thoughts have had a great impact both on anthropology itself and on the cultural and social sciences in general in the late 1960s and the 1970s – even in the 1980s to a certain extent. Geertz is at odds with cognitive anthropology in that he claims that the locus of culture lies in social action. Culture, then, is to be found among the members of a society and it is public. Social action is conceived as a text ('an acted document') that is a bearer of complex networks of meaning:

> The concept of culture I espouse ... is essentially a semiotic one. Believing, with Max Weber, that man is an animal suspended in webs of significance he himself has spun, I take culture to be those webs, and the analysis of it to be therefore not an experimental science in search of law but an interpretive one in search of meaning. (Geertz, 1973: 5)

This culture-as-text the ethnographer has to interpret by making a 'thick description'[22] of the semantic structures it conceals. While cognitive linguistics, especially in the 1960s and 1970s, had a strong affinity with American linguistics, interpretive anthropology had/has relations with hermeneutics and thereby with literary interpretation.[23] So it is also a view of culture that is not blind to the aesthetic dimension of cultural practice.[24]

Interpretive anthropology has been called the expression of a literary turn in anthropology (Spencer, 1996). Because of his literary emphasis, Geertz is highly particularist in his orientation[25], unlike Lévi-Strauss, who is universalist, and unlike cognitive anthropology, which traditionally operates with an abstract concept of the individual (as does the Chomsky tradition).

Practice-oriented Concepts of Culture and Cultural Studies

In the 1970s, anthropology, like many other cultural and social sciences (including culture pedagogy) was to a certain extent influenced by Marxist trends. The concept of culture was typically understood as ideology, and studies of culture were often synonymous with studies of ideological criticism. But from the 1980s the concept of culture becomes salient and now in the practice-oriented form (cf. the discussion in Ortner, 1984), more or less influenced by contemporary postmodern thought (cf. Keesing, 1994).

This orientation towards practice was accompanied by a critique of system thinking in most culture research up till then: Goodenough, Keesing, Lévi-Strauss, Barthes and Geertz all described culture (in their publications prior to the 1980s) as a system or a structure (more or less varied or distributed). There was now increasing scepticism towards, or even a rejection of, the idea of culture as a cohesive system. This anti-system tendency meant, among other things, that cultural theory stopped using analogies to linguistics in its system-oriented forms (cf., for example, Street's critique in Street, 1993), and drew more for inspiration on practice-oriented linguistic philosophy, e.g. late Wittgenstein.

For the period since the 1980s it is difficult to choose between suitable terms to describe the conception of culture – a problem that would seem to be general for cultural and social sciences. It is symptomatic that there are so many competing terms for the epoch itself: postmodern society, late-modern society, second modernity, late capitalism, risk society, information society, post-traditional society, postfordian society, postindustrial society, knowledge society, network society, etc. The discourses on culture and society are polyphonic to such an extent that it is harder than ever to find common denominators.

Since the emphasis in the conception of culture lies on the dimension of practice, this conception of culture is in the main an extension of the interpretive branch. Geertz is a precursor of the practice-oriented concept of culture, and he is sometimes described as 'prepostmodern'. For Geertz, the task of the ethnographer is to unearth the already existing system of symbols via a thick description of symbol-saturated practice. For advocates for the practice-oriented concept of culture, the symbols are created and recreated in 'the negotiation' between people in interaction. Particular emphasis is placed on the meaning-creating individual, with some people also talking of a subject-oriented or subjectivist concept of culture. It is, however, not a matter of the single individual but of individuals in interaction, i.e. of intersubjective processes. Emphasis is placed on the procedural, social and conflictual aspects of the ascription of meaning.

It is popular nowadays to operate with a simplified contrast between the new and the old concept of culture: One speaks of the 'dynamic' concept of culture as opposed to the 'classical' or 'functionalist' concept of culture. In my opinion, this is a variation of 'us' and 'them' at the diachronic level, for – as I have attempted to present in the previous section – the history of the concept of culture prior to the 1980s is extremely varied just within anthropology (and there can definitely not be said to be an academic consensus on the concept of culture at present). It is an indefensible simplification if one seeks to include all earlier anthropological thinking on culture within the term 'the classical concept of culture'. One must refer more explicitly, e.g. to a concept of culture such as Kroeber's (see above) that one can choose to refer to as 'classical' and which stresses pattern and tradition, or be more explicit concerning the various functionalist traditions in British and American anthropology.

An example of a more subtle deconstruction of the concept of culture is to be found in contrasting culture as a substance-concept and culture as an analytical or relational concept (Hastrup, 1989): The earlier anthropological conception of culture as a substance-concept meant that culture was something empirically given, something that one could penetrate and explore (also known as the reifying concept of culture). Hastrup describes another concept of culture, that of culture as an analytical or relational concept, i.e. culture is here an intersubjective category, something that is first identified via an awareness of meaningful differences between one's own world and 'the others'.

Those tendencies that see themselves as part of social constructivism, e.g. many in the Cultural Studies tradition, prefer to criticise what they refer to as the essentialist understanding of culture, i.e. the conception of culture as 'something' that has a particular essence and that can be used as an explanatory factor regarding people's actions and attitudes – a critique that very much runs parallel to that of Hastrup, only formulated in a partially different theoretical context.

Traditional cultural relativism is linked to the understanding of cultures as various substance systems. When one uses the concept of culture as an analytical concept, the question of cultural relativism (here: ethical cultural relativism) is transformed into a more general and philosophical question of particular vs. universal values and the role they play in the concrete analysis of culture.

The Cultural Studies tradition has exerted a strong influence on parts of anthropology. This has led to a shift of anthropological interest towards such subjects as culture and ethnicity in the modern metropolis, subcultures and cultural dominance, multiculturalism and identity politics. In the Cultural Studies tradition a particular brief definition of culture is often cited, formulated by its initiators, including Williams: 'a constitutive social process, creating specific and different "ways of life"' (Williams, 1977: 19). Note that this definition has a holistic tinge, although here it is not normally a matter of national cultures but of youth cultures, worker cultures, gender-specific cultures, etc. This definition came about as a critique of the more exclusive aesthetic concept of culture, as an opening-out of it towards popular culture and everyday culture among various groups.

The Cultural Studies movement intertwines in the 1980s with the post-modern tendency, which generally emphasises capturing differences, heterogeneity, otherness, multiplicity, particularity, complexity and hybridity (e.g. Hall, 1992, 1996). This relativist focus has also partially influenced anthropology; it has, among other things, involved a discussion of the validity of the cultural representations of ethnography and of what form such representations can and ought to assume.[26]

This discussion of ethnographical representations – the conversion of lived life into text – can be seen as an illustration of the kind of meaning that is ascribed to language within the recent practice-oriented tendency: there is considerable interest in linguistic practice, text and discourse in a more general, generic sense, but only relatively sporadic interest in language in the differential sense, including the significance of the various languages for epistemological knowledge (the Whorfian discussion) and intercultural communication.

Running parallel with the practice-oriented conception of culture there is still a cognitive anthropology that is interested in the inner locus of culture: for individuals' cultural models of the world; but this tendency too is moving towards a conception of knowledge of the world as being socially constructed in interaction and discourse. The above-mentioned Keesing, who in the 1970s proposed a cognitive conception of culture influenced by generative grammar, argued in Keesing (1994) in favour of cultural anthropology allowing itself to be influenced more by the Cultural Studies movement – not its relativist and multiculturalist variants but critical variants influenced by Gramsci's ideas. Keesing wishes to work for what he calls 'the political economy of knowledge'.

From the recent cognitive tendency I have found inspiration in the American anthropologist M. Agar (see Chapter 8), who has written about the concept of 'languaculture' in his book *Language Shock. Understanding the Culture of Conversation* (1994). Agar also expresses a procedural and relational conception of culture: 'culture happens to you', as he puts it (Agar, 1994: 20).

Conclusion

It is important not just to base one's understanding of culture on the dichotomy 'the new concept of culture' vs. 'the old or classical concept of culture'. The concept of culture has had an extremely varied history in European and Western development since Roman times. It is in particular the American (cultural) anthropological development that is relevant as a basis for an understanding of the relationship between language and culture, because it is characterised by understandings of culture which in various ways draw on approaches linked to linguistic and textual disciplines. Among the various anthropological approaches it is in particular the types of recent anthropology that have been influenced by the Cultural Studies movement and postmodern thought that are applicable in the analysis of the relationship between language and culture. This is because the recent tendencies focus on modern complex society and its conflicting cultural and identity-related problem areas, a focus that can also accommodate ideas that languages and cultures can be separated from each other and reassembled in new configurations. In Chapter 5, I intend to focus in particular on one of the branches within recent anthropology, that which deals with cultural complexity.

Notes

1. I (and Bauman) am thinking here of the concepts 'etic' and 'emic' description, as presented by Pike. The difference between 'etic' and 'emic' is a generalisation on the basis of the difference between phonetics and phonemics (Pike, 1967: 37ff. (1954)).

2. I am thinking here of the Danish/European etymology and cultural history of the lexeme 'culture' since Roman antiquity. It would be interesting to compare this development with that of near-equivalent Asian concepts, e.g. the Chinese *wen hua* (= culture or civilisation, really, to change oneself through written characters, education) and *wen ming* (= civilisation or culture, civilised) (cf. the dictionary by Cowie & Evison, 1992), and the Japanese (etymologically the same and written with the same signs): *bun-ka* (= culture as opposed to nature, cf. German *Kultur*) and *bun-mei* (= civilisation, cf. English *civilisation*) (cf. the dictionaries by Kindaichi, 1959 and Nelson, 1975).

3. *Col- (colere)* had a very broad area of meaning that can be indicated by such words as: to settle, inhabit (cf. colony, colonisation), to cultivate, care for, provide, praise, celebrate (cf. the other Latin nominalisation *cultus* and the word 'cult').

4. There is a place in Cicero where he writes: '... cultura ... animi philosophia est' (philosophy is cultivation of the soul) (Tusculanae Disputationes, Book II, Chap. V, §13).

5. In Greek the word *politismós* is normally used. After 1974, the word *koultoura* was, however, introduced into Greek, although mostly as a vogue word, so it is possibly on the way out again. *Koultoura* can mean highbrow culture, but also in certain contexts subculture.

6. Fink calls this the social concept of culture, and Márkus talks about 'the societal dimension', while I prefer the term 'collective', which is a more general term.

7. Herder rarely uses the word 'civilisation', although e.g. Herder, 1952 (1782): 284.

8. But it can also mean the same as *Hochkultur* (one cannot, for example, talk about **primitive Zivilisationen*).

9. Böhme (1996) emphasises the spatial associations of this question: the idea of a German-speaking area, the connection with 'the earth'. He calls this aspect of the concept of culture a memory track from the Neolithic leap, when man began to settle and cultivate the land.

10. Cf. Ardener, 1989 (1971) and Leach, 1964.

11. 'classic' because there has also been an evolutionist tendency, especially in the 1950s and 1960s, which interested in the development from less to more complex societies.

12. Tylor was especially influenced by the German Gustav Klemm, and thereby by the German culture-historical tradition (cf. Høiris, 1988: 98).

13. An important exception is B. Malinowski, who also made use of the concept of culture as an overall concept.

14. From the German *Kulturkreis*.

15. Holism is also obvious in the above quotation of Tylor.

16. The society-oriented corresponding theory in British social anthropology is A.R. Radcliffe-Brown's 'structural functionalism', which is based on the conception of society as a functionally structured whole (especially the 1930s).

17. Sapir, who was a pupil of Boas, was also interested in both culture spread (and language spread) and 'culture and personality'.
18. Sapir's chapter can be seen as an elaboration of what Boas writes in his introduction to the study of the Indian languages, e.g. '... anatomical type, language and culture have not necessarily the same fates' (Boas, 1911: 6).
19. Keesing himself has later developed his conception of culture in a postmodern direction, cf. Keesing (1994).
20. 'Toute culture peut être considérée comme un ensemble de systèmes symboliques au premier rang desquels se placent le langage, les règles matrimoniales, les rapports économiques, l'art, la science, la religion. Tous ces systèmes visent à exprimer certains aspects de la réalité physique et de la réalité sociale, et plus encore, les relations que ces deux types de réalité entretiennent entre eux et que les systèmes symboliques eux-mêmes entretiennent les uns avec les autres.' (translation: JI)
21. Apart from the interpretative variant, other researchers can be mentioned who work in partially different symbolic directions and whom I do not intend to examine more closely here: the American D. Schneider, the Frenchman L. Dumont and the Briton V. Turner.
22. The expression was originally coined by Gilbert Ryle.
23. And to the American sociologist Parsons, of whom Geertz is a pupil.
24. In Geertz (1988), Geertz discusses the role of the ethnographer as a (literary) writer.
25. In a later publication Geertz elaborates on e.g. the concept of 'local knowledge' (Geertz, 1983).
26. Cf. Marcus and Fischer, 1986 (and the discussion in Risager, 1999).

Chapter 4

Language, Nation and Culture: The German Tradition

Introduction

This short chapter has been included because it is often claimed that the first people to formulate the idea of a close correlation between language and culture were Herder and Humboldt. This conception, however, needs to be refined somewhat, so I have inserted this presentation of the two German researchers' ideas about language, nation and culture.

The Concept of Nation With or Without a Linguistic Criterion

It can be deduced from recent theories concerning nationality that nationalism has not always included language as a criterion (Anderson, 1991 (1983); Smith, 1986). Benedict Anderson, who has originated the theory of the nation as an 'imagined community' that has arisen in connection with 'print capitalism' – i.e. was created by a reading public, which gradually imagined a community among all those who read books printed in the same language (Anderson, 1983) – deals with nationalism not only in Europe but also for example in Spanish-speaking South America in the 19th century. Here, the various nations were formed on the basis of the identification by the Creole officials with a common administrative area, an 'imagined community', which they felt it was in their interest to realise as an independent state. In this development, reading admittedly also played a part, but language was not a differential element. And in his book *Nations and Nationalism Since 1780* (1990) Hobsbawm, in writing about language as a criterion for nationality, advances a great many examples of nationalist movements through the ages that have not mentioned language at all. The linguistic criterion was not included in the conception of nationality until late: Finnish nationalism did not become linguistic until the 1860s; Catalan regionalism did not become linguistic until the 1880s; Basque nationalism not until the 1890s; and Irish nationalism not until around 1900 (Hobsbawm, 1990: 106ff).

The Concept of Nation With a Linguistic Criterion: Central and Eastern Europe

It is first and foremost in the central and eastern parts of Europe that language originally assumed its defining role in the conception of nation and later of nationalism. This took place on the basis of the particular conditions for German, Italian and east and south-east European development from the 18th century. Both the German and the Italian developments have been influenced by a long-lasting struggle for a definition of and a political gathering of 'the German nation', i.e. all those who speak German, and 'the Italian nation', i.e. all those who speak Italian – a history that has been characterised by many different political, social and regional contrasts (see e.g. Dann, 1996; Hobsbawm, 1990). So it is no coincidence that it was precisely in connection with the emergence of German national consciousness after the 1760s that ideas arose concerning a close correlation between language, nation and culture, most concisely formulated by Herder in 1770 and the following years.

Herder's view of language, nation and culture must be seen in connection with the linguistic and political situation of the German-speaking population groups in Europe at the time. German speakers were spread over a large area in Central and Eastern Europe that would now correspond to Germany, parts of Poland, the Czech Republic, Slovakia, Austria, Hungary, parts of Slovenia, parts of Romania, parts of Italy, parts of Switzerland, parts of France, parts of Belgium, the Netherlands and parts of Denmark. Most of this area lay within the framework of the Holy Roman Empire, which was formed in 962 and dissolved in 1806 in connection with the Napoleonic Wars. (There were also areas outside the empire where German speakers had settled, e.g. in part of Russia and in the Baltic region, just as there were population groups inside the empire who spoke other languages: Polish, Czech, Hungarian, Yiddish, etc.). But even though the area was one empire, powers of government were in practice in the hands of a large number of local princes, kings, dukes, etc., with Austria and Prussia as the two biggest states. The linguistic area was thus very divided with regard to politics (and religion), unlike the West European nation states of France, Britain and Spain.

As there was no particular cultural centre for German speakers, they did not have any common 'national language' in the form of a language standardised from the centre – oral or written. The oral language consisted of a dialect continuum that covered the entire linguistic area, with quite considerable comprehension difficulties between the dialects. The oral language was only just beginning to find certain standards, and it was here that German-speaking theatres played a certain role. The written language had already developed on the basis of Middle German (*Mitteldeutsch*) as a result of Luther's translation of the Bible in the 1520s. So it is possible to speak of a fairly common German written language, although it was, of course, only relevant for those who were able to read and possibly write. And at the time of Herder there were not all that many such people – it has been estimated that there were 3–500,000 German speakers who were able to read (Hobsbawm, 1990: 61[1]). Those able to read, living in the completely or partially German-speaking towns, developed in the course of the 16th, 17th and 18th centuries what Anderson (1991 [1983]) calls 'an imagined community', a community that one can call 'national', but which as yet did not have any political programme.

Johann Gottfried von Herder

In the 1760s, the idea crystallised in to *Die deutsche Bewegung* (the German movement) (Dann, 1996: 52), which was the first movement to express a common-German consciousness. It arose as a reaction to the French-oriented culture of the court and was a movement that was critical of society (of absolutism) and comprised liberal members of the bourgeoisie as well as intellectuals – not a popular movement. In this movement, J.G. von Herder represented the national dimension.

Herder was a central figure in connection with the emerging German national consciousness among the German-speaking liberal bourgeoisie and intellectuals in the period known in literary and cultural history as the *Sturm-und-Drang* ('storm-and-stress') period (1765–85). He wrote what was to become the manifest of the *Sturm-und-Drang* movement, in which he emphasised Ossian, Shakespeare, folk songs and the Middle Ages as important literary and conceptual models.

It is in Herder that we see for the first time a fusion between the concepts of language and nation and – in a certain sense – culture. But it is important to note that the concepts of culture and nation had a different content then from what they have today. As described in Chapter 3, the concept of culture in Herder's age was partly an individual and partly a collective concept, and both were hierarchical: one generally distinguished between individuals/peoples who had culture and individuals/peoples who did not. Herder, as mentioned, was perhaps the first person to de-hierarchise the concept of culture. The word 'nation' was almost synonymous with the word 'people' (*Volk*), and it did not then have the political meaning it was to acquire with the French Revolution. The population of the entire world was seen as consisting of peoples/nations. The concept of nation at the time had, then, similarities with the present concept of 'ethnic group' / 'ethnie'.

Herder expressed a consistently humanist conception of history and humanity. For example, he wrote (in Herder, 1952 (1782)): 141: 'Although the human race appears in such different forms on the earth, it is nevertheless everywhere one and the same human genus.'[2] He believed that all peoples have culture, but to varying degrees; the crucial thing is not quality but quantity:

> The chain of culture and enlightenment reaches ... to the end of the earth. The man in California and Tierra del Fuego also learned how to make bows and arrows and use them; he has language and concepts, practices and arts which he learned as we learn them; insomuch he thus became truly cultivated and enlightened, albeit at the lowest level. The difference between enlightened and unenlightened, between cultivated and uncultivated peoples is therefore not specific but only a matter of degree. (Herder, 1952 (1782): 214)[3]

He also underlined that he did not view European culture as being superior to all others:

> You people from all parts of the world, you who have passed on for eons, you had then not lived and perchance only fertilised the earth with your ashes, so that at the end of time your descendants would be made happy by European culture? (Herder, 1952 (1782): 210)[4]

As did other writers of his time, Herder used the word 'nation' as a synonym for people, and each people had a language that played a decisive role in its degree of culture and enlightenment. He says in this connection: 'Ein Volk hat keine Idee, zu der es kein Wort hat' (Herder, 1952 (1782): 221). As he also advanced in the treatise *Über den Ursprung der Sprache* of 1770, he viewed language as the most important means for human *Bildung*: 'Only language has made man human, by containing the vast surge of his emotions and placing rational monuments in their stead through words' (Herder, 1952 (1782): 221).[5]

By language he understood the mother tongue, the spoken and written 'language of the people'. Since, as mentioned, there hardly existed any common German spoken language[6], he was basing himself – without being aware of it – on the common German written language.

Herder probably did not use the word 'culture' in the plural at any point[7], and he apparently did not explicitly ascribe a particular independent culture to any people. He did not talk about 'Chinese culture', 'Finnish culture', etc. But he did talk about European culture, as can be seen from the above quotation. So he did not use the concept of culture differentially to the extent one does today, although the differential meaning is latent in his views. One could say that Herder thought differentially, not with the aid of the concept of culture but with that of the concept of the nation.

If one looks at what Herder's concept of culture comprised, one can indirectly get the impression of it from the following passage, which speaks of a very broad (generically understood) concept of culture that also includes murder:

> No animal devours its own kind as a titbit; no animal murders its own race in cold blood on the orders of a third party; no animal has language as man has; still less writing, tradition, religion, arbitrary laws and rights; finally, neither does any animal have any of the culture, clothing, habitation, arts, the undetermined way of life, the unfettered urges, the flattering opinions which are the distinctive characteristic of practically every human individual. (Herder, 1952 (1782): 84)[8]

So one can conclude that for Herder it was not the language-culture relationship that was primary but the language-people relationship. He stood for a (German) understanding of nationhood that has subsequently been described as linguo-ethnic, and which crucially differed from the French political understanding of nationhood, which did not imply that one belonged to the French nation only if one had French as one's mother tongue, cf. the following quotation from Hobsbawm (1990: 2) concerning enforced French linguistic orthodoxy during the Revolution, with a reference to Certeau, Julia and Revel (1975):

> ... in theory it was not the native use of the French language that made a person French – how could it when the Revolution itself spent so much of its time proving how few people in France actually used it – but the willingness to acquire this, among the other liberties, laws and common characteristics of the free people of France.

Herder was far in advance of his age by virtue of his humanist, anti-hierarchical conception of culture. This conception does not seriously re-emerge until the first decades of the 20th century.

Wilhelm von Humboldt

Herder's idea of a correlation between language and people/nation was further developed to a certain extent by Wilhelm von Humboldt (especially in Humboldt, 1907 (1836)), although he wrote about the relationship between language and culture/civilisation in a different, more conservative manner.

Humboldt was a politician/diplomat and academic, strongly influenced by the ideas of neo-humanism concerning the value of clarity and harmony in spiritual cultivation (*Bildung*).[9] He was particularly interested in language as a creative activity that was made possible because of the power of the human mind (*Geisteskraft*). He was, then, most interested in the psychological aspect of language, especially in the role of language for thought: 'Language is the formative organ of thought' (Humboldt, 1907 (1836): 53)[10] and for a world view: '… so there lies in every language a particular world view' (Humboldt, 1907 (1836): 60).[11] Humboldt was one of the first to formulate the idea of linguistic relativism.

Humboldt saw language itself as free self-activity and languages as bound to nations, peoples or tribes:

> It is no empty play on words if one represents language as something deriving only from itself in self-activity and as divinely free, but languages as being bound and depending on the nations to which they belong." (Humboldt, 1907 (1836): 17). While languages … are creations of nations, they themselves even so remain creations of individuals, since they can only produce themselves in every individual, in such as way, however, that everyone presupposes the understanding of everyone else and everyone fulfils this expectation. (Humboldt, 1907 (1836): 40)[12]

Civilisation or culture, on the other hand, were for Humboldt something that can spread from language to language; we are not dealing with a direct link between language and culture:

> Java clearly received higher civilisation and culture from India – and both to a considerable degree – but the native language did not because of that change its more incomplete form – one that was less appropriate to the needs of thought… (Humboldt, 1907 (1836): 27)[13]

Humboldt distinguishes between civilisation, culture and *Bildung* in the following way:

> Civilisation is the humanising of peoples in their external institutions and customs and the internal cast of mind that has reference to them. Culture adds science and art to this ennoblement of the social state. When, however, we use the term *Bildung* in our language, we mean by it something that is both higher and more intimate, namely the disposition that surges forth from the knowledge and emotions of man's

entire spiritual and moral striving, exerting a harmonious influence on sentiment and character. (Humboldt, 1907 (1836): 30, italics in the original)[14]

Humboldt distinguishes analytically between civilisation, culture and *Bildung*, and between language as an individual creative activity and language as a national, collective work. He is also interested in what happens to one's world view when one learns a foreign language:

> The learning of a foreign language ought … to entail the gaining of a new standpoint in the previous world view and it is indeed so to a certain extent, as each language contains the entire fabric of concepts and the mode of conception of a part of humanity. Only because one always transfers into a foreign language, more or less, one's own worl view – indeed one's own language view – is this success not experienced in a pure and complete way. (Humboldt, 1907 (1836): 60)[15]

For Humboldt, then, the new language marks a new standpoint, a different approach to an understanding of the world. Here we have a linguistic relativism that does not claim that language determines thought but that it involves a new perspective.

Humboldt was way ahead of his time in his interest in the form of language and for the correlation between language and world view. His posthumously published work on the form of language did not have any major impact before it was turned to account by the neo-Humboldtians.[16] But his thoughts on *Bildung* had a considerable influence on the German education systems, the teaching of classical languages and of German as a first language, and, from the late 20th century onwards, also on the teaching of modern foreign languages (*Neuphilologie*).

Herder, Humboldt and National Romanticism

Neither Herder nor Humboldt were National Romantics, but Herder comes very close in certain respects. He is often referred to as a pre-Romantic: on the one hand, he was influenced by the interest of the Enlightenment in creating the great, objective overview and its interest in humanity and its potential for understanding and forming the world. On the other hand, he placed great emphasis on the emotional dimension of life, and in particular his treatise *Über den Ursprung der Sprache* (*On the Origin of Language*) of 1770 underlines the expressive function of language and the role of the emotions in connection with the origin and development of language – and he was most interested in the potential of national sentiment. Humboldt was a neo-humanist and therefore a non-Romantic.

But there was an important 'interlude' between Herder and Humboldt, namely German Romanticism proper, from c.1795 to 1830. During this period, the idea of a unity between language and people was romanticised (though not by Herder), so that one now spoke of a national soul and a mystical, intimate connection between language, people and national soul[17], as formulated by Fichte and Schelling. This Romantic idea of a fusion between language and people/nation gained considerable general support in connection with the nationalist tendencies that became increasingly strong and widespread in the course of 18th-century Europe, first as a progressive liberal movement and later on in various right-wing nationalist and socialist versions (cf. Hobsbawm, 1990).

Conclusion

To sum up, one can say that Herder and Humboldt were primarily interested in closely linking the concepts of language and people/nation. Humboldt did not place an 'equals' sign between language and culture (in the differential sense), and nor did Herder – with a few isolated exceptions – although subsequent analysis of their work sometimes likes to convey that impression. The identification of the individual language and individual culture is something that belongs to the 20th century. It presupposes the idea of cultural relativism, an idea which, even though it was anticipated by Herder, did not become fully developed until around 1910 in the USA by Boas and his pupils – and they, it should be noted, did not link language and culture closely together; on the contrary, they emphasised that language and culture partially spread independently of each other (cf. section on Sapir in Chapter 3).

As far as I can see, it is not until the 1930s with the work of such people as Whorf, and especially since c.1960 with Fishman's involvement in language and ethnicity, as well as the new culture pedagogy that emerged around the same time, that a thesis is clearly formulated concerning the inseparability of the individual language and the individual culture. So it is wrong to refer to Herder, Humboldt or 'German National Romanticism' when looking for early formulations of the idea of the inseparability of language and culture in the differential sense.

Notes

1. Hobsbawm has the following note at this point: 'Until the "early nineteenth century" *all* works by Goethe and Schiller, jointly and severally, appear to have sold fewer than 100,000 copies, i.e. over 30–40 years', and he refers to Wehler, 1987: 305.

2. 'In so verschiedenen Formen das Menschengeschlecht auf der Erde erscheint, so ist's doch überall eine und dieselbe Menschengattung' (translation: JI).

3. 'Die Kette der Kultur und Aufklärung reicht … bis ans Ende der Erde. Auch der Kalifornier und Feuerländer lernte Bogen und Pfeile machen und sie gebrauchen; er hat Sprache und Begriffe, übungen und Künste, die er lernte, wie wir sie lernen; sofern ward er also wirklich kultiviert und aufgeklärt, wiewohl im niedrigsten Grade. Der Unterschied zwischen aufgeklärten und unaufgeklärten, zwischen kultivierten und unkultivierten Völkern ist also nicht spezifisch, sondern nur gradweise' (translation: JI).

4. 'Ihr Menschen aller Weltteile, die ihr seit Äonen dahingingt, ihr hättet also nicht gelebt und etwa nur mit eurer Asche die Erde gedüngt, damit am Ende der Zeit eure Nachkommen durch europäische Kultur glücklich würden?' (translation: JI).

5. 'Nur die Sprache hat den Menschen menschlich gemacht, indem sie die ungeheure Flut seiner Affekte in Dämme einschloss und ihr durch Worte vernünftige Denkmale setzte' (translation: JI).

6. There hardly does to this very day, either.

7. According to Fink, 1988: 18. But Williams writes that he has found a place where Herder proposes that *Kultur* be used in the plural (Williams, 1988: 89).

8. 'Kein Tier frisst seinesgleichen aus Leckerei; kein Tier mordet sein Geschlecht auf den Befehl eines Dritten mit kaltem Blut; kein Tier hat Sprache, wie der Mensch sie hat; noch weniger Schrift, Tradition, Religion, willkürliche Gesetze und Rechte; kein Tier endlich hat auch nur die Bildung, die Kleidung, die Wohnung, die Künste, die unbestimmte Lebensart, die ungebundenen Triebe, die flatterhafte Meinungen, womit sich beinahe jedes Individuum der Menschen auszeichnet' (translation: JI).

9. Which was realised by his educational reforms as Minister of Education for Prussia, including the establishment of a university in Berlin (now The Humboldt University).

10. 'Die Sprache ist das bildende Organ des Gedanken' (translation: JI).

11. '… so liegt in jeder Sprache eine eigenthümliche Weltansicht' (translation: JI).

12. 'Es ist kein leeres Wortspiel, wenn man die Sprache als in Selbstthätigkeit nur aus sich entspringend und göttlich frei, die Sprachen aber als gebunden und von den Nationen, welchen sie angehören, abhängig darstellt' (Humboldt, 1907 (1836): 17). 'Indem die Sprachen … Schöpfungen der Nationen sind, bleiben sie doch Selbst Schöpfungen der Individuen, indem sie sich nur in jedem Einzelnen, in ihm aber nur so erzeugen können, dass jeder das Verständnis aller voraussetzt und alle dieser Erwartung genügen' (translation: JI).

13. 'Java erhielt höhere Civilisation und Cultur offenbar von Indien aus, und beide in bedeutendem Grade, aber darum änderte die einheimische Sprache nicht ihre unvollkommnere und den Bedürfnissen des Denkens weniger angemessne Form …' (translation: JI).

14. 'Die Civilisation ist die Vermenschlichung der Völker in ihren äusseren Einrichtungen und Gebräuchen und der darauf Bezug habenden innren Gesinnung. Die Cultur fügt dieser Veredlung des gesellschaftlichen Zustandes Wissenschaft und Kunst hinzu. Wenn wir aber in unsrer Sprache *Bildung* sagen, so meinen wir damit etwas zugleich Höheres und mehr Innerliches, nemlich die Sinnesart, die sich aus der Erkenntnis und dem Gefühle des gesammten geistigen und sittlichen Strebens harmonisch auf die Empfindung und den Character ergiesst' (translation: JI).

15. 'Die Erlernung einer fremden Sprache sollte . . die Gewinnung eines neuen Standpunkts in der bisherigen Weltansicht seyn und ist es in der That bis auf einen gewissen Grad, da jede Sprache das ganze Gewebe der Begriffe und die Vorstellungsweise eines Theils der Menschheit enthält. Nur weil man in eine fremde Sprache immer, mehr und weniger, seine eigne Welt-, ja seine eigne Sprachansicht hinüberträgt, so wird dieser Erfolg nicht rein und vollständig empfunden' (translation: JI).

16. L. Weisgerber (who was a supporter of German idealism as well as a Nazi), Trier and others (see e.g. Miller, 1968) and 'the idealist school' (Vossler and the Italian 'neo-linguists': Bartoli and Bertoni and others. Both Vossler and the neo-linguists were inspired by Croce's ideas from around 1900 on language as an aesthetic expression of the individual's intuition and imagination, ideas that can be traced back to Humboldt.

17. And society: During the restoration period's reactionary phase there was implicity an identification of people and social order.

Chapter 5
Cultural Complexity

Introduction

In this chapter I intend to deal with the concept of cultural complexity, using one of the main representatives of anthropological research into cultural complexity as my point of reference: the Swedish social anthropologist Ulf Hannerz. My reason for choosing Hannerz is that his theory of cultural flow in a global perspective offers a good framework for analysing the main idea behind my own work in this book: the idea that 'languages spread across cultures', and 'cultures spread across languages' (Chapter 1). In the following I wish to give an introduction to Hannerz's thoughts on the 'loci' of culture and on the organisation of cultural flow in the global ecumene. Finally, I will express my opinion on some of the points of criticism that have been raised against his approach.

Ulf Hannerz: The Two Loci of Culture and the Cultural Process

In his book *Cultural Complexity. Studies in the Social Organization of Meaning* (1992a), Hannerz describes his theory of the social organisation of meaning, with particular reference to cultural flow and cultural complexity. He begins by giving the following summary of his understanding of culture:

> The three dimensions of culture, to be understood in their interrelations, are thus:
> (1) *ideas and modes of thought* as entities and processes of the mind – the entire array of concepts, propositions, values and the like which people within some social unit carry together, as well as their various ways of handling their ideas in characteristic modes of mental operation;
> (2) *forms of externalization*, the different ways in which meaning is made accessible to the senses, made public; and
> (3) *social distribution*, the ways in which the collective cultural inventory of meanings and meaningful external forms – that is, (1) and (2) together – is spread over a population and its social relationships. (Hannerz, 1992a: 7, italics in the original)

In Hannerz's opinion, then, culture has two loci, an external and an internal. The external locus is meaningful, externalised forms such as speech, gestures, song, dance and decoration. The internal locus of culture is meaning in consciousness – not perceived as an idealised consciousness but as that of concrete human beings. The individual's share in culture he mainly describes with the aid of the concepts of perspective and horizon: each human being is unique in his or her experience-based, socially influenced perspective on the outside world, and his or her horizon is reflected by personal life experiences and education.[1] At the individual level, society is thus seen as a network of perspectives. The two loci of culture are each other's prerequisites, and the cultural process takes place in the interaction between them.

Finally, cultural knowledge and the externalised forms find themselves in a constant distribution process and this means that 'people must deal with other people's meanings' (Hannerz, 1992a: 14), cf. the emphasis placed by the cultural anthropologist Keesing on cultural knowledge being knowledge about what other people know (Chapter 3). This interest in cultural spread can be called a new diffusionism, and Hannerz draws attention to the fact that the interest in cultural diffusion that has lain somewhat at anchor during the functionalist and structuralist period in anthropology from the 1920s onwards is now enjoying a comeback in connection with the discussion on globalisation (Hannerz, 1996: 45).

Hannerz deals with modern, complex society, discussing the concept of complexity, among others, in this connection. Cultural complexity, according to Hannerz, is to be seen in relation to both (1), (2) and (3) in the above. As regards the internal locus of culture, it is a question of the structuring of an individual's personality and cognition. Here, he feels that it is dubious to suppose an increase in complexity through time. For example, people who live in a society that is primitive in the socio-economic sense may very well have a cultural world of ideas that is highly complex. As regards the external locus of culture, one can probably speak of an increase in complexity over time insofar as the forms of externalisation have become more diverse and complex: one could name the development of the written language, the many forms of technological development that enable to a greater extent the multi-semiotic blend of text/speech and images, image manipulation, etc. As regards the social distribution processes, one can also speak of an increase in complexity by virtue of the constant development of communication and transportation technologies.

In relation to the three dimensions of the concept of culture, Hannerz notes that he chooses to make the most out of (3), a little less out of (2) and least out of (1). In doing so, he places the emphasis differently from most other anthropologists, this being based on the desire to strengthen the social and distributional[2] aspect. At the same time, it must be underlined that all three dimensions are important for an overall view of the cultural process, and Hannerz does indeed discuss part of (1) in connection with the individual's perspective and horizon. This is important for the present analysis of the relationship between language and culture, as it requires both (3), (2) and (1) to be included. Language and culture have both an action-oriented, social aspect and a distributional aspect, corresponding to (2) and (3), as well as a personal aspect, corresponding to (1).

American and European Sources of Inspiration

Hannerz's position lies within what I call 'the practice-oriented concept of culture', with links to the interpretive and to a certain extent the cognitive concepts of culture. He has been inspired by Geertz in his choice of the concept of interpretation as one part of his model of cultural distribution alongside externalisation, but apart from that there is a crucial difference, as Geertz insists on the micro-level, the thick description of a piece of cultural practice, the cultural miniature, whereas Hannerz is aiming at combining the micro-level and the macro-level.[3] As regards Keesing's cognitive conception of culture in the 1970s, Hannerz underlines that he is not thinking of idealised individuals but of concrete individuals with specific biographies. One can say that Hannerz unites an individual-oriented approach with the interpretive approach in his emphasis on the double locus of culture, but he does so from a very different, global and complexity-oriented point of view. He is sceptical concerning the question of to what extent 'the cultural' has systemic characteristics.

Hannerz has in particular worked with studies of big cities and he is therefore interested in cultural contact and cultural mixes in present-day complex societies.[4] He derives a great deal of inspiration from the Chicago School, with its interest in micro-sociological studies of life in the metropolis. He has also been inspired by the Cultural Studies tradition, because of its interest in popular culture and the role of the mass media.

Concerning his relation to the postmodern, Hannerz says: 'Postmodernism comes close enough to the view of culture as an organization of diversity which I take here' (Hannerz, 1996: 35). But at the same time he warns against a fragmented concept of identity: 'When it is claimed … that identities become nothing but assemblages from whatever imagery is for the moment marketed through the media, then I wonder what kind of people the commentators on postmodernism know' (Hannerz, 1996: 35). This position is linked to the fact that his preferred reference within social-constructivist theory is P. Berger, especially the book *The Social Construction of Reality. A Treatise in the Sociology of Knowledge* (Berger & Luckmann, 1991 (1966)). This book has its origins in the European sociology of knowledge, which means that Ulf Hannerz combines American approaches with European ones.[5]

Hannerz is interested in linguistic contact phenomena in general, without himself having carried out studies within this field. He refers, for example, to M.L. Pratt, who works within American cultural and gender studies and who, in her classic article from 1987, called for a 'linguistics of contact'[6]:

> Imagine, then, a linguistics that decentered community, that placed at its centre the operation of language *across* lines of social differentiation, a linguistics that focused on modes and zones of contact between dominant and dominated groups, between persons of different and multiple identities, speakers of different languages, that focused on how speakers constitute each other relationally and in difference, how they enact differences in language. (Pratt, 1987: 60, her own italics).

This vision accords very well with my own. I expand Hannerz's model by adding a sociolinguistic perspective that emphasises language spread, and I also want to introduce the concepts of languaculture and discourse. So I want to include certain differentiations into Hannerz's very broad concept of culture.

The Global Ecumene

Hannerz takes interaction at the micro-level as his point of departure, describing cultural flow as a constant alternation between externalisation and interpretation, with the flow passing from person to person in a constant process of distribution and transformation. This process contributes to the production and reproduction of the social system and the single person as an individual and a social being:

> … it is … in part a consequence of the cultural flow through a population that a social system is created and recreated. As people make their contributions to that flow, they are themselves becoming constructed as individuals and social beings. (Hannerz, 1992a: 14)

This cultural process takes place both at the societal micro- and the macro-level. It occurs partly in the concrete interaction between people in interpersonal situations, but also at higher levels, right up to the highest level: the global level, via the distribution of goods and mass communication.[7] Hannerz, then, adopts a macro-anthropological perspective. He studies, among other things, how cultural distribution processes of various, possibly global, extent result in local mixes. He states that he is particularly interested 'in the sources of diversity and in its consequences' (Hannerz, 1992a: 11), or, to use an umbrella concept: 'the organization of diversity'.

One of Hannerz's key concepts is 'the global ecumene'.[8] It is a term by which he seeks to conceptualise interconnections and complexity at a global level:

> Cultural interconnections increasingly reach across the world. More than ever, there is a global ecumene. The entities we routinely call cultures are becoming more like subcultures within this wider entity, with all that this suggests in terms of fuzzy boundaries and more or less arbitrary delimitation of analytical units. To grasp this fact of globalization . . is the largest task at present confronting a macroanthropology of culture. (Hannerz, 1992a: 218)

Hannerz emphasises that cultural flow takes place in real time and has a direction; it is socially organised and characterised by power structures. At the global level, the main cultural flow passes from the world's cultural centres to the periphery, but there is also a flow that passes from the periphery in towards the centres, as people on the periphery create new culture by utilising both imported and local resources. He deals with various forms of transnational migration and with such types as 'the cosmopolitan' and 'the local'. And he includes certain studies of cultural flow in transnational mass media.

Four Frameworks of Cultural Flow

Hannerz suggests that an analytical distinction be drawn between four different frameworks of cultural flow when studying its social organisation: forms of life, the market, the state and social movements.

Forms of life organise cultural flow within the practical spheres of everyday life, where life is reproduced locally from day to day, in the family, at school, at work, in the local area. The various forms of life (e.g. self-employed businessman, student, etc.) leave their special mark on the cultural flow, and they are to a great extent unconscious or implicit, routine, full of repetitions and redundancy.

The market organises cultural flow by distributing goods, by marketing them and via distribution by influencing the lives and self-perception of various groups. All goods presumably have a cultural aspect, some meaning or other, perhaps an aesthetic, intellectual, emotional appeal. This is a fairly central organisation of cultural flow: goods are sent out onto the market, advertising is spread, for example, via the media. But alongside the large monopoly formations there are also many smaller centres, many producers who compete among themselves for the market and the cultural content of consumption. The market can operate over considerable distances across all possible political units, cultural communities and forms of life.

The state is in particular characterised by its power to control and regulate cultural flow within its own territory. Cultural flow is especially from the centre outwards, circulating in the various cultural apparati of the state, the education system, the social services, the judicial system, public-service TV, etc. It can, for example, play a major role in the production and reproduction of ideas concerning distinctive national characteristics, national identity, etc.

Movements – social and cultural movements and subcultures such as environmental movements, feminist movements, religious movements, ethnic and nationalist movements – organise cultural flow in a relatively conscious and explicit way, and flow typically occurs in an outward-going, missionising movement, from individual to individual.

These four frameworks are naturally very general as tools and have to be more precisely defined in a concrete analysis. Here one can also study them in their mutual relations: how they interact with or counteract each other in the global ecumene and the local 'organisation of diversity'. In Chapter 12 I will use the model when analysing the teaching sequence *Tour de France*.

Hannerz vs. Friedman

Hannerz saw the global ecumene as being mainly intended as a culture-theoretical counterpart to the concept of the world system, of which the British historian E. Wallerstein is the chief representative (e.g. Wallerstein, 1974). The world-system theory is a politico-economic theory of how capitalism has gradually created a worldwide system of relations between states of various weight: core, semiperiphery and periphery. In this otherwise important theory the cultural category has a weak position, as culture here is mainly understood as an ideology to defend, or resist, the system (Wallerstein, 1990).

The American-Swedish social anthropologist J. Friedman is one of those who – during the same period as Hannerz – has worked on developing an alternative theory of the global system, in which the analysis of culture is better developed. This tendency is referred to as 'global systemic anthropology'. The main idea of this theory is that the global (capitalist) system of economic relations is expressed partly in certain institutional processes, partly in certain cultural processes. The institutional processes can be the formation of various transnational institutions and organisations such as the World Bank, the Catholic Church or the international tourist industry. The cultural processes can be various forms of meaning-assignment that have to do with the global arena: identities, identifications and other representations that are products of a global cultural awareness, e.g. diaspora identities, the dream of travelling round the world, the formation of concepts such as world music, world citizen, etc.

In the discussion between Hannerz and Friedman, Friedman criticises Hannerz for culturalism and for having an essentialist approach to the concept of culture, while Hannerz for his part is sceptical about the 'systemness' of the world.

Friedman firstly states that Hannerz has culturalist tendencies by virtue of the fact that he does not include his frameworks of cultural flow to any great extent in an understanding of the more material global economic relations. Hannerz replies that if one uses the system concept 'one could get trapped in rather unproductive debates over the "systemness" of the world' (Hannerz, 1996: 172). To a certain extent, I side with Friedman here. Hannerz could be a bit more precise, in my opinion, regarding the historical and politico-economic basis for power structures and centre-periphery relations in the world. A symptom of this is that the existence of transnational companies does not occur at all in his theory of cultural flow. On the other hand, Hannerz, by virtue of his interactionist approach and the network approach, is better than Friedman at conceptualising the relationship between the micro-level and the macro-level.

Secondly, Friedman criticises Hannerz's thoughts concerning cultural creolisation. Hannerz has gained inspiration from sociolinguistic studies of linguistic pidginisation and creolisation processes (he refers to Mühlhäusler, 1986) and reshaped these into his own theory of cultural creolisation. Cultural creolisation he describes as a process that is the result of types of cultural flow that, historically speaking, have been separate but which now coalesce and interact in a mutual centre-periphery relationship:

> Creole cultures – like creole languages – are intrinsically of mixed origin, the confluence of two or more widely separate historical currents which interact in what is basically a center/perifery relationship. (Hannerz, 1992a: 264)

Friedman feels that Hannerz is now thinking of the concept of culture in terms of purity and mixing, i.e. he selects certain cultural identities as being more 'mixed' than others (Friedman, 1994: 208). Friedman is right in this, I feel, and I find the whole concept of cultural creolisation problematic, because it imports an idea about systems and system mixing – an idea which is not totally without foundation within sociolinguistics – into the area of cultural analysis, where such an idea quickly becomes too constrictive: cultural phenomena (that are not linguistically formed) do not have the nature of a system to the same extent as linguistic phenomena have.

Thirdly, Friedman feels that Hannerz has a reifying and essentialist approach to the concept of culture, since he uses the flow metaphor as his central metaphor. This metaphor means that there is something that flows, i.e. a liquid of some kind. In principle, Friedman is right, but the question is: what can be used as a replacement?

The process of globalisation indisputably comprises 'something' that moves purely concretely: people in various forms of migration, goods and currency in circulation. And signals are transmitted via the vibration of sound waves and other forms of 'wave'. The more traditional concepts of 'cultural spread' and 'cultural diffusion' also presuppose 'something' that spreads out. It is probably impossible to avoid reifying metaphors in this area. I feel that metaphors can be highly productive, but they are of course problematic if they distort the discourse. So I feel that one can perfectly well use the flow metaphor if one bears the reifying tendency in mind and is aware of the fact that cultural flow constantly transforms itself in the process of externalisation and interpretation. Hannerz himself says, in reply to Friedman's criticism:

> Perhaps the imagery of flow is a little treacherous, to the extent that it suggests unimpeded transportation, rather than the infinite and problematic occurrence of transformation between internal and external loci. Yet I find the flow metaphor useful – for one thing, because it captures one of the paradoxes of culture. When you see a river from afar, it may look like a blue (or green, or brown) line across a landscapeòË something of awesome permanence. But at the same time, 'you cannot step into the same river twice', for it is always moving, and only in this way does it achieve its durability. The same way with culture – even as you perceive structure, it is entirely dependent on ongoing process. (Hannerz, 1992a: 4).

The flow metaphor has here become a river metaphor, and that too has its limitations: a river has banks on both sides and ends up in a sea or a lake, does cultural flow do that, too? On the other hand, one cannot do without metaphors, and language and culture pedagogy needs, in my opinion, to develop its metaphors. In relation to the usual static image of language teaching as an isolated learning space where linguistic and cultural learning take place, there is at any rate a crying need for metaphors that present language teaching as a practice that lets something 'into' the learning space and lets something 'out' into the outside world – a practice that transforms cultural flow in its special way. Despite everything, I believe that Hannerz's theory is a good starting point for such a development.

Hannerz's descriptive model with its four frameworks is thus not a historical one. It does not say anything about *why* flow takes place, or what impels it. Hannerz distances himself explicitly from the world-system theory as put forward by Wallerstein, and in doing so he is saying that he does not want to refer to explicatory models of a more structuralist, Marxist type. But he does not come up with a really explicit alternative, apart from the rather loose concept of the global ecumene. As I am not concentrating on historical issues in this book, I do not intend to attempt to link the discussion of linguistic, discursive and cultural flow directly to a macro-historical theory of global processes. I will make do with pointing out that I find views like those expressed in Jameson (1984) and Harvey (1990) fruitful insofar as they are trying to explain postmodern cultural development as a result of forms of logic that stem from capitalist organisation – with the emphasis in Harvey's case on flexible accumulation and development in the phenomenon 'time-space compression'.

Conclusion

This chapter has presented the most important culture-theoretical reference for my analysis of the relationship between language and culture. Ulf Hannerz's approach to cultural analysis is macro-anthropological and he stands for a dynamic, network-oriented view of culture, which in many points is in accordance with the sociolinguistic view of language that I develop in Chapters 6 and 7. At the same time, I have certain reservations about aspects of his theory, especially the weak link to economic structures and transnational economic dynamics.

Notes

1.   Hannerz also refers here to Bourdieu's habitus concept.
2.   In this sense, Hannerz is continuing in a cognitive anthropological tradition which emphasises that culture is socially distributed. This is a tradition that is interested in the relationship between culture and personality and that at the same time includes social variation and diversity and includes such anthropol-

ogists as Anthony Wallace and Theodore Schwartz. Wallace has, for example, elaborated another of Hannerz's important concepts: 'the organization of diversity' (a concept whose opposite is 'the replication of uniformity') (Wallace, 1961).

3. He refers to a discussion of the micro-macro issue in Knorr-Cetina, 1981. Knorr-Cetina is a cognitive sociologist who is in favour of a 'representation hypothesis' in the relation between micro- and macro-level: The macro-level is not seen as a special level of social reality: 'Rather it is seen to reside *within* these micro-episodes where it results from the *structuring practices* of agents' (Knorr-Cetina, 1981: 34, italics in the original). This practice is based on the participants' representations of the situation as a whole ('macro-constructions'): expectations, allegations, fear, strategic considerations, etc.

4. Cf. also his books *Exploring the City* from 1980 and *Transnational Connections* from 1996.

5. Hannerz, together with such figures as the Norwegian social anthropologist Fredrik Barth, is among those who took the initiative to set up *The European Association of Social Anthropologists* (EASA), which held its first conference in Coimbra in 1990 (see Kuper, 1992). This association attempts to define a new European synthesis of the two otherwise relatively separate main traditions within anthropology: American cultural anthropology and British social anthropology.

6. There admittedly already was a branch of sociolinguistics in Europe that dealt with contact linguistics (cf. for example Goebl, 1996), but possibly Pratt and Hannerz were/are unaware of this. It is not particularly Cultural Studies-inspired, either, as Hannerz and Pratt are.

7. Hannerz also speaks of 'unfree flow', which one can see, for example, in censorship and industrial, bank and state secrets.

8. *Oikumene* is Greek and in antiquity means 'the known part of the inhabited world'. In modern times the concept has been used by the American anthropologist A. Kroeber (1945).

Chapter 6

A Sociolinguistic View of Language

Introduction

In this chapter I start off with the fundamental view of language. I describe what I conceive to be the two 'natural' loci of language, linguistic practice and linguistic resources, placing these in relation to an 'artificial' locus: the discursive, metalinguistic construction of the language system. An analysis of the relationship between language and culture must therefore start with a basic distinction being made between three points of view concerning language: a sociological, a psychological and a system-oriented view.

Linguistic Practice

Linguistic practice as acts of identity

Among the various functions of linguistic practice which, along with Halliday, one can sum up as the interpersonal, the ideational and the textual metafunction, I would like here to emphasise an aspect of the interpersonal, namely linguistic acts as acts of identity. I would refer to the work of the sociolinguists Le Page and Tabouret-Keller on linguistic acts of identity in their book *Acts of Identity* (1985). Le Page and Tabouret-Keller worked in particular in the Creole-speaking Caribbean area and among West Indian groups in London. In these distinctly multilingual contexts, they have studied the factors that influence the choice of language by various individuals as well as the choice of pronunciation, grammar, etc. in connection with various types of contact and in various ethno-cultural contexts. This focuses on the symbolic value of language choice and its significance for the ongoing constitution of identity in the various contexts. Linguistic practice is seen as 'a series of *acts of identity* in which people reveal both their personal identity and their search for social roles' (Le Page & Tabouret-Keller, 1985: 14, italics in the original).

As Le Page and Tabouret-Keller formulate it, the individual's linguistic resources are a 'repertoire of socially-marked systems' (Le Page & Tabouret-Keller, 1985: 116), a repertoire that places him/her in a position to operate extremely smoothly in a whole range of different situations that make various demands. This individuals do with the aid of a special form of 'projection' that consists in their 'projecting' their inner understanding of the outside world, via their use of language, onto the social world, including their expectations concerning what role their linguistic practice – and that of other people – plays in social interaction. This projection is an invitation to other people to share their special model of the world, and it is a hope of an indication of solidarity on the part of those who wish to identify themselves with it. To the extent that they gain a positive response to their projections, their linguistic practice becomes more regular in the contexts in question – it tends to become more focused. To the extent, on the other hand, to which they are obliged to regulate their linguistic practice and adapt it to others, it becomes more variable, more diffuse. But within a group in which the members identify themselves with each other, total linguistic practice will over time become more focused. This mechanism of linguistic practice will, then, in certain contexts form systems that are more diffuse, in other contexts systems that are more focused.

Even though Le Page and Tabouret-Keller have formulated their theory in multilingual, relatively 'diffuse' language communities, they believe that the theory is also capable of shedding light on more homogeneous, 'focused' language communities – and I agree with them on this. It seems fruitful to me, for example, to view language teaching in this light, including an investigation of the various problems associated with identity in connection with the choice of language (see also Chapter 7).

Constitution of identity is an important part of the field of interest of the Cultural Studies tradition and of the postmodern trend in general, so one can say that Le Page and Tabouret-Keller, by virtue of their particular approach, describe linguistic practice as a form of cultural practice. Thereby, their approach can be related to what I was looking at earlier in connection with Kramsch: the idea that linguistic practice in itself embodies culture (Chapter 1).

Linguistic practice is seen here as constitution of identity, but at the same time it is possible to deduce purely practical aspects of the choice of language. When, for example, one chooses to use English in Scandinavian contexts, this will normally be justified by the desire not to exclude anyone from understanding what is going on. Nevertheless, there is in the choice of English an identity dimension that connects the local choice of English to the status of the English language at a global level. The choice of English is both a practical and a cultural choice. Similar considerations can be made concerning the choice of language in language teaching.

Linguistic practice as normative acts

There is an aspect of linguistic acts of identity that I would like to emphasise: that linguistic practice is a unity of behaviour and unconscious norms. By 'linguistic behaviour' I mean actual linguistic behaviour that can be observed. Linguistic behaviour is always accompanied by unconscious linguistic norms that regulate and develop it.

That linguistic behaviour and unconscious linguistic norms cannot and should not be distinguished is one of the points argued by the British sociolinguist Deborah Cameron in her book *Verbal Hygiene* (1995). She deals with the problem that (socio)linguists shrink from assessing linguistic practice, while the population in general is very interested in linguistic norms and values. She criticises the self-perception of linguistics as a professional field, which operates with a clear distinction between description and prescription, and which calls for the professional linguist to refrain from commenting on what is linguistically speaking more or less correct, good or beautiful, and only to express an opinion on to what extent a linguistic practice is 'appropriate' or not – i.e. whether it accords with the communicative requirements that are made by the concrete situation. Her point is that the concept of 'appropriate' is in itself normative and that not even linguists can avoid dealing with language normatively – like everybody else. The ban on prescriptivism plays a pivotal role in professional linguistic identity: 'Prescriptivism thus represents the threatening Other, the forbidden; it is a spectre that haunts linguistics and a difference that defines linguistics' (Cameron, 1995: 5).

The essential thing is, as Cameron emphasises, to be clear about where these more or less conscious norms and prescriptions come from, who has formulated them, whom they are addressed to, and to what end ('look for the hidden agenda', Cameron, 1995: 226). Linguistic practice always involves linguistic norms. No linguistic practice could exist without such norms, and each time one uses language, the norms are reproduced and reformed and linguistic identity is constituted. Linguistic prescription is part of social practice, and there is a struggle and a negotiation involved as there is for other forms of social practice.

Cameron's book is a contribution to the debate about linguistic essentialism: language is not an organism whose 'natural development' ought to be given free rein ('linguistic Darwinism'). Language users are actors in relation to the development of language, and certain groups of actors have more influence than others. Linguistic norms are historically variable and contingent. In spite of this, there is an unusually strong orthodoxy within this field: norms relating to the standard language are conceived in general as descriptions of what language *is* like.

Cameron deals with linguistic norms throughout the spectrum, from the more or less unconscious to the more or less conscious. In doing so, she glides from a focus on unexpressed norms that accompany and regulate linguistic behaviour to a focus on expressed norms with a metalinguistic content: they have to do with language and its correct usage. The latter are discourses on language – either discourse by language users about their own use of language, or more codified indications of correct language. However, my opinion is that the unconscious, unexpressed forms belong to the description of linguistic practice, while the conscious, expressed norms belong to discursive constructions of language (see later on in this chapter). In regard to the discursive constructions, it is content that is in focus; which language the content is formulated in is secondary. As is known, discourses concerning the right use of, for example, English can be expressed in other languages than English (more about this understanding of discourse in Chapter 9).

Speech and writing; paralanguage and kinesics; social, private and inner speech

In dealing with the relationship between language and culture, it is important to include the various forms in which linguistic practice can manifest itself.

Firstly, it is necessary to distinguish between language as speech and as writing[1], and thus also between spoken language norms and those of the written language. It is well known that the prescription of the written languages has played a particular role in, for example, the building-up of the European nations. And when one looks at the processes of spread it is possible to observe that language does not spread along the same paths when in the spoken form as in the written form. Furthermore, the written language has played an important role in the development of modern-language subjects. The teaching of foreign languages is based historically speaking on a written language tradition, and even though today teaching is usually in both the written and the spoken language, the written language tradition still leaves its distinct imprint.

Secondly, one has to operate with a broad understanding of linguistic practice that also includes paralanguage and (language-accompanying and -complementing) kinesics, which is already usual within anthropological and ethnographical research in oral communication. So, in the following, linguistic practice covers three parts: verbal language in the more restricted sense, paralanguage and kinesics.[2]

The concept of paralanguage refers to the features of pronunciation that are not – as, for example, are individual sounds, stress and intonation –

compulsory elements of the phonological structure of utterances. Paralinguistic features include loudness of voice and pitch, tempo, pauses and hesitating, expressive intonation, sighs, laughter, clearing one's throat, etc. Paralanguage deals then with the role of the speech organs in oral communication (Poyatos, 1993). Vocal qualities contribute to the formation of meaning in various ways. They can reinforce or foreground particular meanings; they can possibly contradict what is being said verbally; they can be used for irony, for communicating emotions, etc.[3] The concept of paralanguage is normally used in connection with the spoken language. But in my opinion it can also be used in connection with the written language. Here, typographical features and handwriting can contribute to the formation of meaning, cf., for example, the use of exclamation marks and underlinings.

Kinesics is part of what is more comprehensively referred to as nonverbal communication. It includes the use of the body (apart from the speech organs) to accompany and expand oral communication. Kinesics can be divided into subgroups such as facial expressions and gestures.[4] Like paralanguage, kinesics consists of a number of expressive elaborations and differentiations which in many instances can facilitate the understanding process, but which can also lead to misunderstandings, cf. research into communication barriers in intercultural communication.[5]

Research into intercultural communication has been quite interested in 'culture-specific' differences in paralanguage and especially kinesics, i.e. differences that can be linked to language differences (e.g. the thought that there could be a particular French form of gesticulating that accompanies French speech, etc.). There is not room here to give an account of that research here; I will make do with underlining the fact that these aspects of linguistic practice can vary considerably both individually, socially and in terms of gender. It would seem doubtful to me that parallels can be drawn to any great extent between the use of a particular verbal language and particular paralinguistic and kinetic features. That verbal language, paralanguage and kinesics form a unity is first and foremost a true assertion at the generic level: the spoken language as such will always be accompanied by paralanguage and kinesics in one form or other. But at the differential level I would think that there are relatively few parallels. If, for example, one takes the fact that for a Danish native speaker 'yes' can be expressed by a nod and 'no' by a shake of the head, this is not *specific* to Danish but to a larger cultural area.

Thirdly, one has – like the Vygotsky tradition – to operate with an extended concept of language which, over and above normal social speech (linguistic interaction, oral and written) also includes private speech, where the individual speaks out loud 'to himself' or 'to herself', and inner speech, which takes place in silence in the individual's consciousness. Ontogenetically speaking, the most important point here is that parents and the young infant enter into a social interaction that is also linguistic, and that this social speech is gradually internalised in the child, first in the form of private speech and later in the form of inner speech. Both children and adults use all three forms of speech in their various activities and learning processes, including the solving of practical and intellectual problems.

The three forms of speech are naturally also used in foreign and second language learning, and this is something that language pedagogues have begun to show an interest in, e.g. Lantolf (1999). One investigates, for example, how learners actively develop their language via self-regulation with the aid of private speech.

This approach is fruitful in my opinion in relation to the multilingual nature of language teaching. For here the target language meets up with learners' inner speech, which for a long time will initially typically be in the first language.

In the next chapter I will place the concept of linguistic practice in a macro-perspective when describing linguistic practice as taking place in social networks of varying sizes.

Linguistic Resources

The individual's linguistic life-history

The individual develops his or her linguistic resources throughout life.[6] Both the first language(s) and possible later additional languages are constantly being developed, if of course they are not forgotten or repressed. The individual moves over the years through a number of more or less variable networks and is thereby influenced when it comes to linguistic practice and the utilisation of the linguistic resources that have been developed. This development takes place in complex cultural contexts (societal structures, networks, linguistic and discursive communities, etc.). This will be dealt with in more detail in Chapter 7.

The linguistic resources are both productive and receptive/interpretive. They include social, private and inner speech as well as paralanguage and kinesics – and in most instances a more or less well-developed written competence. The linguistic resources are integrated into an idiolectal system that comprises the first language and possibly other languages.[7] As Le Page and Tabouret-Keller write, the linguistic resources in the individual are a repertoire of systems that include both his/her own language use and his/her expectations about the language use of others and of other groups. Each person's repertoire contains very rich notions of and expectations about other people's use of language, but the repertoires of these various people coincide only partially. Everyone uses their own idiolectal system in order, among other things, to express and process their own identities, and thus all contribute to the language community becoming more or less focused or diffuse. This also applies, for example, to the small language community of the language class.

It is important to look at a person's entire linguistic biography and at the circumstances under which that person has acquired the various languages. The period when one has language teaching fills in most cases only a small part of life. It is therefore necessary to look at language learning in a second or foreign language as an element of an entire life history. This also means dealing with how learners make use of their other linguistic resources and what use they make of their language proficiencies later on – if they do so at all. In this way, it is possible to analyse what specific role the teaching sequence has/sequences have had for the individual's language learning and general linguistic socialisation – in both a positive and a negative sense.

There are a number of competing terms in this area, including 'resources', 'repertoire' and 'competence'. The concept of competence has been much used within language and culture pedagogy, but I intend not to use it as a general term, as it has a positivist tinge and is too narrow in its view of language. The positivist element lies in the fact that the concept of 'communicative competence' is closely linked to the educational context and to individual assessment and testing in relation to general labour-market requirements. There is nothing wrong with assessment as such, but the multilingual development of the individual comprises more than what can or should be assessed, e.g. the ability to exploit the prestige of the English language by means of a code-switching between Danish and English, or experiences of linguistic prejudices, such as: Arabic is inferior to Danish; German is an ugly language, etc. The concept of competence is thus also based on a concept of language that is too narrow: it does not include metalinguistic attitudes and beliefs, and it does not include private and inner speech. Furthermore, it typically only deals with one (standard) language at a time; it does not contain any sociolinguistic understanding of the multilingual/plurilingual individual. So, for me, competence is a specialised subcategory under resources: when I use the term 'competence', it is with reference to the skills and knowledge aspects of the linguistic resources that it is relevant and possible to assess.

One could well use the term 'repertoire' (as many sociolinguists do), but it too seems to be a bit too limited, as it focuses on linguistic practice and does not clearly include metalinguistic attitudes and beliefs. The concept of resources, on the other hand, can include all of this – and it can more-over be used in relation to the other levels I will be dealing with: discourse and (other) culture, as I use the terms 'discursive resources' and (other) 'cultural resources'.[8]

Collective linguistic resources

Linguistic resources are connected to single individuals and their individual biographies. Single individuals are the elementary social actors. But it is also necessary to operate with collective social actors such as organisations, institutions and companies – and these can be said to have collective linguistic resources: a number of first-language resources and possibly a number of second- and foreign-language resources. These resources can be used and developed by the organisation in a more or less positive way, and thereby contribute to linguistic flows in a particular fashion.

A school class can also be said to develop collective linguistic resources, e.g. in language teaching. Work often takes place in the classroom in small groups and plenum, with an understanding and discussion of texts and perhaps with the production of new texts. Here, the class/teacher can make use of and develop this resource in a more or less positive way in relation to the multilingual resources, in relation to both speech and writing, both verbal language, paralanguage and kinesics, and both social, private and inner speech. One ought to think not only in terms of a number of aggregated individual competences but also in terms of cooperative and mutually complementary resources.

The Linguistic System as a Discursive Construction

All metalinguistic discourse constructs its objects in one way or another with an intention that is more or less conscious. When I write about linguistic resources, we are of course dealing with a discursive construction in which I, among other things, weigh up which of the three terms 'competence', 'repertoire' or 'resource' is the most precise, adequate, elastic, etc. When I write about linguistic practice, we are dealing with a construction of – in this case – a dynamic image of it. But there are certain constructions that have a special status, and which are particularly problematic, and these are constructions of 'language' or 'the language system' as a unity.

As a number of people have advanced in the 1980s and 1990s, the idea of 'language' or 'the language system' is a particular historical construction (Bourne, 1988; Cameron, 1995; Fairclough, 1989; Harris, 1981; Le Page & Tabouret-Keller, 1985; Mey, 1985; Milroy & Milroy, 1985). I am mainly referring here to Roy Harris, who has argued in several publications in favour of the idea that 'language' is a second-order construct in relation to linguistic communication (linguistic practice), which is that which really exists (Harris, 1981, 1998). Harris talks about 'the language myth'. He sharply criticises linguistic structuralism, with reference to, among others, the late Wittgenstein.[9]

That the idea of 'language' is a special historical construction does not mean that one should refrain from developing theories about the language system. But it does mean that one must be aware that 'language' is not an essence that precedes or 'lies behind' linguistic practice and linguistic resources. It is linguistic practice and individuals' linguistic resources that are primary (incl. the unconscious norms), and the idea of 'language' is a secondary construct, a theoretical model, which by the way cannot avoid being normative in some sense or other. One could call it an intentionally created locus for language. It is a locus that has played and plays an important societal role.

The discursive construction of 'language' is, historically speaking, very old, and in most societies an idea has presumably developed about 'our' way of speaking in relation to 'their' way of speaking. But the idea of 'language' has probably developed fully in connection with the development of the various systems of writing and the written language. It has developed as the attempt by various groups to provide norms for and to standardise linguistic practice, especially in its written form.[10]

The discourse on language has – at any rate in many of the European languages – included a conceptualisation that has made it possible to talk about language as 'something': a whole, an object, an organism or a person, depending on the discursive tendencies. An idea has been developed – at least in the European national tradition – of language as a cohesive whole, most clearly developed in the structuralist era from the 1920s to the 1950s.

The conceptions applying at any time to language must therefore be seen as constructions determined by aims and situation. These conceptions can have purely practical justifications, but they will always have at least latent ideological content, because in one way or another they reduce actual complexity in linguistic practice and linguistic resources. A choice is always made among the many variations of linguistic practice, and this choice is nominated as constituting language, i.e. the standard. This activity creates the illusion that it is language that really exists, and that linguistic practice is derived from it. It creates the idea that there is a language that 'is used' and that there exist 'language users'. Language is naturalised and essentialised.

Some of the metalinguistic ideas and theories are relatively objectively oriented and can base themselves on comprehensive empirical studies, e.g. quantitative and qualitative sociolinguistic studies, or corpus-linguistic studies; others are idealisations without any cohesive empirical basis. In the latter case, the constructions are particularly accessible to ideological exploitation, as is clear when one looks at the development of the national language idea in connection with the process of nationalisation, especially in Europe (Anderson, 1991 (1983); Milroy & Milroy, 1985). The generalising assertions of culture pedagogy concerning the inseparability of language and culture belong to this latter category.

The ideas concerning the individual languages (differentially) and language as such (generically) are thus purposive constructions that have been created in particular historical situations by 'laymen' and various groups of 'professionals': philosophers, teachers, authors, translators, philologists, linguists, etc. The individual language has been reified and thereby clearly marked off from other 'things'. It has been described as a totality in grammar books, dictionaries, dissertations on the history of language, etc. The ideological content lies partly in the concrete choice that will always be undertaken regarding when the boundary goes between the one language and the other language, and between language and everything else. It lies partly in the language of which social groups one has selected to represent the language in question: practically always the linguistic practice of the groups that are politically and culturally dominant.

Discourses on language are widespread and diverse (cf. Schieffelin *et al.*, 1998) and they are naturally to be taken seriously, among other things because they have a real significance for the development of people's linguistic practice, both oral and written. They are part of what Cameron calls linguistic hygiene, which she refers to as 'the popular culture of language' (Cameron, 95: 31).

Discourses on language are useful and necessary tools in many practical contexts, even though one can always discuss their ideological content. One of the fields of practice in which discourses on language are absolutely indispensable is language teaching. At any rate, in teacher education and in the personal reflection of teachers on practice, and – many people would now claim – also in teaching itself in connection with the development of pupils' awareness of language, language use and language acquisition. Today, language teaching can hardly take place without the use of reference books such as grammar books and monolingual and bilingual dictionaries.

A central aspect of the view of language in non-sociolinguistic theory and in popular conceptions is the idea of homogeneous, unchanging language. Language is seen as an – idealised – uniform and integrated system, and language change is regarded as decline. This conception is extremely common in the concept of the target language in language and culture pedagogy. The idea of linguistic homogeneity and constancy, which is an important part of the national language idea, is a persistent one, and it contrasts with the large linguistic complexity that can be documented empirically: firstly, all linguistic practice is variable by virtue of its significance for the ongoing construction of identity in social interaction; secondly, linguistic practice is in certain cases so complex that it is hard to conceal that it has several different historical origins: the use of code-switching, the use of pidgin and creole languages, the use of what can be referred to as real mixed languages.[11]

The Loci of Language: 2 + 1

Linguistic practice and linguistic resources in the individual are thus the two necessary and mutually prerequisite forms of existence for language. Linguistic resources can develop only by virtue of linguistic practice, and linguistic practice cannot develop without the existence of linguistic resources in the participants. Linguistic practice represents the basic social function of language, and it is from here that we get our empirical data about language. Linguistic resources are no less real, but they are not accessible to observation, except to a certain extent via introspection.

This mode of thought runs completely parallel to that expressed by Hannerz regarding culture more generally. He distinguishes (as dealt with in Chapter 5) between the internal and external locus of culture:

> Culture has two kinds of loci: in human minds, and in public forms. But it is not in The Mind, or in just any minds. Rather, it is in particular ways in particular minds; and when it is public, it is made available through social life by particular people, to particular people. (Hannerz, 1992a: 7)

To the two fundamental loci for language a third – at least in historical time – must be added, which is a discursive construction that in the last resort rests on observations of linguistic practice, but which even so can be conceptualised as a highly abstract entity. This construction (or family of constructions) has mainly been developed to control and regulate linguistic practice, and it also takes place in the societal process via linguistic prescription and standardisation, language policy, suppression or favorisation respectively of particular languages and language varieties, etc. But they are naturally also indispensable – as I have emphasised – for research and practical work on language.

Within the broader cultural area that Hannerz deals with it is probably not very meaningful to operate with similar constructions. There may be areas of cultural practice that display a pattern that justifies constructing a system for it, e.g. 'the Danish Christmas lunch', 'European pedagogical ideas since Rousseau', 'the world's national flags', or 'organisational culture at Lego'. But, as I touched on in Chapter 3, within modern cultural research, including anthropology, one ceased several decades ago to operate with cultural 'mega-systems' such as a whole 'national culture', understood as a single integrated essence. It is not Hannerz's intention in Hannerz (1992a) to deal with, or directly criticise, conceptions of national cultures as essences. But since his entire approach focuses on (transnational) cultural flow and cultural complexity, it implicitly presupposes a critique of such conceptions.

Linguistic practice is probably that part of the broader cultural practice that is most structured. For that reason, it is hardly strange that thinking in terms of systems or structures is more prominent in linguistics than in perhaps any other social or cultural science. But it is therefore all the more important to deconstruct the tendency to think in systems, especially in its more abstract variants: to show that, even though thinking in terms of systems rests on observable patterns and regularities in linguistic practice, it is in itself a historical construction in which a number of politico-ideological attitudes are embedded. This is not least important in language pedagogy, and especially in foreign-language pedagogy, which has been particularly immune to insights concerning social variation in linguistic practice – and concerning the relationship between language, discourse and power.

Conclusion

In this chapter I have emphasised placing the concept of 'language' in its proper context. It is linguistic practice and linguistic resources that are the primary linguistic loci. But there is also a third locus, the idea of the language system, which is a discursive construction that has had and still has a considerable societal importance – as far as Europe is concerned in roughly the last three centuries, in connection with the standardisation of the various vernacular languages and the development of the national written language. The idea of a national language has been used to ostracise many dialects and sociolects from 'accepted society', but it has also been used to create useful tools – for language teaching: grammar books, dictionaries, etc. Thus it is important for the discussion in the following chapters to distinguish between three points of view:

- the sociological point of view: linguistic practice;
- the psychological point of view: linguistic resources;
- the system-oriented point of view: the linguistic system.

Notes

1. I am speaking here of the absolute difference that consists in whether linguistic practice is mediated via speech (or signs in sign language) or via writing (or derivative forms such as Morse). At the same time, there exists a wide range of speech and writing genres where there is of course not an absolute difference but a gradual transition between many various types of linguistic practice, stretching between two poles: a practice that is decidedly close to speech and one that is decidedly close to the written language (described by Tannen, 1982 as a speech-writing continuum). (I will not be dealing with sign language as such in this book.)
2. Fernando Poyatos, who has worked on paralanguage studies, speaks of 'the basic triple structure of communication' (Poyatos, 1993: 121f.).
3. Gumperz has, among other things, examined the importance of paralanguage in inter-ethnic conversations, where tempo and pauses are among the contextualisation clues that help the conversation partners make inferences and thereby better understand the communicative intention (Gumperz, 1992).
4. Kinesics accompanies oral communication. But there are also written derivatives, such as smileys in electronic communication.
5. Not all kinetic communication is language-accompanying and can therefore be linked to the concept of language. True mime, or pantomime, is not, for example, in my opinion part of the concept of language (the concept of verbal language).
6. As I emphasised in Chapter 1, it is not my intention to deal with cognitive or broader psychological and socio-psychological processes. I therefore do not look at how linguistic resources develop, only (and very briefly) at what they contain.
7. I do not intend here to deal with the comprehensive research into bilingualism and its cognitive and other psychological implications (see, for example, Romaine, 1995 and Pavlenko, 1999).
8. There is an inspiration from Bourdieu concealed here (e.g. Bourdieu, 1977 (1972)). My reason for not using Bourdieu's habitus concept in this connection is that importing part of his theory would involve deliberations concerning the use of other concepts of his, such as disposition, capital, strategy and field. Even though these concepts are fruitful, I feel that the use of them would distort my process-oriented approach, which emphasises linguistic, discursive and cultural flows.
9. It is a post-structuralist criticism, but he does not refer to other representatives of it, e.g Derrida, Kristeva and Bakhtin.

10. Bourne refers, for example, to A. Howatt's studies of how the English (written) language was fixed in 17th century England (Bourne, 1988).
11. For example, a language such as michif, which is spoken by descendants of French-Canadian fur-hunters and Cree and Ojibwe Indians in central and western Canada. The language is made up of elements from French and Cree respectively. Among other things, the vocabulary has a very special composition, since the nouns come from French while the verbs come from Cree. (Bakker, 1997)

Chapter 7

Linguistic Flows and Linguistic Complexity

Introduction

Just as Hannerz places cultural practice within a globalisation framework via the concept of the global ecumene, I would like here to develop the idea of linguistic practice in a global perspective. For that reason, I will consider linguistic practice in this chapter in a larger spatial perspective, as a practice that takes place in social networks by means of which the various languages are spread over greater and lesser distances in the world. After this presentation, I will discuss the contrast between linguistic complexity and linguistic homogeneity in language teaching.

Linguistic Flows in Social Networks

Linguistic practice takes place as a constant process of linguistic production and interpretation, a process in which further construction takes place all the time of intertextual chains of oral and written texts in a particular language – or possibly several. The individual produces texts that are received and understood (in various ways) by other people, and these understandings are then processed and formed in other texts that are sent on, etc. The texts contain a greater or lesser degree of polyphony (Bakhtin, 1981): a diversity of voices that can find expression in the course of the text. The fundamental actor is, as mentioned, the individual, but (s)he can act as part of a greater whole, e.g. an organisation or an institution, and in that way larger social units than single individuals can be linguistic actors.

In the following, I will use as my starting point a network-oriented understanding of linguistic practice: linguistic practice is seen as taking place in social networks of various structures and extents. Such an understanding is also to be found in much of present-day sociolinguistics (J. Milroy, 1992 and many others), but is also shared by many sociologists and anthropologists, including Hannerz.[1]

In the analysis of social networks, one has to distinguish between the description of the nodal points: their social functions, number, etc., and the links between them: the nature, frequency, etc. of the interactions. One must distinguish between the morphological features of the networks: the structure of the links between the various nodal points, and their interactional features: the nature of each single interaction. Networks can be analysed starting with a particular person and his/her networks (an ego-centred network), or with dyadic relations in a particular field, or they can be analysed with a particular thematic focus and a particular organisational delimitation, e.g. teaching conversations in an English class.

The network approach has the advantage of being analytically flexible and offering the opportunity – also when dealing with the macro-level – of retaining the relation to the micro-level: linguistic interaction between single individuals. It enables studies of social relations that develop across societal structures and domains. It also offers the opportunity of studying connections between power relations at the micro-level and macro-level. It can eventually be combined with other approaches, e.g. a Bourdieu-type analysis of linguistic practice and language as a symbolic capital in particular social fields.

Linguistic networks are constituted via actual linguistic interaction and strengthened or weakened by the changing intensity of the interaction and the intertextual chains that are formed.[2] There are spoken language networks and written language networks, with as a rule only little coincidence between them (an example of relatively extended coincidence could be a circle of friends or a family that communicate both orally and via SMS).

Networks exist in some relation or other to the more material societal and institutional structures. For example, the structure of the school and the Danish education system constitutes a framework for the linguistic networks in a school class, but the networks extend beyond the frameworks of the school in many directions and can to a certain extent be traced empirically: networks in relation to TV, the family, the circle of friends, the local newspaper, the chat sites on the Internet, teacher networks, etc.

Moreover, the participants construct communities and identities of a more fluid, provisional nature (S. Hall, 1992): the actors in the actual linguistic networks create communities, both experienced and imagined, local, national and transnational communities built around such things as the subject or profession, family, subculture, religion, lifestyle, etc. With the creation of these communities and identities, boundaries are also created with other communities and identities: differences are set up between 'us' and 'them' (Barth, 1969). The school class, for example, can create cliques and mobbing relations; it can build up an opposition to a parallel class, or it can create a more or less close community with a class in a foreign 'twinned school', etc.

So I distinguish between three levels that develop in a mutual interaction:

- societal structures and domains[3] that are relatively stable, but which in principle are contingent and variable;
- networks that are created and maintained because of the actual interaction in social situations;
- communities and identities that are constituted and formed in (content-oriented) discourses.

A network approach[4] is, as mentioned, analytically flexible, but it can also quickly become extremely complicated. A synchronic description of a network can in itself be complicated, i.e. an individual may participate in various networks at one and the same time (multiplexity). Historically-oriented analyses of networks undergoing change can naturally also become highly complicated, because single individuals ('nodal points') themselves are mobile. Some people move physically over large distances, e.g. in connection with transnational migration, and this naturally influences the range of the networks – and often their intensity as well. It is relevant to include this fact when studying linguistic flows over larger distances – ones that take place when, for example, the language users migrate.

'Linguistic Flows' or 'Language Spread'?

In Chapter 5, I touched on Hannerz's use of the flow metaphor (cultural flow) and discuss Friedman's criticism of it. As I wrote there, I do not believe it is possible to manage in this field without metaphors that have a tendency to reify – the concepts of language spread and linguistic diffusion also assume that 'something' changes its extent or moves. So I intend to retain the term '(linguistic) flows'. It would also have been possible to choose to retain the more traditional term, language spread[5], but I find it more problematic. The concept of language spread induces one to think of spatial movement that has a direction, from the centre to a periphery: from a country/area where the language is a dominant first language to countries/areas where it is not a dominant first language, as, for example, in Kachru's theory of the spread of English in 'the inner circle': Great Britain, USA, Canada, Australia and New Zealand, 'the outer circle': India, Pakistan, Nigeria and other countries that have English as their official language, and the 'expanding circle': the rest of the world, including Denmark (Kachru, 1986). In that way, the theory of language spread becomes a story of the victorious languages. If the theory is to deal with all languages, there must at least be a complementary concept of 'language reduction', or something similar, for there are, as is well known, languages that are on the retreat: the various categories of endangered or moribund languages (Skutnabb-Kangas, 2000).

Unlike the one-sided metaphor of spreading, the network metaphor combined with the flow metaphor enables a more precise description of the relationship between languages and how it develops by virtue partly of language policy decisions at the macro-level, and partly of the choice of language in concrete situations, i.e. more or less conscious language policy at the micro-level. Choices of language in multilingual societies (as, for example, are described by Le Page and Tabouret-Keller) are acts of identity – and via these choices a process takes place that metaphorically can be described as a negotiation between various possible positions, but which have also been referred to as a struggle.[6] The power relations that will always exist in the networks are reproduced and reshaped by the individuals and the other social actors via interaction; in this way, the use of certain languages or language varieties gain ground at the expense of others.

When one focuses on a particular language, some of the networks in which the language is used are clearly more compact and intensive in certain locations than in other locations. The English-speaking network is more compact and intensive in Great Britain than in Denmark. But some networks in Denmark can turn out to be more English-speaking than Danish-speaking, just as there are important non-English language networks among linguistic minorities in Great Britain.

In certain linguistic networks (e.g. in an isolated village) the flow of interactions is relatively stable, and the networks do not change all that much. But what is interesting in the context of this book is the instances where the networks change structure and range. When people migrate, (some of) their linguistic networks become 'stretched' and are potentially linked with new networks in the new location. Therefore, the 'old' networks are potentially weakened, while the 'new' ones are potentially strengthened. When people acquire a new language as a foreign or a second language, they gain access to other linguistic networks that they can combine with those they already participate in. Among other things, they gain access to the written production of the language.[7]

That the linguistic flow moves from the more intensive network, e.g. certain forms of English in England, to the less intensive, e.g. English in various groups in Denmark, can of course be referred to as language spread. But the flow also moves the other way, as, for example, when Danes who have learned English as a foreign language go to England and use the language there. And that would not normally be referred to as language spread.

First Language/Early Second Language vs. Foreign Language/Late Second Language

In this section, I intend to distinguish between various types of linguistic flow, depending on what function the language has for the individual: first language, second language or foreign language. The issue of bilingualism is particularly complex, and I have already (in Chapter 1) mentioned some of the difficulties involved when trying to define the concepts of second language and foreign language in relation to each other. Since biographies of bilingualism can be terribly varied, it is necessary to undertake certain simplifications and to define come canonical instances that make an analytical discussion possible. In the following, I therefore distinguish between two basic types with regard to the function of language for the individual, and – especially in Chapter 8 – argue in favour of the relationship between language and culture being different in the two cases:

- first language / early second language, up to approx. six years;
- foreign language / late second language, from approx. 14 years onwards.

In the first case, the individual acquires the language during an early phase of life mainly independently of instruction. Acquisition takes place as a process that is not only an integral part of but also a prerequisite for the rest of the individual's social and psychological/cognitive development. The first language (possibly first languages) is the primary family language in the home and it is the language that is acquired earliest (although not necessarily the language that the person concerned will be best at, or use most, later on in life). The early second language is a language that is widespread in the environment outside the family and that the child will therefore especially acquire outside the home, among playmates, at kindergarten, etc.

In the second case, the individual acquires, or learns, the language during a phase in life when the fundamental social and psychological/ cognitive development has been completed. Typically, the foreign language is learned at school and at a distance from the environments in which the language is used as a first language. The late second language is acquired as a young person or adult and/or is learned in a teaching context.

One should think in terms of a seamless transition between the two basic types, as is also inferred by the use of the relative concepts 'early' and 'late'. Between them there is a transitional phase which I will refrain from commenting on, as in respect of acquisition it is highly complex (in both linguistic and cultural respects) and contains a much-debated issue concerning critical periods in the language-acquisition process (Ellis, 1994). I will make do with operating with the above-mentioned two basic types in the following.

So I distinguish between two types of linguistic flows: flows of first language or early second language, and flows of foreign language or late second language. Each of these can also be divided into two types: firstly, the acquisition/learning of the language – new language users are added, and they continue to use the language. Secondly, migration: the language users migrate and continue to use the language in their new location. So I therefore distinguish between four situations:

- flows of first language or early second language:
  acquisition/learning and continued use of the language
  migration and continued use of the language;
- flows of foreign language or late second language:
  acquisition/learning and continued use of the language
  migration and continued use of the language.

In these situations we are dealing with the linguistic locus that I have called 'linguistic resources'. There is a focus on linguistic resources that 'flow': People acquire language and thereby develop certain linguistic resources; and/or people migrate, taking their linguistic resources with them.

Flows of First Language or Early Second Language

Acquisition/Learning

Developing one's first language as a child (and as a young person and adult) is a form of linguistic flow, since via the social and cognitive/ psychological acquisition processes, the language gains a new user who can take it further in new networks. The same applies to the second language that is developed at an early age with playmates, etc.

Migration

By means of migration the networks of the individual 'stretch' – one could say that their morphology changes. What happens then with the individual's linguistic resources? When speakers of the first language emigrate, they naturally take their mother tongue with them. But it is not precisely 'language' we are dealing with here but their highly distinctive ways of using the language – their idiolects. They migrate with the special linguistic resources they have developed in the course of their youth: their oral and possibly written resources – productive and receptive. They also take with them the paralanguage and kinesics that they have internalised in the course of their youth – a to a great extent unconscious and important part of their personal identity. They take with them their particular form of private and inner speech. These idiolects develop in the new context, in the partially new networks. They come into contact with other languages, by the individuals involved acquiring a new language that perhaps influences 'the old one'. They probably continue to use the language, possibly in bilingual activities such as translation and teaching. The possibility also exists that they completely drop the use of the language in social interaction in the new networks. That does not necessarily mean that the language disappears from private and inner speech, but it does mean that the social flow of the language has ceased.

Flows of Foreign Language or Late Second Language

Acquisition/Learning

When acquiring a foreign language one already has a first language (or more than one) – and maybe one has a knowledge of other languages. So we are dealing here with an additive and constructive process in which a new language is added to that/those already present. The previous language(s) will probably influence the new language via linguistic transfer, and the new one will perhaps also influence, at certain points, the old one(s) – perhaps via the introduction of words from the new language to the old one(s).[8]

By acquiring/learning a foreign language the individual builds up an interlanguage,[9] that is the person's own idiolect of the target language. Interlanguage displays regularities that are investigated by language acquisition research (cf., for example, Lund, 1997), but it also has its own completely idiosyncratic features, as also applies to the first language. The acquisition/learning process of the single individual has been preceded by a number of specific contexts and learning situations which have left their mark on the final result. Perhaps the person involved has learned to spell perfectly in the foreign language but cannot produce a sufficiently differentiated intonation. Perhaps the person involved has a good grasp of politeness conventions but cannot understand humour in the foreign language. One can have developed fluent oracy and a fumbling literacy, or vice versa. The linguistic identity that is connected to the new language can, then, be highly fragmentary and insecure. But it can also be characterised by the freedom experienced when one is able to express oneself in a language that is not one's first language (Börsch, 1982 and 1987).

When a language is learned as a foreign language in a teaching situation, language learning has, among other things, to do with internalising certain norms, but because of the formal learning situation many of the norms have been conveyed explicitly. Many have with them norms that to a great extent have been verbalised, e.g. 'saucepan inflections' [referring to the paradigm of adjectival inflections] from German teaching.

When one acquires/learns a language as a foreign language, one transfers to a great extent the paralanguage and kinesics that one otherwise normally uses in connection with the first language. The new language is thereby given personal elements that make it one's very 'own' product – as well as to a certain degree a product that one would be able to find in others who are in the same situation as oneself, e.g. those who speak (a version of) the same first language. One also transfers to a considerable extent one's own private and inner speech.

To acquire/learn a language as a late second language has many similarities with acquiring or learning a language as a foreign language. And in cognitive language acquisition research the general attitude is that there is no difference. But when one looks at the social and contextual aspects of second language acquisition/learning, there are of course obvious differences. There are, for example, linguistic networks of a completely different nature and intensity when one acquires the language as a second language, i.e. in an area or a network where the language in question is the dominant first language.

Migration

When one has learned the foreign language, one can of course travel with it – as a tourist, or with the intention of staying longer, possibly emigrating (some foreign-language teaching has, as mentioned, to do more or less directly with preparing pupils for travelling to the target-language countries). Danes who have learned German, for example, can make use of this in 'the German-speaking countries', but maybe also elsewhere in the world, e.g. in Greece among Greeks who have worked in Germany. Or Germans who have learned Danish can make use of this in Greenland. It ought to be pointed out that it is not 'the languages' that flow but the various interlanguages of the individuals involved.

Something similar naturally applies to the language that is acquired/learned as a second language; one may end up using it elsewhere than in the immediate target-language country. Someone with a Turkish background, for example, who has learned Danish as a second language, could move to Turkey and use Danish in the tourist industry there. Or a Chilean who has learned Danish in Denmark could migrate to the USA and use Danish in connection with translation and teaching. Once again, it is the unique interlanguage of the person involved that we are dealing with. The ramifications of, for example, Danish as a second and foreign language thus means in all probability an intensified diversification of the Danish language.

Textual Flows

In the previous section, the focus was as mentioned on the flows of resources. But linguistic practice also flows, first and foremost by virtue of the actual interpersonal oral or written interaction in the social networks, but also in the form of texts (oral and written) that are transported physically or electronically from place to place. It is the latter I am thinking of here – because I am particularly interested in the macro-flows and their impact on the micro-level.

The transportation of texts, e.g. book production and distribution around the world, or film distribution in international mass media, or transfer of text in the virtual space of the Internet, can help develop the linguistic resources around, e.g. in teaching contexts. But the understanding and use of the texts presupposes that there are already language users present who have acquired, or are in the process of acquiring, the language involved – as a first language, foreign language or second language. Before the textual flow can give meaning, there must then be someone 'at the other end' who has a knowledge of the language in which the texts have been composed. One could say that acquisition/learning and migration are initial flows; it is here that the language flow starts, respectively makes its entrance at the new location. Textual flows, on the other hand, are continuation flows; they help keep the use of the language alive. This use will probably be different, depending on whether the receiver speaks the language as a first language/early second language or as a foreign language/late second language, as the various acquisition situations have equipped the receiver with different interpretive resources (see also Chapter 9).

Lexical Flows

As contact language research shows, there are practically no limits to what linguistic features in principle can be spread to other languages (Thomason, 2001; Weinreich, 1953): features of pronunciation, morphology, syntax and genre. But the most common is individual words or short expressions ('chunks'), and that is what I intend to discuss here, partly since the lexical vocabulary is the most culture-relevant part of the language, because of its denotative and connotative potential, and partly because lexical flows only partially move along the same paths as linguistic resources (idiolects, interlanguages) and linguistic practice (texts). For example, a considerable number of words have come to Denmark from various languages as part of the transplantation of various types of food (*karry* (curry), *kaffe* (coffee), etc.), but this lexical flow is not necessarily accompanied by people who speak these languages, or by texts of any length in these languages.

Many loan words[10] can often be revealed in linguistic resources and linguistic practice via lexicological studies, and these loans naturally 'follow along' when people acquire and use the language in question, or migrate. What is more interesting in this connection is the actual borrowing process: that an individual incorporates a word from another language into his or her own language[11], after which this word can continue its flow in social interaction if it happens to be accepted (adopted) into the network. This is a situation where 'language spreads across languages': features from a loaning language spread to the receiving language. The linguistic borrowing process can be part of a contemporary cultural borrowing process: a cultural feature flows from the one linguistic network to the other, and is accompanied by a new loan word that is brought into circulation. But we may also be dealing with a word that, via its use in code-switching situations, is introduced from a particular language more for the sake of its symbolic value, as, for example, when people in Denmark begin to use an English word in connection with a cultural practice one has already had for quite some time.[12]

Global Flows and Local Complexity: Danish and Denmark

The concept of (linguistic) flow is, then, used here as a very comprehensive one. It is a overall concept for acquisition/learning (the development of linguistic resources), migration (language users move with the linguistic resources they have), text-distribution and loans, especially lexical loans.

If one particular language is taken as a starting point, it is possible to follow its ramifications around the world as a first language/early second language and foreign language/late second language, or as texts in the language concerned, or as isolated linguistic features coming from the language involved (especially lexical loans). One can, for example, follow the ramifications of the Danish language in the world: firstly, Danish is the dominant first language within the Danish borders, and it is taught and used as a second language by immigrants with highly diverse linguistic backgrounds (over 100 languages, see below). Danish is further used to a certain extent as a common communication language in the Nordic countries, especially in writing.[13] Danish is a school language in the Faroes, Greenland and Iceland.[14] It is also taught in over 25 countries at more than 100 universities and institutes, including in Japan, Hungary and Uruguay. There are always many thousands of Danish tourists on their travels around the world, on package tours, topic tours, business trips, or backpacking. Many thousands of Danes have settled abroad. There are employees posted abroad in transnational companies, there are development workers in poor countries, there are students on study trips abroad, there are politicians, officials and lobbyists in the European Union and international organisations, there are dispatched soldiers, doctors, clergymen, diplomats and craftsmen. The organisation 'Danes Worldwide' has about six thousand members spread out in practically all the countries of the world.

Danish-language users thus form what one could describe as a global network of Danish speakers. This network is borne by physical individuals and made possible by growing transnational mobility. At the same time, the network also exists as a communications network made possible by teletransmission and the Internet. Every moment, Danish speakers are establishing virtual network connections over shorter or longer distances. Therefore, Danish can be referred to as a 'world language', not by virtue of the number of its users but because of the actual geographical diffusion (Risager, 2004b).

Transnational migration, e.g. from south to north, forms the basis for potentially worldwide networks for a very great number of languages, although those of certain languages will be more closely knit than others. Via the use of information and communication technology the networks even acquire an extraterritorial dimension. This means, among other things, that the concept of 'language area' gains a new content. Normally, the concept is used for the countries where the languages concerned are spoken as first language, e.g. 'the German language area'. But, as part of the network mode of thought, one has to redefine the concept to cover the potentially worldwide networks in which the language is used, and one can then add that the networks are particularly comprehensive and intensive in those states or areas where the language involved is spoken as a first language or second language.

Seen from this perspective, Denmark is a locality where many different linguistic networks meet. The large networks of Farsi-speaking meet with large networks of German-speaking, Dutch-speaking, Danish-speaking, etc. A local linguistic complexity is formed on an ongoing basis, one that is socially structured by means of the power struggles that constantly take place via the language users' actual choice of language in particular situations (Lund & Risager, 2001; Risager forthcoming). Linguistic complexity in Denmark can be described on three levels.

Firstly, many languages are spoken in Denmark. There are, however, no statistics in this area, so one will have to base oneself on an estimate. A possible point of departure can be the number of nationalities in Denmark. For example, in the Municipality of Copenhagen there were per 1 January 2003 people representing 171 nationalities. The list below is my best estimate of which languages are probably spoken as first languages in Denmark at present (the number can constantly be changing, due to immigration and emigration). The list comprises about 110 languages:

Abkhasian – Akan (among others Fante and Twi) – Albanian – Amharic – Arabic (several regional languages) – Armenian – Assyrian – Azerbaijani – Azeri – Bahdini – Bambara – Bengali (Bangla) – Berber – Bielorussian – Bosnian – Bulgarian – Burmese – Catalan – Chin – Croatian – Danish – Danish Sign Language – Dari – Dutch – Edo – Esperanto (yes, also as first language) – Estonian – English – Faroese – Farsi – Finnish – French – Frisian – Fulfulde (Peul, Fulani) – German – Greek – Greenlandish – Gujarati – Hakka – Hassaniya – Hausa – Hebrew – Hindi – Hungarian – Igbo (Ibo) – Indonesian (and Malay) – Irish – Icelandic – Italian – Japanese – Kabyle – Kazakh – Khmer – Kikingo – Kirundi – Korean – Krio – Kurmanji – Latvian – Lingala – Lithuanian – Luganda – Mandarin – Macedonian – Malinké – Mandinka (Mandingo) – Min – Moldavian – Nepalese – Norwegian – Oromo (formerly Galla) – Pashto – Polish – Portuguese – Punjabi – Rohinga – Romani – Rumanian – Russian – Serbian – Sindhi – Singhalese – Slovakian – Slovenian – Somali – Soninké – Sorani – Sorbian – Spanish – Susu – Swedish – Swahili – Tagalog (Filipino, Pilipino) – Tamil – Tatar – Tchèque – Thai – Tigré – Tigrinya – Turkish – Turkmen – Ukrainian – Urdu – Uzbek – Vietnamese – Wolof – Wu – Yue (Cantonese) – Zaza (Kirmanjki).

Secondly, each of these languages (linguistic practice and linguistic resources) appears in various forms that can be related to one or more of a number of theoretical categories such as sociolects, genderlects, youth languages, children's languages, dialects. The differences can also be related to many different types of language register, such as professional jargon, religious language, slang, etc. In addition, there is variation in relation to whether the language concerned is a first language, second language or foreign language – and this does apply only to Danish. A minority language such as Turkish in Denmark can function as a first language, a second language (e.g. for intermarried people who learn Turkish) and a foreign language (e.g. for Danish first-language speakers who study Turkish out of a linguistic interest). The great variation is well-documented as far as the Danish language is concerned as it is spoken and written in Denmark, whereas the nature of the variation is virtually uncharted as far as other languages are concerned.

Thirdly, one can observe many kinds of language 'mixings' that go further than the use of loan words. First and foremost, code-switching[15] is very common among younger Danes, who switch in their speech between Danish and English as part of the expression of their subcultural identity (Preisler, 1999). Code-switching also occurs in conversations between immigrants, who switch between their first language and Danish as a second language (Møller *et al.*, 1998). In addition, one can see a more conscious creative use of code-switching between Danish and English in, for example, commercials or a TV programme like *The Julekalender* (*Jul* = Christmas). This was a daily December TV programme for children and adults (Risager, 1993).

Here I have used Denmark as an example of a linguistically complex society. But in general one should take care not to place an equals sign between the concept of society and that of national state. Traditional sociology is mainly based on a concept of society as being a national state. But this use of the concept has now been toned down as part of an attempt to arrive at a theoretical understanding of postmodern/late-modern society and globalisation, see, for example, Robertson (1992). 'Society' can also be understood at, for example, the global level, and at this level 'multilingual society' has to do with the linguistic process of globalisation and changes in the linguistic world system. Seen on a smaller scale, multilingual society has to do with multilingualism in an international organisation, a transnational company, a multinational formation such as the European Union, at an educational institution, in a school class. In connection with all these societal structures, crisscrossing multilingual networks and multilingual communities can be identified. Take, for example, transnational school networks where pupils develop together their foreign language knowledge via e-mail, etc.

Linguistic Complexity and Homogeneity in Language Teaching

As I have already touched on in Chapter 1 when describing the example *Tour de France*, I consider language teaching as a linguistic contact zone, one that is a result of the union of various linguistic flows. So the idea is to take a teaching sequence as a point of departure and look at its role in the historical process:

- Where do the linguistic flows come from?
- What happens to the linguistic flows in the teaching sequence?
- Where do the linguistic flows go?

As regards the first question, it is a matter of tracing the flows backwards in time and out of the learning space: how have the teacher's linguistic resources been formed, where do the written texts come from, what have the students seen on television in the language involved, what types of loan words have they been in contact with, etc.?

The second question has to do with studying, at the micro-level, how the various languages/language varieties are used and mixed in the ongoing interaction taking place in the learning space: with studying how multilingualism develops in the specific context, e.g. via ethnographic studies.

With the third question, attention is drawn to what comes out of the specific linguistic configuration of the teaching/learning process: to looking ahead and out of the learning space. This issue can be studied at two levels: either one can look at the pedagogical intentions that are built into the pedagogical method, e.g. ideas about particular communicative needs that are potentially satisfied by virtue of the teaching, or one can – in a retrospective light – look at what results actually emerged from a teaching sequence already given. One can, for example, carry out life-historical interviews that focus on the individual's (own conception of his/her) use of the target language and other languages as a result of the specific learning process (s)he has been through.

Tour de France and linguistic complexity

In the following I wish to outline how linguistic flows can be analysed in connection with the imagined German sequence: *Tour de France*. I would like just to recapitulate certain main features of the composition of the class: we are looking at a Class 10 in German in the Danish Folkeskole (i.e. 16–17 year-olds in a municipal school). The students are both girls and boys, most of them are Danes, and there is also a boy with an Iranian background and a girl with a Dutch background. The teacher is a Danish woman.

The target language

The target language, 'German', functions here as a foreign language, not a second language, for the students. In this example, it is also a foreign language for the teacher.

The teacher's version of German is influenced by her personal experiences with German speakers in Denmark and in particular social environments and particular localities in German-speaking countries. She has very good knowledge of the German written language, especially parts of the literature and the daily press, while she has never, for example, read a periodical in German about cars and leisure pursuits. She has a definite idea about what 'the German language' is all about.

Apart from the input the teacher is capable of giving, there is in this instance also input in the form of German-language newspapers and magazines. Language teaching is a context in which many highly different written texts are often used to provide an all-round insight into various ways of using the target language; preferably, so-called authentic texts that come from a target country and have not been produced with language teaching in mind. In the *Tour de France* example, magazines produced in Germany have been used, and the texts have been written by German (?) journalists on the basis of material from international news agencies. Their texts contain many voices: there are interviews with cyclists (which were originally in German? English? French?) and with other participants such as organisers, doctors or sponsors from many countries, employed in certain cases by transnational firms.

The students have to a varying extent experience with German-speaking practice, and some of them probably have definite ideas as to what 'German' is. On the basis of these experiences and the interaction in the class the students develop their individual German interlanguage, productively and receptively. Linguistic practice is characterised in one sense or other by the specific input: for example, the sequence would look different if the teacher had had German as her first language, in some version or other. It would also look different if the material had been written by school students from a multicultural school in Berlin (but still about *Tour de France* and still with a 'German' perspective), or by French school students at a school in southern France, as part of a transnational e-mail network, and with a 'French' perspective.

The sociolinguistic perspective on interaction in the German class will be able to shed light on whether or how the students, via their mutual interaction, influence each other's interlanguage. In some cases it might be the teacher who is the model, but it can be some of the students, depending on the social relations in the class. Other students will perhaps be used as 'anti-models', with their comrades more or less consciously thinking: 'I don't want to speak like that, at any rate'. In the linguistic networks in the class the students (and the teacher) make ongoing use of the language as an identity marker – if we introduce Le Page and Tabouret-Keller's perspective in this context.[16]

First languages

In the class involved, there are three first languages represented: 'Danish', 'Farsi' and 'Dutch' (idiolects of these). During the sequence, the mother tongue of the Danish students is strengthened within certain areas: they learn, for example, about German grammar in Danish, they translate between Danish and German, their private and inner speech in Danish has a certain place in their German teaching – and naturally also when/if they have homework between lessons. From time to time, the class actually has to carry out comparisons between 'German' and 'Danish', and it is quite all right for Danish to be used in the teaching from time to time if it is necessary for the content to be understood – this is underlined at several points in the Danish curriculum guidelines. They do not, however, take account of the fact that an explanation in Danish does not necessarily help those students who do not have Danish as a first language but as a second language, and who have perhaps not yet developed a satisfactory Danish for grammatical explanations.

The Iranian boy's Farsi can find expression only as private and inner speech, and broadly speaking only when he is working on his own. Farsi has great importance for him in his acquisition of German, but it is a hidden resource that does not become public in the class. The Dutch girl, on the other hand, can use various Dutch words and expressions in the class, for the teacher is able to decode them and is interested in the historical relation between German and Dutch.

Other languages

Other languages in this case are 'Danish' as a second language, 'English' as a foreign language and 'French' as a foreign language.

The Dutch and Iranian students may have their Danish strengthened as a second language[17] by following this German sequence, but we do not in fact know if the use of Danish has made their learning of German more difficult, or confused them – perhaps the Iranian in particular, for whom Danish and German can appear to be fairly similar as regards grammatical structure and word formation. The possibility of resorting to English in order to explain certain things, which in some cases can be relevant, would be virtually unthinkable in a lesson of German as a foreign language.

English loan words are quite numerous in the German coverage of *Tour de France*: 'team', 'power', 'sprint', etc., as well as French ones: *étape, cham-*

pion, etc. The teacher points out some of the English loan words, but not the French ones. She could possibly have encouraged the Iranian student by looking for German loans in Farsi and trying to explain why they are there.

Code-switching

Language teaching is mainly presented as being single-language teaching in curriculum guidelines, and in most academic literature. The point of aim is the 'target language', and the fact that those taking part use their eventual common language (here: Danish as first language and second language) from time to time is seen as a necessary evil – or maybe as a positive chance to develop linguistic awareness via a comparison of languages. But, in fact, language teaching is always bilingual or multilingual. It is precisely characteristic for this context of linguistic practice that there is always at least one other language 'present'. Even when all teaching is carried out in the target language – using the so-called direct method – the first language still exists in the students' universe, and they use it, if nowhere else, in their private and inner speech while they are acquiring the target language. There will in addition be some degree or other of language transfer from the first language (and possibly other languages the student may happen to know) to the target language (Ringbom, 1987).

Language learning (and language acquisition outside the teaching context) can thus include more or less constant code-switching between two or more languages. This can occur directly, as translation in the class, but also in the form of communicative strategies where the first language and other languages are included in order to make the meaning clearer. There is a kind of code-switching in inner speech: 'I wonder what "issue" means here?'. A foreign-language class can prove to be a good example of a relatively compact bilingual or multilingual network (and – let us hope – a community) in which experiments are made in creating bilingual or multilingual intertextual chains, e.g. cohesive conversations about cycling in German and Danish, with use of such expressions as *das gelbe Tricot,* which invites comparisons with the Danish *den gule trøje,* English 'the yellow jersey' and (perhaps) the French *le maillot jaune.*

It would be interesting to shed light on the code-switching of language teaching using Le Page and Tabouret-Keller's approach. What kind of linguistic identity constructions take place when the teacher and the students switch between target language and first language/second language? On the surface, the switch is most often based on practical

considerations to do with intelligibility and level of formulation, but identification is also included – e.g. concerning national identities or group
identities in the class. What kind of identities does language teaching try
to establish, among other things via the generally-used comparative
method? What does it mean to identify oneself with 'the target language' –
i.e. those who speak this language? What processes of 'diffusion' and
'focusing' take place in language teaching?

Another question that it might be interesting to highlight is whether any
real borrowing processes take place in connection with language teaching.
When there is code-switching, does a word then become a loan that is
taken out of the learning space and put into circulation outside, e.g. in the
family or circle of friends?

A research tradition is developing that focuses on multilingualism in
second-language teaching – see, for example, Bourne (1988) and the overview
in Martin-Jones, (1995). Efforts are also being made to develop a didactics of
multilingualism, especially in Germany (*Mehrsprachigkeitsdidaktik*), a didactics that to a greater or lesser extent attempts to develop awareness of the
multilingual society and the multilingual class in foreign- and second-
language teaching (Nieweler, 2001; Oomen-Welke, 2000). See also the previ-
ously mentioned Rampton (1999) on the German-English code-switching in
a multicultural school in London, and my own article *Buy some petit souvenir
aus Dänemark* (Risager, 1993) on potential cooperation between foreign
languages.

Linguistic homogeneity in language pedagogy discourse

Against a background of linguistic complexity – which may be more or
less pronounced, depending on the specific situation – it leaps to the eye
just how much general language pedagogy discourse is dominated by
conceptions and concepts that conceal this complexity. There are recom-
mendations that students should be presented with various regional and
social varieties of the target language (e.g. in the curriculum guidelines for
English and, to a certain extent, also for German, in the Danish
Folkeskole), but no conclusions are drawn concerning the students'
construction of their own interlanguage. When, for example, may they
imitate the varieties in their own speech, and when are they to be prepared
only to perceive and understand them? Practically all discourse in curriculum guidelines is characterised by a view of the target language as a
homogeneous system. It seems as if it is the written language, the most
standardised, homogeneous and stable part of the language, that is the
paradigm for the concept of the target language.

Furthermore, the concept of the target language is narrow, as it normally refers to the language in its capacity as a first language.[18] In my opinion, one ought to broaden this perspective so that language teaching deals consciously and systematically with the target language both as a first language and as a second language (typically in the target-language countries) and as a foreign language (typically outside the target-language countries). So there is a need for a more inclusive target-language concept in this respect, too.

An example of a first-language-oriented conception of the target language is a passage in the guidelines for English in the Danish Folkeskole. The only place where the term 'second language' is mentioned is in connection with the status of the English language as the official language in certain states:

> Pupils shall work with the culture and living conditions of countries where English is the mother tongue … At a later stage, countries such as Ireland, Australia and Canada ought also to be included. They can also work with conditions in the countries where English is a second language or the most used common language, e.g. India, African countries or other former British colonies.
> (English, a subject in the Danish Folkeskole, 1995: 33)

This passage ignores the fact that English is an important second language in Great Britain, the USA, Australia, Canada, etc.

A parallel situation is seen in the discourse on the students' 'own language', e.g. the occasional use of Danish in French teaching. This discourse also has to do with a homogeneous standard language, and it marginalises possible linguistic minorities in the class in the sense that the expressions 'the pupils' own language', 'the pupils' first language' and 'Danish' are treated as synonymous. Here, 'language' is only spoken of as 'the language as a first language'.

In the theoretical discourse of language pedagogy, and, for example, in the discourse on Danish curriculum guidelines, there is a very slender awareness of social hierarchies between languages and between linguistic norms. A discussion is lacking of the ideological content in the abstract constructions of 'the target language' and the students' 'first language'. This, though, seems to me to apply more to foreign-language pedagogy than to second-language pedagogy. Whereas second-language pedagogy has been the subject of a politicisation that has forced researchers and practitioners to develop a certain awareness of politico-ideological dimensions of their activity (cf., for example, Cummins, 2000), foreign-language pedagogy has been more unambiguously characterised by a technical epistemological interest that focuses on the question of how one can support language learning as effectively as possible. There is admittedly a growing awareness of politico-ideological dimensions, but it is more peripheral and deals broadly speaking only with English (Pennycook, 1994; Phillipson, 1992).

In practical language teaching there is, then, a pedagogical dilemma between on the one hand the actual linguistic complexity in every language class, and on the other hand the necessity – especially in the first phases of language learning – of reducing the complexity so as not to create uncertainty concerning the aim of the teaching. But how much reduction of the complexity is pedagogically justifiable? The concrete decision often rests with the individual teacher, who thus has a not inconsiderable language-political role, not only in connection with the students' linguistic competencies but also in connection with their images of the target language and of languages in the world.

Conclusion

I adopt a macro-oriented and historical view of linguistic practice: linguistic practice flows in small and large social networks, and people create within this social interaction intertextual chains that, seen in an overall perspective, constitute the (world) history of linguistic practice. Many languages now flow in very large, more or less global, networks, partly as a result of transnational migration. At the same time, linguistic resources are also being seen in a larger, life-historical perspective.

Linguistic flows look different, depending on whether they are flows of a first language/early second language or flows of a foreign language/ late second language – and one can furthermore speak of textual flows and lexical flows. All of these linguistic flows are relevant to an analysis of language teaching. I see language teaching as a place where, among other things, linguistic flows unite and blend, e.g. via code-switching that has a specific nature because of the special learning context. Language teaching is therefore potentially highly complex when seen in purely linguistic terms, whereas the discourse of language pedagogy often emphasises homogeneity rather than complexity.

An analysis of the relationship between language and culture must have its point of departure in a view of language in which the idea of the homogeneous and static language system is deconstructed. 'Culture' must be seen in relation to linguistic practice, linguistic resources and the discursive construction of the language system.

Notes

1. Hannerz discusses among other things the use of network approaches in anthropological studies of metropolises in Hannerz, 1980.
2. And linguistic practice changes at the same time (Le Page & Tabouret-Keller, 1985; Milroy, 1980). Here, however, it is not the temporal process that is in focus but the spatial.
3. I am referring here to Fishman's concept of the domain: 'a cluster of social situations typically constrained by a common set of behavioral rules' (Fishman, 1972: 452). A domain is a construction on the basis of empirical investigations of regularities in linguistic practice, e.g. code-switching. It can coincide with a societal, institutional structure, but does not necessarily have to do so.
4. It is usual to refer more or less vaguely to the idea of networks in sociolinguistics, and it has been methodically elaborated in the main by Lesley and John Milroy (e.g. J. Milroy, 1992). But the latter focuses on local networks and their role in connection with the emergence and spread of linguistic innovations. They do not look at spreading in larger networks, and they limit their focus to oral interpersonal communication. They do not, for example, investigate the possible significance of mass media in the process of linguistic change.
5. This term is used by, among others, Cooper (1982), who otherwise has a different approach from mine, since he is primarily interested in the communicative aims people can have for acquiring a new language. He stands for a functional point of view and attempts to operationalise the question: Who adopts what, when, where, why, and how?
6. Calvet (1987) directly uses the war metaphor: *'La guerre des langues'*.
7. If there is a written language, but this is normally the case when we are dealing with languages that function as second languages or as one of the common foreign languages.
8. This many-sided and integrated linguistic competence is called 'plurilingualism' by some, e.g. in *Common European Framework* 2001.
9. I would refer readers here to the meaning of the concept 'interlanguage' used by Færch *et al.*: 'An interlanguage is a variety of language which exists in a contact situation between a learner's L1 and L2. According to this, an interlanguage typically has features in common with both a learner's L1 and with the L2' (Færch *et al.*, 1984: 272).
10. It is usual in Danish lexicology to distinguish between heritage words (*arveord*), loan words and foreign words (e.g. Hansen & Lund, 1994). Both loan words and foreign words are imported words, but differ in that the loan words (no longer) differ from the language in their phonological structure, spelling or inflection from the heritage words, while the foreign words do so. In this book, however, I will use the term 'loan word' for both groups of imported words.
11. I am speaking here of direct loans, not indirect ones. The vocabulary of a language is always structurally integrated into the rest of the language system, which is conceptualised in, for example, the Halliday school's term 'lexicogrammar'. Despite this, however, words can also be isolated and integrated into other language systems (other idiolects) – depending, though, on what language we are actually dealing with, since the word structure of certain languages makes the process more difficult than that of other languages.

12. The first type Myers-Scotton calls 'cultural loans', the second 'core loans' (Myers-Scotton, 1997; Myers-Scotton & Okeju, 1973).
13. Cf. Haberland 1993.
14. Iceland, the Faroes and Greenland are former Danish colonies. Since 1944, Iceland has been an independent republic, while the Faroes and Greenland (Kalaallit Nunaat) are now parts of the Danish kingdom, with a special home rule arrangement.
15. Code-switching can be divided into intersentential and intrasentential code-switching (Saville-Troike, 1989). The latter, which is also called code-mixing, takes place within the individual sentence, typically at a syntactic boundary. In the following I use the code-switching concept for both types.
16. One can also refer to social psychological studies in linguistic accommodation, e.g. Giles, 1994.
17. Which, as mentioned, can be more or less similar to the first language.
18. Unlike teaching in classical languages such as Latin, which is nobody's first language.

Chapter 8
Languacultural Dimensions

Introduction

In Chapters 6–7 I have dealt with a social view of language. I have focused on linguistic practice as acts of identity and normative acts in social networks, and I have drawn attention to the spread of languages in a global perspective. But at the same time I have dealt with language as a pure code, without taking account of the fact that linguistic practice conveys and creates meaning in meaningful contexts.

In the following chapters I will deal with a cultural view of language. I will describe language (with its three loci: 2 + 1) as a meaning phenomenon, and in this chapter I would like to start by introducing the concept of languaculture. I will attempt to give an impression of the many aspects of the concept of languaculture, including its three dimensions:

- the semantic-pragmatic dimension;
- the poetic dimension;
- the identity dimension.

As an introduction to the discussion of the concept of languaculture, I first present Agar's concept of 'languaculture' and Friedrich's concept of 'linguaculture', after which I give an account of my conception of how one can use the languaculture concept in relation to linguistic practice, linguistic resources and the discursive construction of the linguistic system. Once again, it is important here to distinguish between the functions of language as a first language/early second language and a foreign language/late second language. The chapter ends with a concluding commentary on my interpretation of the Whorfian hypothesis.

Michael Agar: Languaculture

The American (cognitive) linguistic anthropologist Michael Agar has described the concept of 'languaculture' in his book *Language Shock. Understanding the Culture of Conversation* (1994). The book is an inspiring introduction to the connection between language and culture (in a differential sense), providing many examples and indications as to how the layman can investigate culture and language.

In his book, Agar presents the linguistic and anthropological basis for ideas about the interrelation between language and culture, especially in connection with the Whorfian discussion. He deals with the misunderstandings and cultural awareness that can arise in connection with conversations, both when it is a question of 'the same language' and when it is a question of 'different languages'. He refers, among other things, to Gumperz's work on interethnic conversations and to R. Scollon and S.W. Scollon's work on intercultural (interdiscursive) communication, and also to Hannerz.[1]

In his book Agar distinguishes between two conceptions of culture. On the one hand, there is the widespread conception that culture is something one 'has'; on the other hand there is the conception of culture of which he himself is a spokesman, that culture is something that happens to the individual in everyday life:

> Culture is ... *what happens to you* when you encounter differences, become aware of something in yourself, and work to figure out why the differences appeared. Culture is an awareness, a consciousness, one that reveals the hidden self and opens paths to other ways of being. (Agar, 1994: 20, italics in the original)

Culture, then, is something that belongs to the individual's consciousness – and this conception is an extension of the cognitive tradition within American cultural anthropology. Agar places special emphasis on the changes of consciousness or change potential that lie in linguistic practice, and his assignment is not least to criticise what he calls 'the number-one mentality', the ethnocentrism one can find among many Americans (but which he stresses can also be found elsewhere).

Agar introduces the concept of 'languaculture' in order to be able to sum up culture and language in one word. 'Languaculture' refers to 'the necessary tie between language and culture' (Agar, 1994: 60). He has in general a highly language-oriented conception of culture, as he says 'Culture starts when you realize that you've got a problem with language, and the problem has to do with who you are' (Agar, 1994: 20). Culture is personal and relational: it arises in concrete situations and has to do with differences between concrete individuals.

Agar expresses a clearly integrative view of language that focuses on the semantics of language and its use in linguistic practice, especially in conversations (here he uses the term 'discourse', as do Tannen, Gumperz and Scollon & Scollon). He says about language that it is loaded with culture:

> Language, in all its varieties, in all the ways it appears in everyday life, builds a world of meanings. When you run into different meanings, when you become aware of your own and work to build a bridge to the others, 'culture' is what you're up to. Language fills the spaces between us with sound; culture forges the human connection through them. Culture is in language, and language is loaded with culture. (Agar, 1994: 28)

The term 'languaculture', then, stresses two relations: 'The *langua* in languaculture is about discourse, not just about words and sentences. And the *culture* in languaculture is about meanings that include, but go well beyond, what the dictionary and the grammar offer' (Agar, 1994: 96, italics in the original).

Agar spends some time explaining what the Whorfian discussion is about, including ethno-semantic research into lexically carried conceptual systems such as the terms for colours in various languages (Berlin & Kay, 1969; Brown & Lenneberg, 1954; Kay & Kempton, 1984). He is in favour – as are so many people within modern linguistic anthropology and socio- and psycholinguistics – of the so-called weak version of the Whorfian hypothesis, with such formulations as: 'Language carries with it patterns of seeing, knowing, talking, and acting. Not patterns that imprison you, but patterns that mark the easier trails for thought and perception and action' (Agar, 1994: 71). Agar proposes that what Whorf was really talking about was 'languaculture'.

The places in conversation where people misunderstand each other are referred to by Agar as 'rich points'. It is there that there is the opportunity to glimpse 'culture', to become conscious of cultural differences. He talks about 'the Whorfian Alps' in linguistic communication in the sense that between people who have different 'languacultures' (which ultimately everyone has) a number of cultural differences rise up – some small, some large – and that it is a question of bringing these out into the open and trying to go beyond them. So there are three phases on the way to 'culture': 'mistake, awareness, repair'.[2]

Agar mixes metaphors from various parts of linguistics: on the one hand, he uses the surface/deep structure metaphor that has become well known because of generative grammar, since he says that words are the surface of culture: 'Culture is a conceptual system whose surface appears in the words of people's language' (Agar, 1994: 79). At the same time, he also uses the structuralist contrast between expression (*signifiant*) and content (*signifié*) when he says that 'Language is the signifier of culture concepts' (Agar, 1994: 89).

The book indicates how as a layman one can build up one's cultural awareness by collecting rich points and investigating whether they form patterns, by investigating linguistic practice in certain situations in order to define frames (the typical example is what are also referred to as 'scripts', e.g. concerning typical sequences of acts when visiting a restaurant): 'Frames take language and culture and make them inseparable. The 'and' disappears, and we're left with *languaculture*' (Agar, 1994: 132, italics in the original). One ought to work inductively, empirically, and build up an increasingly comprehensive set of interrelationships between frames. He warns against taking abstractions such as 'American culture' at face value, but otherwise borders on a somewhat culture-relativistic view of culture:

> You begin to find the *coherence* among the different frames, the weave that pulls them together into ever more elaborate ideas about the new languaculture, ideas that tantalize you with that elusive 'feel' for the people you're trying to understand. That 'feel', once you've articulated it, teaches you some grand differences between you and them, differences that go by the name of history, of fundamental premises of existence, of politics, of economics. Coherence brings to life all those foggy abstractions. With coherence, you don't just handle rich points; you sense what it's like to lead a different kind of *life*, to see and act with a different *mentality*, to move through a fundamentally different kind of *world*. (Agar, 1994: 190ff., italics in the original)

It is important for Agar to make it quite clear that 'languaculture' is not simply something one can create in an instant: 'Languaculture is a social fact. It sets limits on what you can say and sets up expectations of how you're supposed to talk' (Agar, 1994: 209). But it also involves struggle and renewing potential:

> The new languaculture is something you invent, something you win in a struggle with the old, something that tears down the old social fact walls and lets new discourse in. The new languaculture is a way to change the world by changing what it is that can be thought, said, and done. (Agar, 1994: 209)

Agar does not deal very much with globalisation and the transnational – he does not actually use such terms. He does believe, however, on the one hand that both nations and states are 'languacultures' (Agar, 1994: 215), but that the concepts of 'nation' and 'state' on the other hand both conceal differences 'inside the languaculture' and similarities 'across languacultural boundaries'.

Paul Friedrich: Linguaculture

Agar has taken the concept of 'languaculture' from Paul Friedrich, who calls his concept 'linguaculture'. Agar justifies his alteration of the term as follows: 'I modified it to "langua" to bring it in line with the more commonly used "language"' (Agar, 1994: 265).[3] Friedrich, who is an American linguistic anthropologist who is interested among other things in poetics and linguistic relativity (cf. Friedrich, 1986), introduced the term 'linguaculture' in connection with an article from 1989 on the relationship between political economy, ideology and language (Friedrich, 1989).[4] In it he wrote that 'the many sounds and meanings of what we conventionally call "language" and "culture" constitute a single universe of its own kind' (Friedrich, 1989: 306), and he describes the concept of 'linguaculture' in these words:

> a domain of experience that fuses and intermingles the vocabulary, many semantic aspects of grammar, and the verbal aspects of culture; both grammar and culture have underlying structure while they are constantly being used and constructed by actual people on the ground. I will refer to this unitary but, at other levels, internally differentiated domain or whole as *linguaculture*, or, concretely, Greek linguaculture, rural southern Vermont linguaculture, and so on. (Friedrich, 1989: 307, italics in the original)

Friedrich adds that this terminological innovation can contribute to getting rid of decades of confusion about the concepts of 'language' and 'culture': How much of language is bound up with culture? How much of culture is bound up with language? Is language part of culture? Is culture part of language, etc? These questions imply that Friedrich is not an advocate to the same extent as Agar of a holistic concept of culture, where culture stands, so to speak, for 'the whole lot'.

Languaculture: Three Cultural Dimensions of Language

Agar then, uses the term 'languaculture' to emphasise the inseparability of language and culture: 'languaculture' stands for language + culture. Friedrich also speaks of 'a single universe of its own kind', but points out that one can use 'linguaculture' to show a way out in relation to the traditional, unclear fusion of the concept of language and that of culture.

In the following, I will choose Friedrich's strategy, but in a way that Friedrich himself would probably be unwilling to follow: I will use the languaculture concept to argue in favour of the assertion that the inseparability of 'language' and 'culture' *by and large* can be reduced to an assertion of the inseparability of 'language' and 'languaculture' for the person who speaks the language as a first language or early second language. The reduction implies that there is some 'culture' that is not 'languaculture'.

Languaculture can be understood in both a generic and a differential sense. The generic sense is found, for example, in the subjects that universal pragmatics deals with. But in this book I want to focus on the differential sense, i.e. I want to say that 'the individual language' (with the three loci: 2 + 1) has a 'languaculture' (with the same loci). So: the English language has its special languaculture; Newcastle English has its special languaculture, etc. This differential concept of languaculture will, as mentioned, be analysed in three dimensions:

- the semantic-pragmatic dimension;
- the poetic dimension;
- the identity dimension.

My languaculture concept thus covers a wider area than those of Agar and Friedrich. Broadly speaking, Agar's text deals only with the semantic-pragmatic dimension, with the main emphasis on the semantic. Friedrich writes about both the semantic and the poetic dimension. Neither of them, though, links sociolinguistic research into language and identity to their concept. In my opinion, however, this is an obvious thing to do, as the issue of identity is one of the most central ones in contemporary cultural analysis inspired by the Cultural Studies tradition.

The semiotic nucleus of language: Content and expression, structure and substance

At this point, I would refer to the concepts of content and expression, structure and substance in the sense given them in functional grammar by 'The Copenhagen School' (Harder, 1996). I do so because my position can be said – with many reservations – to be a poststructuralist, sociolinguistic and culture-oriented version of theirs.

The Copenhagen School argues in favour of a language theory that is functionally oriented by taking as its point of departure the communicative needs of language users, and that at the same time is based on a reinterpreted version of Hjelmslev's distinctions between content, expression, form and substance (the school prefers, however, the word 'structure' to the easily misunderstood word 'form'). Linguistic practice in this theory is synonymous with linking elements of content with elements of expression, and this applies to all linguistic phenomena above the morpheme boundary: linguistic phenomena within the morphological-syntactical and the lexical area. Advocates are of the opinion that one must operate with both a content-syntax and an expression-syntax. Language is perceived as formed (= structured) substance, on both the content and the expression sides, and the commutation test is ascribed a central function in deciding where the boundary goes between linguistically formed substance ('structure', 'invariance'/'constancy') and non-linguistically formed substance ('variance'). With its functional point of departure, the Copenhagen School argues in favour of an integrative, non-autonomous, view of language and linguistic structure (Harder, 1996).

The representatives of the Copenhagen School in functional grammar thus use the commutation test to delineate the outer boundaries of language's structural nucleus, and it is this nucleus that constitutes the focus of the grammar theory. In an extension of the Saussure tradition, they work on the basis of a Durkheimian view of language as a social institution, but with a functional interpretation. At the same time, they are inspired by cognitive grammar, although the cognitive perspective is subordinate to the functional.

Concerning the semantics/pragmatics pair of concepts, Harder describes the functional perspective in this way:

> ... all linguistic meaning, including ordinary descriptive meaning, is functional in nature. The expression *horse* means 'horse' only because members of the speech community recognize that it has the canonical function of mobilizing the concept 'horse' in the mind of the addressee. Membership of a speech community is constituted by attunement to the structured set of conventional functions which together make up a whole language. Ordinary descriptive meaning is therefore just as surely dependent on 'pragmatic' facts about actual speakers in an actual community as those more elusive and situation-dependent aspects of utterance meaning which are associated with the word 'function' when it is understood in contrast to 'meaning'. (Harder, 1996: 430f.).

I believe it is right to emphasise, along with Harder, that semantics and pragmatics ought not to be conceived as separate and hierarchically ordered components in the theory of language but as coordinated aspects of the description of content, in which semantics is directed towards conceptual content and pragmatics towards situational content.

As can be seen from Chapters 6 and 7, my professional point of departure differs in many ways from that of the Copenhagen School: I adopt a sociolinguistic starting point, so I have a (variance-oriented) approach that emphasises individual and social variability in linguistic practice and linguistic resources. Furthermore, I investigate the interface between these phenomena and the rest of culture from a point of view that has been inspired by post-structuralist ways of thinking. But by referring to the Copenhagen School I also wish to indicate that I, when it comes to the conception of the basically semiotic nature of language, am developing further the European structuralist tradition – that of Saussure and Hjelmslev.

Languaculture: Variable and constant. Relational and absolute

A characteristic feature of languaculture in all its dimensions is enacted between relative constancy and relative variability, between the aspects of languaculture that are constant by virtue of the structure of language and the aspects that are characterised by social, individual and situational variability.[5] Within semantics it is, for example, a question of the interaction between denotation and connotation in lexical meaning. It must be stressed that the boundary between constancy and variability is not fixed. It is always subject to negotiation in linguistic practice, but there are considerable differences as to how easy it is to change it. It is in particular the variable side of languaculture that is interesting from a culture-theoretical point of view.

Languaculture is both absolute and relational. One can study the languaculture of a language 'in itself', or one can include another language and carry out an investigation of what happens in the meeting between languages, i.e. what happens between people who perhaps use 'the same language', e.g. Danish, but with their different linguistic and cultural backgrounds. As Agar emphasises, it is particularly the aspects that feature as rich points in a language encounter that are interesting when investigating languaculture. And these rich points can arise both in the meeting between various 'languages' and in that between various ways of using 'the same language'. The concept of languaculture deals then with that which is language specific, and focusing in particular on linguistic differences. This should not be understood in a language-systematic sense, as in traditional contrastive linguistics (e.g. Lado, 1957), but precisely relationally, as it is expressed and processed in linguistic practice.

Three culture-theoretical approaches to language

Languaculture seen as the semantics and pragmatics of language has its point of departure in the content side of language – its communicative and psychological/cognitive functions – and describes how a structuring of the expression side corresponds to the structuring of the content side: the phonological, grammatical-lexical and textual structure. By underlining the languacultural in the semantics and pragmatics of the individual language the language-specific is underlined and also possibly the relational – and thereby there is a connection to the Whorfian discussion and the linguistic anthropological tradition.[6] This is a tradition that in particular operates with a collective and differential concept of culture (Chapter 3), and to which Agar also belongs. A link is also made to Cultural Studies, including contemporary culture-oriented translation theory (Bassnett, 2002; Venuti, 1992).

Languaculture seen as the poetics of language has its point of departure in both the expression and the content sides of language at one and the same time. This in itself leads one's attention away from the content side towards the expression side and its connection with the content side. The poetics of language has to do with language play, ritual and art (cf. Cook, 2000), with special reference to the effects that are specific to the individual language. By underlining the poetic languaculture a link is made to an aesthetic-literary tradition that operates on the basis of an aesthetic and often individual concept of culture (Chapter 3). Parts of this tradition are also strongly inspired by the Cultural Studies movement and its focusing on popular-cultural forms of practice.

Languaculture seen as the identity dimension of language has its point of departure in the expression side of language, more specifically in the choice of language (or variety of language) (cf. Le Page & Tabouret-Keller). By underlining the languacultural here a clear link is made to the Cultural Studies tradition, which is characterised by a particular interest in how various forms of identity (ethnic, social, religious, linguistic, etc.) are formed and processed in relations and conflicts between various groupings in complex societies (Chapter 3) – a collective and differential but also politically reflected concept of culture.

The three dimensions of languaculture are analytical and cannot be treated completely separately in investigations of concrete linguistic practice. The semantic-pragmatic dimension can be linked to the poetical in connection with a more or less conscious aestheticisation of linguistic practice, and this connection can be important for how the identity dimension is utilised and interpreted.

An example of this could be work done by students on a song in the *Tour de France* sequence: A group of students are given the task of translating the Danish[7] children's song *Ti små cyklister* (Ten small cyclists) into German (*Zehn kleine Fahrradfahrer*) and of singing it afterwards. The song has ten verses, in nine of which one of the small cyclists makes a stupid mistake in the traffic and is 'out'. Finally, there is only one cyclist left and, as it says, 'han kørte helt korrekt, så ham kan vi li' (*Er fuhr nach allen Regeln, den mögen wir also gern*) (He rode as he should, so he's the one we like).[8] This translation task is not easy, and it demonstrates a number of translation problems to do with the meaning of words and expressions as well as the possibility of transferring rhythm and rhyme. As to the identity dimension, the translation into German in the class awakens certain ideas about rules and punishment that the students had not thought of in connection with the Danish version, i.e. connotations that have something to do with what the language of German is identified with in certain contexts in Denmark.

The Loci of Languaculture: 2 + 1

By introducing the concept of languaculture one gains a way out of the all too far-reaching claim concerning the inseparability of language and culture. But it is important not to end up with a simple claim concerning the inseparability of language and languaculture – which would be an essentialist conception in line with the claim concerning the inseparability between language (the linguistic system) and culture (the cultural system). One must therefore distinguish in an analysis of the languaculture concept between three points of view, as in Chapter 6:

- the sociological point of view: languaculture in linguistic practice;
- the psychological point of view: languaculture in linguistic resources;
- the system-oriented point of view: languaculture in the 'linguistic system'.

Furthermore, it is still necessary to distinguish between language in its function as first language/early second language and foreign language/late second language respectively, as stated in Chapter 7. But so that the following presentation does not become too clumsy, I intend in the following to shorten these terms to *first language* and *foreign language* respectively.

If one crosses the various categories presented with each other, 18 different aspects of the languaculture concept emerge, as can be seen from Table 8.1. In the following, I intend to go through these 18 aspects one by one[9].

Languaculture in Linguistic Practice

(1) Linguistic practice – first language – semantic-pragmatic dimension

Linguistic interaction has at all times a fluid nature, no matter whether it is spoken or written. When a text is produced, certain languacultural intentions are laid down in the text, certain intentions about how this text is to

Table 8.1 Aspects of the languaculture concept

Linguistic practice		Linguistic resources		Linguistic system	
first language	foreign language	first language	foreign language	first language	foreign language
1 sem.-prag. dimension	4 sem.-prag. dimension	7 sem.-prag. dimension	10 sem.-prag. dimension	13 sem.-prag. dimension	16 sem.-prag. dimension
2 poetic dimension	5 poetic dimension	8 poetic dimension	11 poetic dimension	14 poetic dimension	17 poetic dimension
3 identity dimension	6 identity dimension	9 identity dimension	12 identity dimension	15 identity dimension	18 identity dimension

function semantically and pragmatically in the situation: what language act is meant, what references to the context have been undertaken, what ideas about the world does one wish to conjure up?[10]

These languacultural intentions are narrowed or widened by the text being received, i.e. being grasped and interpreted by the addressee or the various addressees[11], with the inclusion of their knowledge of the context in a broad sense. The receivers make use of all their personal languacultures in order to interpret the text. The intertextual chain will thus undergo greater or lesser transformations from link to link. If there is a large distance in time and space between text production and text reception, the differences in languacultures will come to mean a great deal – this is a widely known hermeneutical problem area.

This way of looking at linguistic interaction is based on a post-structuralist conception that meaning is not something that is given simply because of the semantic and pragmatic structuring; (Bakhtin; S. Hall; R. Harris; Kramsch; Vološinov). Meaning is changeable and comes into existence in each new act of production and interpretation. Normally, the meanings that have the greatest power behind them win, since linguistic practice is seen as being integrated in – and a constituent part of – more general social processes.

But on the basis of this accentuation of variability it is, as mentioned, also important to point out the relative constancy of linguistic practice. The semantic and pragmatic structuring always sets boundaries for variability: once one has said 'cat', one cannot make it mean 'dog'. But there will be nuances in the understanding of what, for example, 'cat' involves, and at the structural boundaries – especially those of a gradual nature – there are ongoing negotiations and attempts at fixing meaning: where, for example, does the boundary go between 'yours' and 'yours affectionately', between 'adult' and 'elderly', between 'entertainment' and 'information', between 'semantics' and 'pragmatics', between 'language' and 'culture'?

The relational languacultural fixing of meaning takes place via the various forms of intercultural communication, e.g. in translation, where it is the translator's personal languaculture that is employed in order to interpret and reproduce the semantic potential laid down by the author(s) in the source text. In the translation process the rich points appear to the translator, i.e. the relative difference between the two personal languacultures is actualised.

(2) Linguistic practice – first language – poetic dimension

The poetics of language is utilised in, for example, repetitions, alliterations, hyperboles, contrasts, special rhythms and patterns of intonation, proverbs, songs and declamation, and the use of paralanguage in personal performance in speech and writing. There is an especially large variability in the poetic use of language due to the exceeding of the everyday language conventions and the picture of reality that is normal for poetic language. At the same time, there is greater constraint, because this part of languaculture is connected to the expression side of language. There can be clear structural limitations to what directions poetic use of language can develop in – for example, limitations imposed by the sound and syllabic structure of the grammatical (expression) structure: only if the language is a tonal language is there a possibility of making use of the interplay between tones and sentence intonation. Only if the language distinguishes between grammatical male and female gender is there a possibility of making use of this distinction semantically in connection with gender symbolics (think, for example, of the various narrative possibilities in German, where the sun is feminine and the moon masculine, as opposed to French, where the sun is masculine and the moon feminine).

For this reason, the poetic languaculture can be said at certain points to be more constrained than the semantic and pragmatic languaculture, as can be seen from the difficulties that can arise when translating poetry and other genres that make use of poetic effects, such as advertisements (Friedrich, 1986; Jakobson, 1987 (1959); Scherzer, 1987). One could say that in the poetic dimension of languaculture there is an especially strong structural binding to one particular language.

(3) Linguistic practice – first language – identity dimension

As Le Page and Tabouret-Keller have touched on, linguistic practice is one long, varied identity construction. Through linguistic interaction people construct linguistic identities.

That part of languaculture that contains the identity dimension is closely linked to linguistic practice in precisely that language. This relationship can be observed in translating from one language to another. For example, it will normally be possible to confirm that it is very difficult to translate linguistic identity acts that presuppose a specific knowledge of social and historical conditions. It calls for particular sociolinguistic considerations to translate for example a conversation in which code-switching has been used as an ethnic identity marker if one wishes to retain this identity dimension in the target text.

(4) Linguistic practice – foreign language – semantic-pragmatic dimension

In situations where the language is used as a foreign language (or late second language) there are many opportunities for adding an even greater variability to it than when using the language as a first language (or early second language). Kramsch (1993) is among those who make use of this in foreign-language teaching, as she emphasises that work on the texts in the class can actualise many different readings and help create 'third places'.[12]

Agar, too, pays attention to this openness in textual interpretation through his discussion of rich points that emerge in communication between people using the same language, but where the language for some is a first language and for others a foreign language. Agar discusses, for example, how certain words are candidates for functioning as rich points, because they play a central role in the cultural self-perception of the language users (the first language speakers). He says it is characteristic of such words that their meaning is particularly difficult to define for the language users. He discusses, among other things, the Austrian word *Schmäh*, which is used in connection with situations where there is a reason for referring to something in the direction of black humour.[13]

The relative lack of semantic isomorphism that one can note between first-language speakers is even more pronounced when the language is spoken by people with different first languages, i.e. with possibly very different languacultural backgrounds. When using a language as a foreign language, it is not certain, however, that the languacultural difference is immediately registered in the expression of the language (as particular interlanguage and transfer phenomena). But at some point in the interaction possible rich points may appear and require clarification via metalinguistic negotiations or disagreements. This problem area is similar to that within intercultural pragmatics (e.g. Blum-Kulka *et al.*, 1989), but the investigation of the meeting between languacultures would do well, in my opinion, to link itself more clearly to other research into culture and society, including anthropology and Cultural Studies, which operate with a more process-oriented and variable concept of culture.

The above implies that a language is never culturally neutral in the sense 'languaculturally neutral'.[14] When a language is used in a lingua franca situation, i.e. typically in a situation where it is used as a foreign language by all participants because they do not have any other common language, it is used with contributions from all these participants' own languacultures. This produces a considerable elasticity in this language's semantics and pragmatics, but it also leads to a potentially lesser degree of precision. The conversation partners will probably adjust to each other and end up with some ad hoc compromises characterised by, among other things, power relations and levels of competence. In the lingua franca situation, it is therefore often the intersection of the various languacultures that is made use of, so that few politeness markers, for example, are used, as well as words with a more situation-determined meaning.

(5) Linguistic practice – foreign language – poetic dimension

What does it mean to make use of a language's poetics when one uses the language as a foreign language? When one learns a new language, one sometimes uses it in ways that are poetic or ludic: repetitions of words and phrases, experiments with new sentence structures (in relation to the first language), new ways of creating language acts, dramatisations in which both verbal language, paralanguage and kinesics are included, etc. Some language-pedagogical approaches include methods such as creative writing and other tasks in connection with particular texts and topics, language games, etc. This might, for example, consist of writing a haiku poem in the target language, making an acrostic[15] in the target language, or designing an advertisement with both pictures and text in the target language. Guy Cook has written an exciting book about *Language Play, Language Learning* (2000), in which he suggests that one should start to think about the ludic function of language as a central function in human cognitive development and social life and as an important aspect of foreign- and second-language teaching.

(6) Linguistic practice – foreign language – identity dimension

To participate in linguistic practice as a foreign-language speaker normally involves completely different identity dimensions from when one is speaking one's first language. As a foreign-language user one is – also in one's linguistic form of expression – a 'foreigner'. This identity as a foreigner can easily overshadow other aspects of one's social and personal identity – and make an ongoing development of identity difficult. The study of this issue can draw on research into foreignness such as, for example, that of Simmel (1908) and Wierlacher (1993), but these researchers do not deal directly with the linguistic dimension. The use of a foreign language can also be linked to going beyond boundaries, greater freedom or greater unfreedom, depending on, among other things, one's personal mental constitution (cf. Sabine Börsch's research into the motivation of male and female students to study foreign languages (Börsch, 1982, 1987)).

There is, incidentally, very little research specifically into the identity aspects of the use of a foreign language, although research is now getting under way within the use of language as a (late) second language, cf. Norton (2000) and Cummins (2000). One must assume that there is quite a large difference between talking about foreign languages and second languages. The user of a second language will typically be in a minority position in the society where he or she lives and uses the language, while the foreign-language user will typically be a relatively resourceful tourist or a visitor abroad, who is therefore not so exposed to social discrimination or stigmatising.

Languaculture in Linguistic Resources

(7) Linguistic resources – first language – semantic-pragmatic dimension

When talking about linguistic resources, it is the life-perspective of the individual person that is centre stage. That so much emphasis can be placed on variability in languacultural practice in the previous sections is owing to the fact that languacultural resources will always differ to a certain extent, developed as they are under different social and personal circumstances. The way the individual uses the language, the meanings that are placed in linguistic practice in the various situations, are idiolectal and characterised by the individual and social experiences of the person involved. At the same time, each individual, within his or her own experiential horizon, has a wide spectrum of ideas about various linguistic communities, and expectations as regards the languaculture of other persons and groups – expectations about what their particular semantic and pragmatic use of the language looks like.

When the individual migrates, individual linguistic resources, including languaculture, are part of the luggage. In the new context a more or less profound transformation (a resemanticisation or resignification) of parts of the languaculture will probably take place, depending on the new linguistic needs and the eventual meeting with a new language in the new location. So the idiolect and its semantic-pragmatic languaculture form a unity in the individual that constantly develops and that can undergo relatively drastic changes if the cultural and linguistic context becomes another one.

When one wishes to describe an individual's languacultural resources, it is necessary to use an integrative approach, one that emphasises the simultaneous development of linguistic, languacultural and other cultural resources in the individual, as part of his or her socialisation in a complex cultural context. The individual's verbal language, paralanguage and kinesics are all influenced by the personal languaculture – as well as social, private and inner speech. It must be stressed that the personal languaculture is not to be understood as a stable, well-integrated whole. It is constantly developing, and it may very well contain discontinuities and contradictions.

So we are dealing with a psychological (sociocultural) approach to languaculture. In this connection, I would like to mention a publication that also adopts an integrative point of view, but which is cognitive (i.e. not sociocultural) in its approach: *Toward a Theory of Cultural Linguistics* (1996) by Gary B. Palmer. Palmer does not advance sociological points of view but deals partly with universally human cognitive structures and processes, and partly with specific ideas about language on the part of individuals in various 'cultures'. His task, as he sees it, is to describe a new research area that can be called 'cultural linguistics':

> I have proposed a synthesis of anthropological linguistics with the newly emergent field of cognitive linguistics. The approach centers on linguistic imagery, which is largely defined by culture. Therefore, I call the approach cultural linguistics. The term invokes the anthropological tradition that culture is the accumulated knowledge of a community or society, including its stock of cognitive models, schemes, scenarios, and other forms of conventional imagery. (Palmer, 1996: 290)

This approach offers a basis for investigating how people construct various models of the world and of language. But as it completely lacks a sociological dimension, it does not observe, for example, socially conditioned differences, nor does it ask questions that have to do with power and ideology. It does not adopt the historical, dynamic perspective that I use in this book. Palmer's approach is based on a fairly traditional view of culture, one that was typical of American cultural anthropology until the 1960s, especially cognitive anthropology (the accumulated knowledge of a community). So Palmer is an advocate of a particularly cognitively oriented cultural linguistics, whereas I feel it is necessary to develop a sociological and historical cultural linguistics that can also form a framework around cognitively oriented investigations.

(8) Linguistic resources – first language – poetic dimension

Here the focus is on the development of poetic resources and competences in a life-perspective. Depending on their social and personal circumstances, the individuals develop various poetic resources in connection with their first language, both receptively and productively. If they migrate, they naturally take their poetic resources with them, and these perhaps gradually change as they come into contact with other poetic traditions. An example could be the poetic, lyrical production of exiled authors (in their first language) under changed cultural circumstances and perhaps with an altered audience composition.

(9) Linguistic resources – first language – identity dimension

Individuals develop their linguistic identities throughout their lives on the basis of the choice of language(s) and language varieties in the social environments they frequent. But the linguistic identity acts only have their meaning within the language community in which they function. If the first-language speaker emigrates to another environment where the language is not spoken as a first language, perhaps to another country, the identity dimension of the language can suddenly change quite decisively. Those who are at home in the new location cannot differentiate socially in the same way as the first-language speaker can, and the language involved is typically the subject of quite other metalinguistic conceptions than it is in the first-language context. Somebody who speaks French as first language can, for example, in Denmark encounter Danish stereotypical conceptions of the French language and thereby the person involved is ascribed other linguistic identities than (s)he is used to. The person concerned will find it hard to maintain an inner feeling of linguistic identity under the new conditions. The relationship between the person's linguistic resources and his/her new linguistic identity has been transformed to a greater or lesser extent.

(10) Linguistic resources – foreign languages – semantic-pragmatic dimension

When a person acquires a new language as a foreign language, (s)he involuntarily uses his/her own languaculture a lot of the time. As yet, (s)he is unfamiliar with the languacultural potential of the new language and adapts his/her own languaculture to the target language. This also applies to large sections of the structural core of the target language, especially in the first phases of the acquisition process, the word-collecting phase and the filling-in phase (Lund, 1999). The target language thereby has its languacultural potential enlarged considerably: all those who are in the process of acquiring or learning it expand and transform the target language and add new variability to it. So it would not make sense, when acquiring and using a language as a foreign language, to say that the language and its languaculture are absolutely inseparable. The target language is used with the inclusion of languacultures from other languages.

In research into bilingualism the question is sometimes raised concerning 'biculturalism' (e.g. in Grosjean, 1982). In his article '*The biculture in bilingual*' (Agar, 1997), Agar has directly argued in favour of biculturalism resulting from bilingualism. However, I feel it is important to distinguish between languaculture and the rest of culture here: when we are dealing with two languages, there are also two structurally defined (first-language) languacultures. So in that sense the individual involved can develop into being 'bicultural'. But this is only in a languacultural sense, and one could use the expression 'bilanguacultural' in this connection. What the relation is to the other cultural relations is another (empirical) matter (see also Chapter 12).

(11) Linguistic resources – foreign language – poetic dimension

The person acquiring a new language on the one hand has a lot of latitude when it comes to linguistic experimentation, but on the other hand has to take over to a great extent the poetic potential of the new language, especially that which is delineated by structures such as the syllabic and sentence structures already mentioned.

No matter whether one finds oneself in a learning situation or is acquiring the language independently of it, one will probably transfer poetic patterns from one's first language to the new language. Probably the poetic potential of the language will be widened by being used as a foreign language, but it may be at the same time that the individual cannot or does not have the opportunity to utilise this potential. Perhaps it is not accepted in the environment that (s)he, as a foreign-language speaker, uses the language in a poetic, aesthetic or literary way. This has to do with the fact that the language in its capacity of foreign language is usually not recognised as a special linguistic form that has value in itself, but only as a transitional form in relation to something better: native competence, or, in a weakened form, near-native competence. Generally speaking, one will not be accepted as an author, or something similar, before one has acquired at least near-native competence.

(12) Linguistic resources – foreign language – identity dimension

When one acquires / learns a language as a foreign language, certain special conditions apply regarding linguistic identity. Firstly, it is characteristic for, in particular, foreign-language teaching that one learns to use (productively) a language variant that, in some vague sense or other, is characteristic of relatively educated people, with a regional accent mainly coming from major economic centres: capital or similar. It is possible to assume this social identity without realising it: perhaps one simply believes that the language one is learning is, for example, English. A Dane who has a social background in a fishing environment on the North Sea coast, and who has a distinct Western Jutland identity in his spoken Danish, learns, for example, a form of English that is most characterised by the leading social strata in London and its environs. The student in question may have no awareness of this considerable social reidentification resulting from the language learning, and may be incapable of taking this into account in his use of English when at some point he takes part in union meetings with fishermen from the east coast of England.

Languaculture in 'The Linguistic System'

(13) The linguistic system – first language – semantic-pragmatic dimension

As I touched on in Chapter 6, the idea of 'the language' has been a central one in metalinguistic discourses for many centuries, and during the past 300–400 years in Europe it has centred on the notion of the national standard language as the norm one could and ought to describe. As an extension of this, one has to say that the structuralist tradition has mainly been interested in language as a first language and not as a second or foreign language – a result of the earlier-mentioned widespread first-language bias in linguistics (Chapter 1).

If the personal languacultures are so different, because of the individual connotations that each individual has developed in the course of his or her life, is it then possible to describe 'the language' as a common, unified languacultural system? I do not believe it is, but for practical purposes one can of course decide to construct a system that contains an intersection of the languacultural potentials one can imagine in a language community. An example of this is the dictionary *Longman's Dictionary of English Language and Culture* (Summers, 1992). The assignment here seems to have been to imagine the knowledge connotations of a more general (collective) kind that well-educated people who speak English as a first language could conceivably have in connection with each of the headwords – a somewhat vague assignment, but not completely useless because of that.

The construction of the semantic and pragmatic potential of language will always be capable of being placed on a kind of continuum that stretches from a minimalist description of the relatively constant semantic and pragmatic potential – the denotative core of the language – and a maximalist description in the form of a huge encyclopedia, combined with a huge manual of linguistic social conventions. And what language users are represented in such works? In practice, it would be a question of reproducing (more general sections of) the personal languaculture of every article-writer, unless (s)he has included some control groups or built on other material that can widen the perspective.

The idea of the homogeneous linguistic system (implied here: first language) is based, as mentioned, on the idea of a homogeneous written language, and from here the link to the national – the national community, national history – is just waiting to be made.

(14) The linguistic system – first language – poetic dimension

Constructions or descriptions of the linguistic system that emphasise its poetic potential are to be found in rhyming-word dictionaries, synonym dictionaries and manuals in rhetoric, etc., which are also mainly based on the written language. This dimension will also typically be linked to the national, especially the national-literary, lyrical tradition.

(15) The linguistic system – first language – identity dimension

Every act of identity is both a confirmation of oneself as a unique being (personal identity) and an identification with some group or other (social and cultural identity). Among the groups one can refer to in the modern world there is the imagined community referred to as 'the nation' and thereby, indirectly, 'language' seen as a national common language (cf. e.g.

Pratt, 1987). In connection with this side of the national construction of 'the language', writers, politicians etc. have contributed to the national consolidation by producing a whole series of identity symbolics in connection with the language, including some 'us' – 'them' contrasts in the form of stereotypes about one's own first language and that of certain others, especially those who are geopolitically interesting. This practice, also called 'language ideology' (Schieffelin *et al.*, 1998) contains discourses about various languages (e.g. English, Spanish, Japanese) that can have a significant impact on language learning.

(16) The linguistic system – foreign language – semantic-pragmatic dimension

In this instance, one normally speaks of an interlanguage: a mainly individual and variable phenomenon that can be studied in connection with analysis of student language. But there are some who also operate with a common 'system', or at any rate certain regularities across interlanguage developed by people with the same first language. This can be seen from such expressions as 'Danes' interlanguage in German', 'Danish school English', 'French with a Danish accent', etc. Here there is a vague link to the national, but without the National-Romantic connotations that are traditionally linked to the first languages.

(17) The linguistic system – foreign language – poetic dimension

As far as I know, there are no systematic descriptions (dictionaries or other aids) that deal in particular with the poetic potential of interlanguages. Generally speaking, there does not seem to be any research interest in the field. But, as already mentioned, many language-pedagogical methods actually utilise the poetic skills of their students.

(18) The linguistic system – foreign language – identity dimension

Do treatments of interlanguages exist that draw attention to their identity dimensions? One could perhaps point to studies of attitudes to languages used as foreign languages, possibly as a lingua franca such as 'immigrant Danish', 'pidgin English', 'airport English', etc. One could also point to the discussion of the concept of native speaker and that of to what extent one ought to upgrade and include non-native speakers as linguistic models in language teaching and linguistic practice, cf. Widdowson's discussion of *The Ownership of English* (Widdowson, 1994), and Kramsch's similar discussion in relation to German, *Wem gehört die deutsche Sprache?* (Who does the German language belong to?) (Kramsch, 1996).[16]

Research is sadly lacking into languacultural aspects of the interlanguage phenomenon. Research into second-language acquisition has in particular cultivated the problem area that deals with acquisition sequences within morphology and syntax, including the discussion of what drives this acquisition forwards (Lund, 1999). Research into interlanguage pragmatics has cultivated the problem area that deals with how interlanguage is used in intercultural interaction (Blum-Kulka *et al.*, 1989). Projects are getting under way on English as a lingua franca with special reference to grammatical, lexical and phonological characteristics (Seidlhofer, 2001). But we still lack research into the languaculture of interlanguages: semantics/pragmatics, poetics and identity dimensions. Research is also lacking into the sociolinguistics and sociology of interlanguages. These lacunae are remarkable in the light of how widespread the interlanguage phenomenon is.

The Whorfian Hypothesis and the Concept of Languaculture

The Whorfian hypothesis deals first and foremost with the relationship between language and cognition. That it is also presented as dealing with the relationship between language and culture is because one implicitly assumes a parallelism between the individual language and 'its' culture. I feel it would benefit greatly if we could make it quite clear that the Whorfian hypothesis has to do with language, *languaculture* and cognition, and that in that connection one must distinguish between the three loci for language/languaculture and acknowledge the importance of the idiolect.[17] In the following, I will briefly summarise how the Whorfian discussion can be structured if one makes use of the languaculture concept, as once more I divide into linguistic practice, linguistic resources and the idea of the linguistic system.

Linguistic practice and its languacultural variability has been researched in the more recent versions of the Whorfian discussion that gain inspiration from pragmatic and interactional tendencies within linguistics, sociolinguistics and anthropological linguistics (e.g. Gumperz & Levinson, 1996; Kramsch, 1993; Stubbs, 1997). This form of linguistic relativity Lucy (2000) refers to as discursive relativity.[18] In linguistic practice, the various participants make use of their personal languacultures, and a negotiation of meaning takes place – a negotiation that at a certain point contributes to fixing or 'closing' certain meanings, but which can always continue and create new meanings and new understandings of the outside world (here it is very much a question of the semantic-pragmatic dimension). The languacultural resources of the participants in one or more languages play a role in the development of the intertextual chain in the social networks. I would call this interpretation a sociolinguistic version of the weak Whorfian hypothesis.

Linguistic resources and their languacultural variability have not yet been researched all that much, but there are early signs in socioculturally oriented researchers such as Lantolf (1999). On the other hand, there is considerable research in a more cognitive direction that focuses on those parts of language that are common to the entire language community – what I have called the denotative core – and here I am especially thinking of the type of categories that have to be activated in practically every sentence: tense, aspect, countability, etc. (depending on which language we are dealing with). There have been a number of experiments in recent years that indicate that such categories play a role in people's habitual thinking and in how one describes the world in terms of language (languaculture), cf. Berman & Slobin (1994), Kay & Kempton (1984), Lucy (1992a and b), Palmer (1996). I would call this a psychological, cognitively oriented version of the weak Whorfian hypothesis.

This brings us over to the system-oriented approach, which as is known is the oldest one, and which has always had a psychological angle. It is also Whorf's own approach – and it dates further back to Humboldt and his successors, cf. Chapter 4. Whorf's classic structuralist version had to do with the importance of the linguistic (grammatical) categories for gaining knowledge of physical and social reality – and here he was thinking in particular of broad epistemological categories of a Kantian nature (time, place, cause, etc.). A more recent representative of the structuralist approach that looks in particular at the lexical semantics of various languages is Wierzbicka (1997). It is, however, necessary to deconstruct Whorf's abstract idea of language seen as a system and culture seen as a system that is analogous in some sense or other. Whorf (like many other anthropologists of his time) talked about language and world view, a thought he had taken over from the German idealistic tradition: Humboldt talked about the special *Weltansicht*[19] that lies in the individual language.[20] This general notion is, in my opinion, an indefensible abstraction in relation to the many more or less different personal languacultures, linguistic identities and understandings of the outside world one would be able to carry out empirically in complex linguistic communities and comprehensive linguistic networks.

Furthermore, it must be stressed once again that the Whorfian discussion until now has broadly speaking dealt with language only in its capacity as first language. What role language might possibly play for cognition when we are dealing not with a first language but with an early/late second language or foreign language has only begun to be looked at in recent years in connection with reflections on what constitutes the multilingual subject (Kramsch, forthcoming) and what the relationship is between the bilingual subject's linguistic resources and his/her conceptual representations (Pavlenko, 1999 and forthcoming).

The Term 'Languaculture'

It is remarkable that the concept of 'languaculture'/'linguaculture' has given rise to so little interest, with the exception of Agar. Kramsch touches on it in Kramsch (1989), but apart from that it is only mentioned *en passant* in e.g. Kramsch (1993), and not at all in Kramsch's *Language and Culture* (1998a). And the above-mentioned book on linguistic anthropology based on a cognitive perspective (Palmer: *Toward a Theory of Cultural Linguistics* from 1996) mentions it only very briefly twice. Is this because the introduction of the concept of languaculture paves the way for a new question that is perhaps even harder to pin down: what is the relationship between languaculture and the rest of culture? Or is it because one is thinking more along psychological than sociological lines? For it is from the *sociological* point of view that the concept is particularly useful.

The English term 'languaculture' (and the Danish *sprogkultur*) does not have any direct equivalent in for example German or French. The word *Sprachkultur* exists in German, but it means something different from what I mean by languaculture. *Sprachkultur* means care of the language, language planning, language criticism – i.e. cultivation of the language or cultivated use of the norm, especially the written norm, cf. Daneš, 1988; Oksaar, 1985; Weinrich, 1985. This meaning is already to be found in Humboldt: 'Durch die Cultur der Sprache fallen nun entweder diese blossen Ausfüllungsworte hinweg, oder …' (Via the culture of the language these mere fill-in words either drop out, or…) (Humboldt, 1906 (1824–26): 379). This is also the meaning we find in the Slavonic languages, e.g. the Russian: *kul'tura reci*. We are dealing here with an aesthetic, hierarchical concept of culture. As regards French, I do not think that there exists such a term as, for example, **linguaculture*. French prefers to use the expression *culture dans la langue* (e.g. Galisson, 1991, who is thinking here of the semantic dimension). And within English one finds the expression 'culture-in-language' (e.g. Crozet & Liddicoat, 2000 and Murphy, 1988; who are thinking in particular here of the pragmatic dimension). And in German one would translate languaculture as *Kultur* *in der Sprache.*[21] Even so, I feel that if the structure (and languaculture) of the language otherwise permits it, it would be a great advantage to have an independent lexicalisation here, since it makes it easier to develop more sophisticated concepts at the border between language and culture.

Conclusion

At this first stage of the analysis of the relationship between language and culture I have undertaken a shift of perspective from a sociolinguistic to a culture-theoretical look at language and emphasised certain culture-theoretically interesting aspects of language: the variable and relational side of language's semantics-pragmatic dimension, poetics and identity dimension. I have argued in favour of the idea that language (in the three loci 2 + 1) is always a bearer of culture and that language is never neutral in terms of languaculture – not even when it is used as a lingua franca, as, for example, English. I have underlined the idiolectal nature of languaculture as an aspect of the life history of the individual.

One could perhaps come to the immediate conclusion that 'language' and 'languaculture' are identical – and Agar and Friedrich are apparently of that opinion. But this is only correct at the generic level ('language' always implies 'languaculture'). If we keep to the differential level – and leave the first-language bias – it is incorrect to operate with such an identification.

When a language is used as a foreign language/late second language, certain transfer phenomena occur. The language in question is used with contributions from the languacultures of *other* languages. So there is a kind of language mix in the linguistic resources that, for example, makes use of the expression side of the one language (the target language) and of the content side of the other language (the first language). When one migrates to another country, one takes this particular, more or less individual, language mix with one. This means that the linguistic flows and languacultural flows do not move along precisely the same paths. If I, with Danish as my first language, travel round the world, I take my Danish idiolect with me, with the personal languaculture I have developed during my life. But I also take my special forms of English, French and German with me – the languages I have learned as foreign languages. My foreign-language resources are, without a doubt, influenced to a great extent by my Danish languaculture. So I contribute to the spreading of Danish languaculture, but to a lesser extent to the spreading of English, French and German languaculture. In the *Tour de France* example, the Dutch girl and the Iranian boy contribute with elements of Farsi and

Dutch languaculture respectively, and the teacher contributes to a certain extent with Danish languaculture in her use of German as a foreign language.

To use the languaculture concept is synonymous with saying that there is some 'culture' that is not (just) 'languaculture'. In the next chapters I will therefore introduce some conceptual distinctions that are to be used in the subsequent analysis of the complex relationship between language and culture. I intend to begin with a particular interpretation of the concept of discourse.

Notes

1. Agar writes in a footnote: '… I'm hardly the only one tangling with culture with an eye toward what the world has turned into. A few of my favorite allies in the struggle are Ulf Hannerz, Cultural Complexity …' (Agar, 1994: 267).
2. These Agar sums up in the acronym MAR: the art of swimming in the cultural ocean (Agar, 1994: 42). *Mar* means 'sea' in Spanish. Agar has relations to California and Mexico.
3. And he also says that the word 'linguaculture' reminds him of pasta (Agar, 1994: 60). He does not say why, but my guess is that he is thinking of the kind of pasta that is called *linguini*. In Agar (1997) he writes that the word 'linguaculture' creates problematic associations to 'agriculture' for English speakers.
4. He also used the term 'linguaculture' in a manuscript from 1988. In 1986, he used the expression 'language-culture' (Friedrich, 1986).
5. I am deliberately using the word 'variability' and not 'variance'. The concept of variance is linked to a discourse that emphasises systemness (e.g. the Labov tradition in sociolinguistics). Instead, I wish to emphasise the individual, experience-based, more or less willed variability – a variability that can be explained only partially by referring to social structures and processes.
6. But also to the German tradition within linguistic relativity: Humboldt and the subsequent Humboldtian tradition.
7. The idea of the song with the cyclists is probably originally Swedish.
8. There are parallel texts in various languages, including German: *Zehn kleine Negerlein* (with special variants in the Nazi period), and in Yiddish: *Zejhn brider sennen mir gewesen* (Klaus Schulte, personal communication).
9. I wish to stress that via the sections that now follow I do not intend to provide an overview of 'pragmatics', 'semantics', etc. – that would of course be impossible within the scope of the book. The purpose of the sections is just to show that it is important to distinguish between the three points of view seen in relation to language as first language/early second language and foreign language/late second language respectively.
10. I also believe that unconscious factors are involved in text production and reception, but there is not room to develop this subject here.
11. And possible other participants: chance passers-by, analysts, etc.
12. Part of this variability is of course involuntary to the extent the learner is trying to attain a 'native' reading.

13. Wierzbicka touches on something similar in her contrastive investigation into semantic/pragmatic relations in various languages (Wierzbicka, 1997: *Understanding Cultures Through Their Key Words*). But Wierzbicka does not adopt the relational view as Agar does (and I do), preferring to deal mainly with 'linguistic systems' separately, without introducing considerations about social and individual variation. She refers to Geertz's system-oriented conception of culture from the 1970s and concentrates on the (essentialist) concept: 'core cultural values'.

14. This also applies, for example, to such a language as Esperanto, which is a living language with a particular languaculture with regard to the semantic-pragmatic, poetic and identity dimensions.

15. A poem whose initial letters form a word.

16. Cf. also Haberland (1989), and the discussion in the journal *The European English Messenger*, e.g. Modiano (2000) (who favours the development of a special English for European communication (Mid-Atlantic English or Euro-English).

17. Cf. that I mentioned earlier in this chapter that Agar suggests that what Whorf is really talking about is (what Agar understands by) languaculture.

18. Unlike 'linguistic relativity' (the forms of relativity I discuss below) and 'semiotic relativity', which deal with language in a generic (semiotic) sense. This latter form I will not be dealing with, as my focus is on language in a differential sense.

19. Not to be confused with *Weltanschauung*, which is a philosophical concept that does not immediately have anything to do with the individual language.

20. The neo-Humboldtian Weisgerber talks about *das Weltbild der deutschen Sprache* and about *eine sprachliche Zwischenwelt* (the world-picture of the German language... a linguistic interworld) (Weisgerber, 1953–54).

21. This was at any rate the expression that was used in a translation into German of one of my articles on languaculture (Risager, 2000).

Chapter 9
Discourse and Double Intertextuality

Introduction

In both the former chapter on languaculture and this chapter on discourse I see *culture as meaning*, i.e. I make use of an understanding of the concept of culture that is also used by Hannerz.

The concept of languaculture has to do with meaning that is linked to a particular language in a differential sense. But what we are to deal with in this chapter is meaning that is not linked to a particular language, but which is formed by (verbal) language nevertheless. The transition from languaculture to discourse is thus the next step in the analysis of the relationship between language and culture. We are dealing here with a shift of perspective from the individual language in the differential sense to 'language' in the generic sense.

A Concept of Discourse that is Content-oriented, Yet Still Linguistic

In the various linguistic uses of the concept of discourse it is typical for it to be used to conceptualise the process of linguistic practice, the more or less cohesive chains of spoken and written language. The linguistic approaches are interested in the content side and the thematic content, but first and foremost with the aim of studying the way in which the content develops and is structured with the aid of the linguistic effects in relation to the context.

This purely linguistic concept of discourse, however, is not all that useful in the construction of a model for the analysis of the interface between language and culture. We need a mediating concept between language and culture – and here the concepts of discourse that are based on theories of culture and society are more useful, because they focus more clearly on content at the textual macro-level and relate it to ideological and political positioning and to the actors' perspective and horizon of understanding. I am thinking here of the conceptions of discourse inspired by Michel Foucault's work on discourse, knowledge and power in a historical perspective.

Among these conceptions of discourse it is most relevant to point to the theories that connect this culture-oriented interest to a linguistically oriented analysis, i.e. the various forms of interdisciplinary critical discourse analysis (van Dijk *et al.*, Fairclough, Jäger, Wodak). In the more general context concerning the relationship between language and culture it is not crucial which branch one actually chooses to work in relation to. In the following I intend to take Fairclough's approach as my starting point, because he has been relatively explicit regarding his own position vis à vis the other positions based on theories of culture and society, and because – as I did in Chapter 7 – he operates with the concept of intertextuality and with intertextual chains in social networks, also thought of in recent years as global discursive flows.[1]

Fairclough's concept of discourse focuses almost exclusively on content and on the perspective shaping of it:

> a discourse is a particular way of constructing a subject-matter, and the concept differs from its predecessors in emphasizing that contents or subject-matters – areas of knowledge – only enter texts in the mediated form of particular constructions of them. It is helpful in this regard to choose terms for particular discourses which designate both the relevant area of knowledge, and the particular way it is constituted, for example 'techno-scientific medical discourse' ... or 'feminist discourses of sexuality' ... (Fairclough, 1992: 128)

Fairclough emphasises the dialectic relationship between discursive practice and societal structures and processes of change. He stresses that language is both constituted and constituting: that at one and the same time it is subject to societal, historical conditions and has an important role as regards changing them. Discursive practice must therefore be analysed as a social practice among other social practices in society.

Fairclough's concept of discourse is predominantly linguistic, as he restricts the concept to mainly dealing with verbal language texts (spoken and written) – summed up by the abbreviation TODA: *Textually-Oriented Discourse Analysis* (Fairclough, 1992). Fairclough expresses himself somewhat variedly in different publications as to how well defined this limitation is. In Chouliaraki and Fairclough (1999), for example, the authors define the concept of discourse as follows:

> We shall use the term 'discourse' to refer to semiotic elements of social practice. Discourse therefore includes language (written and spoken and in combination with other semiotics, for example: with music in singing), non-verbal communication (facial expressions, body move-

ments, gestures, etc.) and visual images (for instance, photographs, film). The concept of discourse can be understood as a particular perspective on these various forms of semiosis – it sees them as moments of social practice in their articulation with other non-discursive moments. (Chouliaraki & Fairclough, 1999: 38)

Here they are operating with an expansion that runs parallel to the one I have stressed earlier: verbal language plus language-accompanying phenomena: paralanguage and kinesics. But it is still verbal language discourse that is the pivotal element.

A Non-differential Concept of Language

Discursive practice in Fairclough's model, then, always includes linguistic practice, and this will of course always be expressed in some specific language or other (or in some form of language mix or other). But Fairclough does not take account of what specific language the discourse is expressed in. In his close-language textual analyses he does not reflect on what particular expressive means and ideological possibilities the English language, for example, can give rise to, as opposed to other languages. One could say that in his theory of discourse Fairclough expresses a conception of language that belongs to the generic level: the theory always treats 'language' as a social phenomenon in general.[2] This is quite common in the cultural and social sciences that are interested in growth and changes in the significance of language in modern and modernist developments, and that stress 'the linguistic turn'.[3] And Fairclough obviously chooses – in his dialogue with the other cultural and social sciences – to ignore language differences in the differential sense, i.e. he implicitly distances himself from linguistic relativity.[4] At the beginning of Fairclough (1992), he objects to the widespread notion of the transparency of language: 'while linguistic data such as interviews are widely used, there has been a tendency to believe that the social content of such data can be read off without attention to the language itself' (Fairclough, 1992: 2). But the content of the rest of the book shows that he is only thinking here of the generic sense.

   Critical discourse analysis (here in Fairclough's version, although it also applies more generally) thereby ends up concealing multilingualism in the world, including that in 'English-speaking' countries.[5] It ends up functioning ideologically, by reproducing a monolinguistic conception of society. Critical discourse analysis does not thematise the question of the semantics and pragmatics of different languages, or of the identity – and thereby also political and ideological – dimensions of the choice of language. In order to do this, one has to connect critical discourse analysis (language at the generic level) to the analysis of language and languaculture (language at the differential level).

Double Intertextuality

In Fairclough's version of critical discourse analysis the flow metaphor is on the point of being introduced: '… a global-local dialectic wherein disembedded language practices increasingly flow across linguistic and cultural boundaries …' (Chouliaraki & Fairclough, 1999: 83). In this passage, 'language' and 'culture' are linked together in the same expression – something that would indicate that Chouliaraki and Fairclough conceive language and culture as possibly being (partially) coterminous. But the most important point here is that discursive flows move across languages – to an increasing extent, according to Chouliaraki and Fairclough.

However, Chouliaraki and Fairclough do not discuss the consequences of the thought they just touch on here. The idea that discourses and languages flow across each other has certain interesting consequences for language theory. It means that in every textual analysis and analysis of discursive practice one must adopt an intertextual perspective that is double: the text is always a meeting between two flows, a linguistic flow and a discursive flow. The actual concept of intertextuality has to be analysed in these two highly different yet mutually connected forms.

The German teaching sequence on *Tour de France* is full of examples of this: a class conversation about professional cycling in German (the students' German interlanguages) is a meeting between on the one hand the flow (spread) of the German language to this class by virtue of the learning processes here and their possible use outside the class, and on the other hand the discursive flow that carries knowledge and perspectives to do with international cycling, professionalism, etc. This discourse is transnational, but it will always be tinged by the language in which it has been formulated – and this has to do with the languaculture(s) that is / are connected to the language involved. The students' conversation about cycling will be influenced by the fact that it is conducted in a German interlanguage that is partly supplemented with Danish languacultures and maybe also with Dutch and Farsi languacultures. What do the various students associate, for example, with the word *Fahrrad* (bicycle)?[6]

The discourse on international cycling is transnational. It is channelled in a structured way in the global communication system and may be assumed to be mediated more often in certain languages than in others.

This issue I will return to in Chapter 12, in connection with a more societal analysis of the relationship between linguistic, discursive and (other) cultural flows.

Apart from the concept of intertextuality, Fairclough also makes use of the concept of interdiscursivity when he wishes to focus on relationships between discourses rather than between specific texts in the form of references, direct or hidden quotations, etc. (Fairclough, 1992: 85). Both these concepts are at what I would call the discourse level, as they have not been defined in relation to a differential concept of language. In the following, I will make do with the concept of intertextuality, which, on the other hand, will include both a discourse level and a (differential) linguistic level. Every text is the result of a meeting between discursive practice and (individual) linguistic practice, and in the following I will stress this by talking about 'linguistic, discursive practice'.

So there are two fundamental perspectives on the linguistic sign:

- The concept of 'language' (and 'languaculture') comprises both expression and content, but has the expression side as its point of departure, i.e. the primary focus is on (various forms of) a specific language, e.g. 'Danish', or possibly on code-switching between specific languages. The semantic-pragmatic and thematic content is not excluded, but it is of secondary importance: what is spoken or written of is not irrelevant, but this aspect plays a subordinate role.
- The concept of 'discourse' comprises both expression and content, but has the content side as its point of departure, i.e. the primary focus is on the specific perspectival content, e.g. discourse about the French language, or nationalist discourse. The expression is not excluded, but it is of secondary importance: which specific language (and languaculture) the discourse is expressed in is not irrelevant, but this aspect plays a subordinate role.

In concrete linguistic, discursive practice there is of course always both an expression side and a content side, and the relationship between them is solidary, to use Hjelmslev's term. One could say that discourses flow around in the world, but never without being linked to the expression side of some language or other. Conversely, languages flow around in the world, but never without being linked to a discursive content – perspectival knowledge – of some kind or other, in a more or less fragmentary form.

One can on the one hand adopt a linguistic (sociolinguistic) perspective and be interested in the choice of language and the linguistic expression, and in how the linguistic expression is linked to the linguistic content in various ways (arbitrariness, iconicity, etc.). This perspective is characteristic of more linguistically oriented discourse analysis. On the other hand, one can adopt a more culturally and socially oriented perspective and be interested in the content and genre of the discourses, and in how they find expression in the particular thematic structure, text genre and style of the verbal language text – as one would do within the various forms of critical discourse analysis. In my opinion, both perspectives are important in all text and conversation analysis – and they are necessary in an analysis of language teaching if one wants to take seriously that language teaching is both work on developing linguistic competencies (with the expression side as the point of departure) and work on discourses (with the content side as the point of departure).

As can be seen, I prefer a content-oriented discourse concept, but that does not mean that a specific discourse has of necessity been defined by its subject matter ('global theme', as Tomlin *et al.* [1997] would say) and the textual macrostructure ('Macrostructure is the global semantic structure of a discourse and may be expressed by its title or headline or by summarizing sentences,' Tomlin *et al.*, 1997: 90). A discourse can also be defined by more implicit structures, perspectives and positions – as when one can understand 'national discourses' both as discourses that explicitly deal with the national and as discourses that implicitly lay certain national conceptual frameworks over some other subject, e.g. the weather: 'Danish weather', 'domestic weather', etc.

Translation of Discourse from Language to Language

Within the flow metaphor, one can say that discourses flow from language to language, and conversely that language flows from discourse to discourse.[7] The latter is perhaps not so interesting: all languages are multidiscursive in the sense that they either have or can develop the necessary semantic and pragmatic potential to express every discourse.[8] But the former raises the question of multilingual discourse.

A discursive practice can be multilingual at two levels: at the macro-level one can follow the path of a discursive flow through a number of linguistic communities (linguistic networks), mediated via translation and other methods of transfer (retelling, adapting, etc.). At the micro-level, one can follow a discursive flow through a multilingual conversation in which various forms of code-switching are used. In both cases, there is good reason to enquire as to which elements of linguistic, discursive practice are language-specific, and which not.

This question can be clarified only via translation, and thereby the translation process gains a central position in the analysis of the two layers of linguistic, discursive practice and the intertextuality phenomenon as such. Only via translation[9] can one hope to distinguish between the two layers. And since the translation process always takes place between language pairs, the question of the relationship between the two layers is a relational one: in a translation from Danish into English the border area between the two layers presumably looks different from in a translation from Danish into Chinese, because of the greater linguistic/languacultural distance between Danish and Chinese.[10]

In the single linguistic event the two layers have melted together to form one unity, and it is difficult, not to say impossible, to distinguish language-specific elements from language-neutral ones, i.e. to mark off where languaculture 'ends' and where discourse 'begins'. This methodological problem applies both to the single monolingual text and to the larger monolingual text corpus.

One can, for instance, ask how one is to mark off languaculture from discourse in an example such as this one: I can refer to my television in different ways and thereby draw on various (interlingual) discourses in combination with Danish languacultural elements. I can use the Danish compound word *fjernsyn* and have a relatively neutral discourse on the well-known mass medium (*fjern* means 'distant' and *syn* means 'vision'). At the same time, we are dealing with a lexical compound that links the Danish languacultural elements *fjern* and *syn* together, in terms of both denotative and connotative elements. I can also refer to it as *dummerkasse* and draw on a critical discourse that involves a reduction to a state of stupidity (*dum* means 'stupid' and *kasse* means 'box'). Or I can talk about a *husalter* and thereby also draw on a discourse that is critical but which furthermore makes use in an ironic way of a religious comparison (*hus* means 'house' and *alter* means 'altar').[11] Here, too, a lexical compound has also been used, this time drawing on the Danish languacultural elements *hus* and *alter*, which – like the other elements mentioned – separately awaken a number of notions that can be related to the life experiences, perspective and horizon of the individual Danish-speaking language user.

In each of the three instances, it will be by virtue of the translation process (to a specific language where ideally the reference and the discourse are to be preserved as intact as possible) that one can distinguish the relatively language-specific from the relatively language-neutral.

It is quite possible to imagine a discourse that circulates exclusively within a particular language community. Perhaps there are particular subjects and points of view that are reserved to those who can speak the language, and via this practice it is confirmed that they can speak the language, that they have something in common, as opposed to those who cannot.[12] So discourses may exist that are simply not translated or are not to be translated.

It should be noted that in the above section I have dealt only with the semantic/pragmatic side of languaculture. There are, of course, particular sets of problems involved in translation when dealing with the poetics of a language. And in connection with the identity dimension certain significant transformations take place: when, for example, one translates from Danish into French, one may perhaps be successful in retaining both the specific references and most of the discourse, including creative reformulations of metaphors etc.; but because the target text is now in French, the reception of it will probably be tinged by the receiver's attitudes to the French language in general.

Discursive Resources

The discursive process takes place in an interaction between discursive practice and the discursive resources of the individual. These comprise, among other things, knowledge of a whole world of verbalised themes, points of view and positions; insight into which subjects are taboo; knowledge of who can be expected to be of the opinion and express what in which situations; greater or lesser ability oneself to express, formulate and develop discourses within a wide range of subject areas; reflexive capacity to understand one's own and other people's positions in relation to social and political reality; strategic abilities to shape and administer one's own subjectivity in collaboration or conflict with others, especially with the aid of language (cf. the discourse psychologists Potter and Wetherell (1987), who focus on the subject's manifold discursive practice and interpretative repertoires).

A central question in this context is to what extent the eventual bilingualism or multilingualism of the individual is of significance for the discursive resources. I do not intend to analyse that question in more detail here, only to mention that it may well be that certain discourses are easier or more natural for the individual to express in one language than in another (cf. Agar, 1997). It may also be that certain discourses are easier to express in a foreign language (or late second language) than in the first language (or early second language).

Under all circumstances, we are dealing with a more or less integrated co-development of linguistic and discursive resources, and these resources accompany the individual should he or she possibly migrate. But what the development can actually look like is an open question, one that research has not to date shown any interest in – and this has to do with the interdisciplinary nature of the question.

Order of Discourse

If we now turn to the system-oriented view of discourse, then Fairclough operates here with a central concept: the 'order of discourse', translated from Foucault's *ordre du discours*. Fairclough has defined the concept in this way:

> I see the order of discourse of a particular social domain as the structured totality of discursive practices – genres and discourses – used within that domain. The emphasis is both on the diversity of practices, and on the social structuring of diversity, in terms of, for example:
> — boundaries of flows between practices (and between orders of discourse)
> — relationships of complementarity, tension, struggle between practices
> — hegemonic structuring and relations of dominance between practices. (Fairclough, 1997: 11)

In recent years, Fairclough has also expressed himself a little about the global level and, *en passant*, he uses the concept 'global order of discourse', e.g.:

> The orders of discourse of different nation-states are interconnected, and this network of practices – an emergent global order of discourse – constitutes the horizon against which the orders of discourse of particular nation-states are formed and transformed... But globalization of discourse should be seen as a global-local dialectic, not as a simple international spread of globally dominant practices. International practices are taken up and reacted to in vastly different ways, depending upon the internal dynamics of particular societal orders of discourse. (Fairclough, 1997: 11ff.)

The concept of the order of discourse[13] has been discursively constructed, as has the concept of the linguistic system – and thus also has an 'artificial' locus. I am of the opinion, however, that it is well suited for describing discourse relations and conflicts within clearly defined social fields if one does not think of it in too static a way. The concept of the global order of discourse can also possibly be linked to something concrete, but it appears mostly to be a postulate at the moment – or, if you like: a draft of a research topic. It should be noted that the concept of 'global order of discourse' is completely different from 'the linguistic world system' (de Swaan, 1993): the global hierarchy among the various languages, see Chapter 12.

Conclusion

Both Chapter 8 on the concept of languaculture and this chapter on that of discourse serve to neutralise the dichotomy between 'language' and 'culture'. Both of them are mediating concepts between language and culture, and, by introducing them, three linking interfaces arise between language and culture:

- between language and languaculture;
- between language/languaculture and discourse;
- between language/languaculture/discourse and the rest of culture.

As regards the second interface, that between language/languaculture and discourse, this chapter has described a shift of perspective that consists in shifting one's gaze from language in the differential sense (language and languaculture) to language in the generic sense (discourse). The main point of this stage of the analysis is that linguistic flows are not identical with discursive flows, but that discursive flows move across linguistic communities or linguistic networks. This does not, however, exclude the possibility of there being discourses that exclusively circulate within one particular linguistic network and are never translated or transformed in some way or other.

Seen from this point of view, the concept of intertextuality comes to consist of two layers: a discursive layer and a linguistic layer. Research into intertextuality has until now dealt with the discursive layer, i.e. how discourses develop in a socially structured interaction and form textual chains of various kinds. But this has taken place without any special interest in which individual language is involved. In my opinion, one ought to think in terms of a combination of critical discourse analysis, sociolinguistics and translation theory: one ought to be interested to a greater extent in the linguistic translation and transformation processes that discourses go through. It is perhaps particularly apposite to emphasise this in an English-language context, where there can be a tendency among monolingual English speakers to underestimate all other linguistic flows than the English ones.

Notes

1. But Siegfried Jäger's approach is also interesting in relation to the present analysis, because of the explicit reference to the flow of texts in society (Jäger, 1993).
2. John Lucy would call this the semiotic level, cf. the section on the Whorfian discussion in Chapter 8.
3. including S. Hall, who, as mentioned, is thinking about the broad metaphorical concept of language (e.g. Hall, 1997).
4. In Fairclough (1989: 47ff.) there is a discussion of interethnic communication, so linguistic differences do at some point feature in his theory.
5. This lacuna in critical discourse analysis sometimes unfortunately results in its being forgotten that the analysed texts are actually in English and not some other language – or that 'the English world' is not identical with the whole world. Cf. the following passage: '… while we recognize that systemic functional linguistics is the one major linguistic theory within the English-speaking world capable of productively connecting with sociology, we believe that CDA has a crucial mediating role between them' (Chouliaraki & Fairclough, 1999: 106). The authors possibly believe that the English-speaking world is the only 'world' one needs to think about. I would further claim that whatever good sides systematic functional linguistics might have, they are not due to the fact that this branch of research has developed on the basis of an English-speaking environment, or that it has been developed with the particular aim of analysing texts in English. But this conception apparently underlies the following statement: '… the version of CDA which we work with would gain from extending its so far limited relationship with SFL (essentially just using a systemic grammar of English as a method in text analysis) …' (Chouliaraki & Fairclough, 1999: 139).
6. The Dutch girl will know two different words: 'rijwiel' (a very formal word used mainly on signs) and 'fiets' (the everyday word, of obscure origin) (JI).
7. This should not be taken to mean that discourses occur sharply separated from each other. On the contrary, it is normal for discourses and themes to be interwoven and to influence each other in an incredibly complex interaction, as is emphasised, for example, by Fairclough and Jäger.
8. This does not mean that all human experiences can be 'translated' into verbal language – I do not believe that they can.
9. Ranging from word-to-word translation to pragmatically oriented text mediation, and from transference (taking over words from the source language) to rendering on the basis of semantic componential analysis, cf. Newmark (1988).
10. By studying translation it may perhaps be possible to clarify a recurring difficulty in various approaches to critical discourse analyses and critical linguistics: the concept of genre and its relationship to textual analysis. By analytically separating the two layers it might perhaps be possible to distinguish between on the one hand discourse genres that are typical ways of organising particular discourses in a *language-neutral* action perspective, and on the other hand text genres that are *language-specific* ways of organising texts as language acts, in speech and in writing.
11. All these translations are of course approximations, near equivalents.

12. Hartmut Haberland, for example, is of the opinion that he has noticed the existence of a particular 'Faroese discourse' that is used among the Faroese only when speaking the Faroese language, as opposed to when they speak Danish (personal communication).

13. Scollon and Scollon (1995) operate with the concept of a *discourse system*. It is used in particular to characterise the way in which organisations act, and is really a reformulation into discourse terms of a fairly traditional concept of culture: a differential and collective concept of culture with roots in Kroeber and Kluckhohn (1952) (see Chapter 3) Cf. the discussion in Søderberg (1999).

Chapter 10
Cultural Contexts

Introduction

As mentioned, the single linguistic event is a fusion of linguistic, langua-cultural and discursive practice. It is *this fused unity* that I intend to use as my point of departure in this chapter and the two succeeding ones.

In this chapter I take a look at a macro-oriented problem area concerning the relationship between language and culture. I use as my starting point a notion that is more or less implicit in much discourse linked to language and culture pedagogy: language cannot be separated from its cultural context. Or, expressed normatively: language must not be separated from its cultural context. The aim of this chapter is to argue in favour of linguistic practice actually being able to move from one cultural macrocontext to the other, and of language and culture in this respect thus being able to be separated.

The Linguistic Concept of Context

The relationship between language and context – especially at the micro-level, but also sometimes at slightly higher levels – is a subject that has preoccupied large sections of linguistics over the past two to three decades, such as linguistic pragmatics, interactional sociolinguistics and (linguistic) discourse analysis, the ethnography of communication and linguistic anthropology[1], and ethno-methodologically oriented conversation analysis.

Nevertheless, the actual concept of context has been insufficiently clarified. There is no linguistic theory of context, as emphasised by Quasthoff and van Dijk. Quasthoff begins an encyclopedia article on 'Context' with the following statement: ' "Context" is one of those linguistic terms which is constantly used in all kinds of contexts but never explained' (Quasthoff, 1994: 730). Van Dijk also discusses the as-yet absent theory of context, and makes do with the following interim definition: '… we may provisionally define a context as the structure of those properties of the social situation that are systematically (that is, not incidentally) *relevant* for discourse' (van Dijk, 1997: 11, italics in the original).

In Schiffrin (1994), there is an overview of various ways of understanding the concept of context in linguistics.[2] Schiffrin distinguishes between a cognitive and a social/situational understanding of context: linguistic speech act theory and universal pragmatics see context as a type of knowledge that is linked to linguistic competence, i.e. a cognitive approach. Disciplines such as interactional sociolinguistics and (linguistic) discourse analysis, the ethnography of communication, linguistic anthropology and ethno-methodological conversation analysis operate with a concept of context that is at one and the same time both social/situational – since context is perceived as part of the reality between the interactors[3] – and cognitive. Some of these disciplines operate to a varying degree with a concept of context that also comprises the text itself, such as ethno-methodological conversation analysis, where a central research interest concentrates on showing how people via the course of conversation create and reshape the social situation and interpret and reinterpret in an ongoing way what has already been said – and thereby also what is expected to be said. My own position most resembles those for which the ethnography of communication and linguistic anthropology stand – although placed in a macro-context, as will be apparent from the following.

Linguistic thinking on the concept of context deals *either* with a completely openly conceived cognitive context that can comprise any *ad hoc* knowledge whatsoever of the world in more general terms, *or* with the social micro-context: the immediate social situation in which the linguistic event is embedded, and which it also helps to constitute. On the other hand, linguistics has precious little to say on the concept of context at the social macro-levels.

Cultural context in a systemic functional perspective

Halliday, as are representatives of systemic functional linguistics in general, is among those who for some time have operated with the macro-concept 'context of culture', which is a further development of the concept 'context of situation' (cf. Halliday, 1978; Halliday & Hasan, 1989), a distinction taken over from the ethnographer Malinowski (1920s and 1930s). But while the 'context of situation' has been thoroughly dealt with, the 'context of culture' has been only very loosely described and at times equated with a social system that is not described in any further detail. In Halliday and Hasan (1989) there is a passage that describes the content of the concept 'context of culture':

> The context of situation, however, is only the immediate environment. There is also a broader background against which the text has to be

interpreted: its context of culture. Any actual context of situation, the particular configuration of field, tenor and mode that has brought a text into being, is not just a random jumble of features but a totality – a package so to speak, of things that typically go together in the culture. People do these things on these occasions and attach these meanings and values to them: this is what a culture is.

The school itself provides a good example of what in modern jargon could be called an 'interface' between the context of situation and the context of culture. For any text in school – teacher talk in the classroom, pupil's notes or essay, passage from a textbook – there is always a context of situation: the lesson, with its concept of what is to be achieved; the relationship of teacher to pupil, or textbook writer to reader; the 'mode' of question-and-answer, expository writing, and so on. But these in turn are instances of, and derive their meaning from, the school as an institution in the culture: the concept of education, and of educational knowledge as distinct from common sense knowledge; the notion of the curriculum and school 'subjects'; the complex role structures of teaching staff, school principals, consultants, inspectorate, departments of education, and the like; and the unspoken assumptions about learning and the place of language within it.

All these factors constitute the context of culture, and they determine, collectively, the way the text is interpreted in its context of situation. (Halliday & Hasan, 1989: 46f)

As can be surmised from earlier chapters, I am critical of this understanding of culture: Halliday and Hasan have as their point of departure a conception of culture as being a (here implicitly understood in a national way) cohesive system of meanings (values, conceptions, etc.), an essence that determines the way in which texts (language use) are understood.

The concept of context in systemic functional linguistics is typically abstract and purely language-derived, and this understanding of context causes its supporters to project the systemness of language increasingly farther out into the context. One of the results of this is that 'genre' in one version (Eggins & Martin, 1997) is understood as a potential of acting intentions that are directly linked to the cultural context. In their own words:

> The terms *register* (context of situation) and *genre* (context of culture) identify the two major layers of context which have an impact on text, and therefore the two main dimensions of variation between texts. (Eggins & Martin, 1997: 251, italics in the original)

This truncated and ahistorical conception of context is unsuitable for forming the basis of an analysis of the relationship between linguistic practice and cultural context, first and foremost because it does not adopt any concrete attitude to interactional networks and intertextual processes in historical time. It is necessary to operate with a more concrete concept of context, since text production and understanding take place in and presuppose concrete contexts, and are carried out by concrete individuals. Systemic functional linguistics focuses on the relationship between the individual text and the context; one could metaphorically speak of a 'vertical' relationship. On the other hand, it finds it hard to conceptualise movement, spread, intertextuality and hybridity: the 'horizontal' relationship. Chouliaraki and Fairclough also touch on this. They criticise systemic functional linguistics for finding it difficult to deal with hybrid texts: texts that mix discourses, genres or registers (Chouliaraki & Fairclough, 1999: 143).

Cultural Context Seen As a Complex Historical Macro-context

However, in my opinion it is not possible either to create a theory about the cultural context based exclusively on a linguistic perspective. It calls for an interdisciplinary approach, e.g. a link with Hannerz's approach to cultural complexity and cultural flows. Such an approach must take an interest in the linguistic and the cultural and societal perspective at one and the same time. If one is interested only in the linguistic aspect, the understanding of the context will have an ad hoc touch. An example of this is Sperber and Wilson (1986). Their theory of relevance – of how language users make elements of the micro- and macro-context relevant by utilising their knowledge of the many different ways to produce and understand language – is important as a theoretical framework for the study of the conditions for linguistic communication and for the pragmatic analysis of spoken and written text. But their concept of context is insufficient, because it is derived from language. To achieve a more systematic understanding of the concept of context one has to abandon the idea that the sole aspects of the context that are interesting are those that one can decode from the text, or which one must assume are known by language users for them to be able to understand the text, via inference.

Linguistic/languacultural and discursive practice (bound together in the same linguistic event) always takes place in a concrete historical, societal context that can be described at various different levels, from the lowest micro-level (the situational context in relation to the individual communicative event) to the uppermost macro-level (the global, world-historical context). The context contains dimensions that one can describe as economic, technological, political, etc., depending on one's professional point of view. In Chapter 7 I mentioned which theoretical levels I myself find necessary in the present analysis: societal structures and domains, networks that exist by virtue of the actual interaction, and communities and identities that are constructed discursively on an ongoing basis. An analysis of linguistic practice must always contextualise this practice, i.e. point out the structures and domains, networks, and communities and identities that are considered necessary in order to achieve an overall understanding. This is also important in language and culture pedagogy.

When I here use the concept of *cultural* context, it is in order to emphasise the side of every context that conveys meaning. In my opinion, all societal life can be seen both as social life and cultural life. While the analysis of social life will typically be interested in the relational aspects of activities and institutions, the analysis of cultural life will typically be interested in the aspects that convey and create meaning. These two sides cannot be separated from each other. All social life conveys and creates meaning, and all exchange of meaning is relational, inscribed in power relations of various kinds. The context is always culturally complex – which is something I will discuss in greater detail in Chapter 12, where I deal with Hannerz's theory of cultural complexity and frameworks of cultural flow. As I have already pointed out, the cultural context also includes language: since most communities are multilingual, the context will as a rule comprise linguistic practice in a number of languages.

So as not to operate with a too idealistic conception of the concept of context, it is necessary to distinguish between its objective and subjective dimensions. The objective[4] dimension has to do with the concrete, material anchoring in time and space (setting), and with the actual social organisation, the material interests and power relations. The subjective dimension has to do with the conception of the situation (scene)[5], with the ascribing of meaning, with how people and groups interpret the world.

Linguistic/languacultural and discursive practice mainly contributes to characterising the subjective dimension, because it creates (constructs) images of culture and society, models of situations and roles, etc. It can also contribute to changing the material conditions, but this again calls for power if it is to be effective. The development of society contributes to a great extent on the other hand to language users developing and differentiating their linguistic/langacultural and discursive resources, including their conceptual potential and linguistic behaviour patterns.

First-language Context, Foreign-language Context and Second-language Context

Linguistic practice flows in social networks because of the elementary process: linguistic production and interpretation created by individuals and other collectives on the basis of their linguistic resources. These networks form complex networks of networks (Hannerz, 1992a, 1992b).

In relation to a particular language, the network can develop in a first-language context, a foreign-language context and a second-language context[6], or a combination of these. These concepts do not necessarily have to be understood in national terms, e.g. Denmark as a first-language context for Danish, etc. One must be more specific. When a person chooses for example to speak French as a foreign-language in Aalborg (a Danish city), (s)he may perhaps be in a foreign language context. But if (s)he visits a French-speaking family, then we are dealing with a first-language context embedded in a foreign-language context. If (s)he travels to Lyon and speaks French there, we can then speak of a first-language context. But it can also be a second-language context if (s)he is with Portuguese who speak French as a second language. This second-language context is embedded in a larger first-language context (the French-speaking areas of Western Europe, etc.). So one has to imagine contexts within and across contexts.

Some of these contexts can be called minority contexts to the extent that they develop under political and cultural dominance. This is nearly always understood in national terms: the 'minority' is dominated by the 'majority' within the political and cultural frameworks of a territorial state. But it does not have to be the case; Italy, for example, can be referred to as a minority context in the larger European political context that is now taking shape.

When people migrate, larger or smaller parts of the context can accompany them, especially its subjective dimensions: if a Danish upper-secondary class in English goes to Scotland on a study trip, they take their Danish school context with them in the form of certain frameworks for interaction and understanding. This accompanying Danish school context (a first-language context) has potential meaning for what they do in Scotland. But when they speak with their Scottish counterparts in English (Danish school-English), they are acting in another first-language context that is linked to the English language (or more correctly to a Scottish variant of it). Here the students can enter into other frameworks of understanding and agendas.

Another example of a context moving can be the situation in which half a village migrates (e.g. chain emigration) from one country to another, taking with them a varied cultural space, which is a first-language context in relation to the language they use. Yet another example can be the situation of a text being 'packaged' within its context, e.g. a film in which the linguistic practice is embedded in a visual and auditive micro- and macro-context adapted to the medium of film.

It is important to keep the social angle – which I am making use of here – apart from the individual-oriented one. If one took the latter as one's point of departure, the nature of the context would be defined by the role it plays for the individual: if I speak French as a foreign-language, then all contexts are foreign language contexts for me in relation to French. If I speak German as a second-language, then all contexts are second-language contexts for me in relation to German. The concept of linguistic flows (flows to do with the first language or early second-language, etc.) is based on the individual-oriented angle: the language is first language or early second language for the person who migrates. But when I am talking about contexts, I am basing myself on the social angle: the social function or status of the language in society.

Cultural Contexts in Language Teaching

In language teaching, the first-language contexts of the target language have enjoyed a privileged role. Generally speaking, attention has been directed at first-language contexts (understood in a national-state framework: Great Britain, USA, Brazil, Japan, etc.) and this still applies, even though there is a certain reaction taking place, especially in English teaching. Textbooks mainly strive to illustrate linguistic practice as it takes place in first-language contexts, so that students can gain an impression of a broader cultural context. One uses so-called 'authentic' materials from first-language contexts, and one invites first-language-speaking guest teachers to the classes so as to be able to demonstrate 'authentic' language use. The preferred destinations in connection with study trips and exchanges are also countries in which the target language is spoken as the first language.

But, as emphasised by Kramsch (1993), one must also deal with the contexts of language teaching where it actually takes place. Here we can once more make use of the *Tour de France* example.

To the extent that teacher and students use Danish in this sequence, they are in a context that is primarily a first-language context. And when they use German in the class, they are of course in a foreign-language context and are to a certain extent linking Danish languacultures (plus maybe Farsi and Dutch languacultures) to the German-speaking practice. The students are therefore perhaps more easily able to understand each other when they speak German in Denmark than when they travel to Germany and use the language there, even though the language in both cases is, in terms of structure, generally speaking German.

The two students with a Dutch and Iranian background respectively speak Danish as a second language. For them it means something whether the context is conceived (contextualised) on the part of the school and the teacher as a purely first-language context, or whether it is conceived as a mixed first-language and second-language context. In the latter instance, we will be dealing with a relatively inclusive norm for the Danish language, and this means that it is not merely tolerated but also accepted that the two students speak Danish in special second-language variants, and that their languacultures are slightly different from those of students who are native speakers of Danish – also when they speak German.

In the class, German-language magazines are also used that have been produced in Germany. So one could say that the German language 'flows' to Denmark and is utilised in new ways in the new cultural context. It becomes assimilated to some extent or other into the Danish school context, its agendas and frameworks of understanding. This takes place at the personal level via the learning process and at the social level via the teaching process in the particular institution that the school constitutes – a teaching process that mixes the various versions of German and Danish in many ways.

This class might also have travelled to Germany and experienced German there in first-language contexts. It might also, via contact with linguistic minorities in Germany, have experienced German in second-language contexts, where the linguistic/languacultural use of German is different and perhaps stigmatised. The class might, as part of internationalisation, in principle also have travelled to France and visited a German school or class that lay on the *Tour de France* route. There they would perhaps have encountered different attitudes to the German language among the French students and their teachers. So the potential cultural contexts of language teaching are many.

Life Context

The life history of the individual can be considered as a special type of macro-context: a life context that can be analysed in an objective dimension – the actual life course in real time – and a subjective dimension – the self-experienced life history that is constantly being retold and reinterpreted to a greater or lesser extent. The life context has to do with the social and personal development of the individual in a sociocultural perspective, and so it differs from the cognitive understanding of context I have been looking at above.

The linguistic development of the individual has taken place in this life context, and thereby a fusion of the individual's linguistic experiences has taken place with the rest of his or her life history. The personal linguistic/languacultural resources – in one or more languages – and the discursive resources are interwoven with this life context. Linguistic practice can thus be considered from two different perspectives that do not exclude each other: partly as taking place in a social network and embedded in a complex historical, societal context, and partly as embedded in the implied different life contexts of individuals, with the ensuing different meanings in their respective life narratives and life projects.

Some people in Denmark, for example, may have life experiences in which English plays a major role – they may possibly be children from bilingual families where English was spoken. Others may have life experiences with very little exposure to English if, for example, they are refugees from a country where there is little or no access to acquiring a knowledge of English. For some people, English plays a major role in their life project, for others a lesser role.

This complex ontogenetic development will not be further analysed here; it should merely be underlined that while linguistic/languacultural and discursive practice can be separated from its cultural context and transferred to another one, it cannot be so from its life context – we are always dealing with an additive, integrative process. The relationship between linguistic development and life context can of course be reconstructed and reinterpreted on an ongoing basis. We may be dealing with a traumatic break in a life history, or with a more or less split and fragmented self. But, all in all, one has to say despite this that linguistic/ languacultural and discursive resources cannot be separated from the life context as a whole in the individual.

Does 'Language' Have a Cultural Context?

By 'language' I mean the discursively constructed idea of the linguistic system discussed in Chapter 6. Firstly, it must be said that it is *practice* that has a concrete, historical and societal micro- and macro-context, no matter whether this practice is linguistic/languacultural, discursive or otherwise cultural/social. Furthermore, practice has a life context in an ontogenetic perspective – including language acquisition and learning. 'Language' does not have such concrete contexts. 'Language' is a metalingual abstraction, an artificial locus[7], and can only be ascribed just as abstract a context. The less abstractly one imagines 'language', the less abstract does the understanding of context also become.

One can, for example, attempt to base the concept of 'language' on a practice-oriented understanding: one can imagine that 'the Danish language' is identical with 'all' the intertextual chain of spoken and written texts in 'Danish'[8] that have developed through time and space up to the present day (not to mention the hypothetical projection into the future). In that case, the macro-context will be almost global, for Danish is spoken in most parts of the world. Naturally, it will be possible to confirm an extra close-knit network within the (historically shifting) territorial frameworks of Denmark, but the network does not cover the whole of Denmark, for a whole range of other languages are also spoken there. One of the questions that arise here is: do we mean only Danish spoken as a first language, or do we also mean Danish spoken as a second language and as a foreign language? I myself would choose the inclusive approach.

Within such a practice-oriented understanding one could focus on the possible common basis in the form of the total text corpus in 'Danish', i.e. the written layers of the intertextual chain through the ages. Here, a large amount of languacultural material has amassed that has developed along with the social and cultural development in the macro-contexts, including the various first language contexts in Denmark and elsewhere. But in that case one would focus on the written tradition, which is more homogeneous than the spoken languages, and one would tend to focus on constancy rather than on variability. So one will not grasp all that much of the languacultural variability.

One can also attempt to base oneself on a resource-oriented understanding of 'language'. One can, for example, imagine that 'the Danish language' is identical with the union of the various linguistic resources among all those who speak or have spoken Danish anywhere in the world. This will be reminiscent of a cognitive distributional understanding: linguistic resources are seen as socially distributed knowledge. Here the context might be described as the union of the many life contexts spread over most parts of the world, naturally with a particularly strong concentration within Denmark's borders. Here too we have to think of people who speak all types of Danish, as first language, second language and foreign language.

I am of the opinion that both conceptions are relevant; one must see 'language' both as more or less abstracted from practice (the external locus) and as more or less abstracted from resources (the internal locus). And one can correspondingly look at the more or less abstract context both as a cultural macro-context and as (a number of) life contexts. But in all cases we are dealing precisely with notions, abstractions, and it is an important point that, no matter how one conceives the context, it does not coincide with 'Denmark'. The linking together of 'Danish' and 'Denmark' is a construction that immediately springs to mind, but is no less erroneous for that – if one considers today's general 'banal nationalism' and its genealogy over the past couple of centuries (Billig, 1995).

By means of this construction, two imagined communities are linked together: on the one hand, the national language, understood in terms of practice or resources respectively, and, on the other hand, national culture, understood in an analogous way as a comprehensive cultural context or a number of life contexts respectively. It is this ambiguous construction that in the culture-pedagogical discourse assumes the form of the expression 'the country/countries where the language is spoken' – a discourse that until now has favoured the languages as first-languages and the countries as first-language contexts.

Conclusion

If one takes *the sociological point of view* as one's point of departure and looks at linguistic/languacultural/discursive practice in relation to the cultural macro-context, one has to conclude that it is quite common for language/languaculture/discourse to be separated from the first-language context and, via migration or acquisition/learning, be transferred to a foreign- or second-language context and there undergo a process of change (which might possibly end up being a nativisation process, as seems to have happened, for example, to the English language in India (Kachru, 1986)). In this respect, language and culture can be separated.

If one takes *the psychological point of view* as one's point of departure and looks at linguistic/languacultural/discursive practice, one has to conclude that these resources in the single individual, are inseparable from his/her life context. In the single individual language and culture are thus inseparable, but their mutual relations can be changed in the life history and be restructured and reinterpreted in the individual's self-narrative. In this respect, language and culture cannot be separated.

If one takes *the system-oriented point of view* as one's point of departure and looks at language as a system, one has to conclude that we are dealing with a construction of constructions, where the construction of the imagined linguistic community is linked to the construction of an analogously imagined cultural community. This community is mostly thought of as national, not least in Europe (the language is a symbol of the people/country), but there are also many examples of formulations that avoid the national understanding via a use of such expressions as 'area' or 'community'. In this respect, the link between language and culture is thus an ideological construction that can be used for various political aims – these can be nationalistic aims, but also aims linked to the struggle to preserve threatened languages, where an important element can be to underscore 'the intimate connection between language and culture' (Fishman, 1982).

Notes

1. Or anthropological linguistics. There is no particular difference between saying 'linguistic anthropology' and 'anthropological linguistics', since there is a high degree of fusion in this discipline of linguistic and anthropological approaches. Cf. Duranti (1997: 1) and Foley (1997: xiv).
2. See also the discussion in Goodwin and Duranti (1992).
3. An important example of this is Hymes' SPEAKING-model (Hymes, 1974) and its later elaborations. S: setting and scene, P: participants, E: ends, A: acts, K: key, I: instrumentalities, N: norms, G: genres.
4. 'Objective' understood as the result of an objectivisation in Berger and Luckmann's sense of the term. Social life is generally conceived by Berger and Luckmann as an interaction (a dialectic) between the three elements: externalisation, objectivisation and internalisation, summed up in the dictum 'Society is a human product. Society is an objective reality. Man is a social product.' (Berger & Luckmann, 1991 (1966): 79).
5. This distinction between the objective and subjective dimension is reflected in Hymes' distinction between 'setting' and 'scene', but this difference is not found in Scollon and Scollon (1995), which treats 'setting' as an aspect of 'scene' and thereby reinterprets the entire model in a subjective (idealistic) direction.
6. Cf. the expressions: EFL country (English as a Foreign Language country) og ESL country (English as a Second Language country).
7. It must naturally be said that the actual construction process, e.g. the drawing up of a grammar, takes place in a particular context.
8. In itself naturally a terribly difficult concept to define, cf. dialect continuum, constant language change, etc.

Chapter 11
Cultural Contents

Introduction

In this chapter I move on to another macro-oriented issue concerning the relationship between language and culture. Here I begin with a conception often encountered in discourse within language and culture pedagogy, including official requirements and guidelines for foreign- and second-language teaching: language and culture are inseparable, therefore language teaching must primarily deal with cultural and societal relations in the countries where the language is spoken. Here we are dealing with the thematic content of the texts in a broad sense (oral and written, films, images, etc.). But what is the relationship between language and culture here?

Cultural References and Representations: Internal and External

The thematic content of linguistic/languacultural/discursive practice can be directed at all possible kinds of subject and perspective, but in this context I wish to focus in particular on those that are related to cultural and societal conditions in various places in the world (without this having to be understood in national terms). When it comes to an analysis of the relationship between language and culture, it is of particular interest to look at references to and representations of first-language contexts: in what sense is there, for example, a closer relation between German and discourses on cultural and social conditions in Germany than between German and discourses on cultural and social conditions in Denmark? In what sense does knowledge of a particular language presuppose knowledge of cultural and social conditions in contexts in which the language is spoken as a first-language?[1] In the following I therefore intend to introduce a distinction between *internal* and *external* cultural references and representations. The internal relate to first-language contexts; the external relate to foreign-language and second-language contexts. When one talks in French about (first-language contexts in) France, one uses internal references. When one talks in Danish about France, one uses external references. In language teaching it is especially *the target-language internal references and representations* that are centre stage: work on the target-language countries in the target-language.

Michael Byram, who is among those who have written most about the cultural dimension of foreign- and second-language teaching, writes in Byram (1989) – a book that has been of great importance for culture pedagogy, at any rate in Europe[2]:

> The meanings of a particular language point to the culture of a particular social grouping, and the analysis of those meanings – their comprehension by learners and other speakers – involves the analysis and comprehension of that culture... The tendency to treat language quite independently of the culture to which it constantly refers, cannot be justified; it disregards the nature of language. (Byram, 1989: 41)

Here, Byram is not talking about pedagogical necessity but about a general necessity which derives from the very nature of language. But what is the nature of language? As has been shown, I believe that (at an overall level) a distinction must be made between three loci for language (2 + 1), and in the light of my discussion of the relationship between these loci it is possible to single out one of the problems in Byram's discourse in the above text: because Byram does not base himself on a deconstructionalist approach, as I do, he does not clearly distinguish between linguistic practice and the discursive construction of 'language'. This results in an ambiguity as to what 'language' stands for: it can stand for what I would call linguistic practice and the references one can make to reality in connection with this practice. But it can also stand for what I would call 'language' and an imagined connection between the meanings of 'language' (the meaning potential of langua-culture) and 'culture', a connection that is open to discussion – as will be dealt with below.

Saville-Troike is among those who have explicitly emphasised that a given language may well be used to express cultural relations 'in many domains of communication' in other language communities (she does not refer to Byram):

> There is no intrinsic reason that the structures and vocabulary for one language cannot be used in many domains of communication within other speech communities to express the cultures of those communities, and in ways in keeping with their rules of appropriate behavior ... Although language is unquestionably an integral part of culture, to assume specific cultural experiences and rules of behavior as invariable correlates of specific linguistic skills is a naïve oversimplification of the relationship of language and culture. (Saville-Troike, 1989: 35)

In this passage, in which Saville-Troike furthermore talks about culture as both context and content, she distinguishes between an understanding that I – in pursuance of the above – would call generic ('an integral part of culture') and an understanding that I would call differential ('specific cultural experiences and rules of behavior'). She outlines the problem area – though only *en passant* – in a way that resembles mine. But she too glides from 'one language' (the system point of view) to 'specific linguistic skills' (the sociological point of view) without reflecting on this.

To get a bit closer to a differentiated understanding of language and culture at this point, one has to distinguish between on the one hand cultural references and on the other hand cultural representations.

Cultural References and Cultural Words

Within translation theory one speaks of 'cultural references'. With the cultural turn in translation theory since the late 1980s, more systematic interest has been shown in the cultural dimension of translation (Mailhac, 1996; Snell-Hornby, 1988), including cultural references. These are references to cultural phenomena that are specific for 'the source culture' (the culture-pedagogical tendency to identify language and culture has its parallel in translation theory). Translation theorists have in particular been interested in translation strategies in connection with the rendering of cultural references that one can predict that the target group in 'the target culture' will not immediately be able to understand. It is, for example, in many cases easy to transfer a reference to 'London' from an English-language to a Danish-language text, but it is less easy to transfer a reference to a *julenisse* (a kind of Christmas pixie) from a Danish-language text to an English-language text. One could say that the problem of cultural references has particularly to do with how one is to translate 'unmatched elements of culture' (Mailhac, 1996: 132).[3] I do not intend to deal with translation strategies here but with how the concept of cultural reference can contribute to shedding light on the relationship between language and culture.

Firstly, it should be said that it is a problem in the tradition to do with cultural references that no distinction is made between reference and denotation (as, for example, in Lyons, 1995). In my opinion, it is important to include that distinction here. Lyons uses the term 'reference' for an act in which the language user with the aid of language refers to or 'points at' something in the outside world (the real world or an imagined world). It can, for example, be a reference to 'London'. The act of reference is thus a part of linguistic practice. Opposed to this, Lyons uses the term 'denotation' for meaning, e.g. the meaning of the Danish word *julenisse*, and this denotation can be used to make a specific reference to a particular *julenisse* in the outside world. Denotation is then a meaning potential that *can* be utilised for reference. It does not have to be so.

It must be added that Lyons is working within a structuralist not a sociolinguistic tradition. Translated into my discourse, one can say that the denotation of a word cannot clearly be demarcated from its connotations; denotation and connotation are analytical concepts. Furthermore, one can say that the meaning potential of a word – denotation(s) and connotations – have developed differently for different language users, depending on the personal and social circumstances, including whether the language is the first-language/early second-language or foreign language/late second-language. Every individual has a more or less comprehensive knowledge of what denotation(s) and connotations other people and groups can be expected to activate in connection with a particular word, e.g. *julenisse*.

The above quotation from Byram (1989): '... The tendency to treat language quite independently of the culture to which it constantly refers' represents an example of the mixing up of denotation and reference: is Byram talking about denotations that are characteristic of the English language, or is he talking about (constant) internal references to 'English culture' in English-language practice?

One must, then, distinguish between the (language-specific) meaning potentials that language users are bearers of and the internal and external cultural references they regularly undertake in linguistic practice: in texts, spoken or written. The language-specific denotations and connotations are a part of the languacultural resources. They have accumulated through linguistic practice in (especially) fairly small first-language communities and spread via various networks, including such cultural apparati as the national school. It can be words such as *julenisse*, *geheimeråd [Privy Council]*, *klasselærer [class teacher]* and *pølsebrød [rolls for sausages]*. It is important to stress that these words can of course be made relevant all over the world. In connection with a trip to China, for example, one can refer to a particular item of food and say: *Yes, this tastes quite like Danish 'pølsebrød'!* The Danish denotations do not then have to be used as *references* to reality in Denmark.

Conversely, references to Danish conditions do not have to make use of language-specific denotations. A typical example would be pure proper names, which do not have denotation (but lots of connotations). One can refer to Hjørring (a Danish town) in any language, but the reference has perhaps to be explained to the target group – and perhaps a comment has to be added about relevant connotations. One can refer to *Copenhagen* in any language, but there can be language-specific forms of this proper name *(København, Kopenhagen,* etc.).

A text about old Copenhagen in the time of King Christian IV does not, of course, have to be in Danish, and cultural references to street names, dates, buildings and shops, social groups, guilds and city government can be made based on any language, only under different languacultural conditions – here in particular of a semantic nature. No matter whether the text is in Danish or some other language, there will, depending on the previous knowledge of the target group, be a need for more or less detailed supplementary information or explanations.

Cultural references belong to the textual micro-level, i.e. they are normally undertaken by the language user with the aid of referring expressions, often (in such languages as English, German, French), nominal or adverbial phrases filled out with lexical words, possibly proper names (the head of the Roman Catholic Church, the Pope, the Vatican State, in Rome, at Easter 1998, etc.) Further eventual references in the same text are connected via cohesion mechanisms and via the building-up of coherence from both the producer's and the receiver's side, while activating their respective languacultural resources and their knowledge of the world in general.

Even though cultural references can in principle be expressed or explained in any language, there is a difference in how 'easily' this can be done, depending on which language and which references one is thinking of. References to the first-language contexts of the given language will normally be 'easier' to carry out than in another language, depending mainly on the lexical borrowings and lexicalisations of the various languages. In connection with the process of change in linguistic practice in the linguistic networks, language users borrow words from other languages if necessary, or form new lexicalisations for the concepts that are in use in the various communities. New words are coined, primarily by the formation of new compounds or by semantic differentiation (poly-semy).

Words such as *julenisse, pølsebrød* etc. are sometimes referred to as cultural words *(mots de civilisation, Kulturwörter* etc.). Within the discipline of translation, cultural words are an important concept, and cultural words (words and expressions) have been classified in many different ways, e.g. in head categories such as ecology, material culture, social culture, social organisation – political and administrative, gestures and habits – with many subcategories (Newmark, 1988: 95). The prototype of a cultural word is a word that can be used to refer to phenomena that are more or less specific to the linguistic area concerned, e.g. *folkeskolen* (the Danish primary and lower-secondary school) or *julegrød* (special rice pudding served on Christmas Eve). Such cultural words can involve translation difficulties, but Newmark also stresses that it can be even more difficult to translate certain words with an apparently more general meaning, for example words for morals and feelings (Newmark, 1988: 95).

Cultural words and cultural references are typically thought of in a national framework: the reference is to an element in the source culture (within translation theory), and the target-language culture (within culture pedagogy). It is indeed sometimes relevant to contextualise nationally, namely in the instances in which the reference is to an element in a national state system, such as the French national school system, the French national justice system, etc. References to such systems *(les collèges, les juges d'instruction* etc.) ought to be contextualised in a national-state framework in order to create an overall understanding (and furthermore it will in many cases be relevant to supplement with a contextualisation in relation to the European Union). But, when referring to local flora and fauna, to local products and craft traditions, etc., it will typically be less relevant to articulate a national understanding.

In fact, the concept of a 'cultural word' is problematic, for in my opinion all lexical units can be linked to culture-specific connotations. Even so, it can be useful to operate with a continuum ranging from relatively local denotations such as *sønderjysk kaffebord* (ritual involving coffee and many kinds of small cake, typical of Southern Jutland) to less location-bound denotations such as 'primary number'.

Internal Cultural References: Are Language and Culture Inseparable?

When one focuses on internal cultural references, are language and culture inseparable? Over time, first-language users have developed lexicalisations that have made possible precise references to elements in the contexts in which the language was used. These lexicalisations are part of the common languacultural resources that have been developed in the various social networks. Linguistic practice can therefore not be separated from its previous social and cultural history. The development that linguistic practice has gone through in its first-language contexts and in other contexts elsewhere in the world have taken place and can partially be empirically reconstructed on the basis of written texts.

But the linguistic/languacultural resources that language users are bearers of are accumulated potentials: the word *Berufsverbot* exists in

German, but this does not necessarily mean that the phenomenon *Berufsverbot* exists in the real world. The words *geheimeråd* (privy council) and *paradis* (paradise) exist in Danish, but the phenomena do not have to be actualised.

When one looks backward in time, one will then be able to trace co-developments of linguistic/languacultural and discursive practice, especially in first-language contexts. When one looks forward in time, this picture will of course develop, and it is important to underline that there is no determining relation between linguistic practice in a particular language and its potential to refer to specific cultural and social conditions: linguistic flows can go anywhere and link up with any form of context and discursive content. The languacultural potentials will mix with the languacultures of other languages and change in the process, by developing the meaning of existing words and by new lexicalisations.

Cultural Representations

Cultural representations belong to the textual macro-level, and cultural references can be part of them. Cultural representations are built up in discourses, and they convey images of or narratives of culture and society in particular contexts.

One must distinguish between two different ways of understanding the concept of cultural representation: it can either be a representation *of* 'culture' in a particular context, or a representation that adopts a particular cultural point of departure or *perspective*. One could refer to two kinds of look: a look at culture, and a look out from culture.

The former way of looking is the one in which culture pedagogy in particular has been interested. It has been in the form of practical and theoretical issues concerning the choice of themes and texts that communicate important images of the target-language countries (e.g. Byram, 1997). It has also been in the form of more critical approaches that make use of analyses of textbooks in terms of discourse and ideology (Dendrinos, 1992), or which discuss how production and reception of textbooks in language subjects can be linked to anthropological difficulties in ethnographical representation (Risager, 1999).

The latter way of understanding cultural representation is often seen in the materials that base themselves on the choice of literary texts. Here the selection has traditionally concentrated on authors that speak (write) the target-language involved as a first-language, and the rationale for such a selection can be double: this author has been included because (s)he is a first-language speaker, e.g. Danish, and is (therefore) assumed to represent a particularly Danish perspective on the world. The literary text does not need to base itself on material about life in Denmark; it can, for example, deal with travel and thereby convey a Danish view of the world outside Denmark – e.g. a travel account by Hans Christian Andersen.

Tour de France is also an example of the latter way of looking at cultural representation. This sequence does not deal with Germany as such, but adopts a German perspective insofar as the magazines are in German and have been produced for a German-speaking market. There is also a German link via Jan Ullrich and the German *Telekom* team.

As already stressed, a narrative that takes place in old Copenhagen can be expressed in any language, only under different languacultural conditions: semantic and pragmatic, poetic and identity-related. It is important to emphasise that I am not of the opinion that it 'doesn't matter' in what language the representation is expressed. Both the semantic-pragmatic, the poetic and the identity-related dimension of languaculture will probably influence the understanding of and relation to the representation concerned in the specific reception context. If one reads, for example, about old Copenhagen in Swedish, one's experiences with and attitude to the Swedish language will colour the overall reception of the text.

Internal Cultural Representations: Are Language and Culture Inseparable?

When one focuses on internal cultural representations, are language and culture inseparable? Since any language can link up with any discourse, i.e. with any subject, my opinion is that, at this macro-level, language and culture are separable. When many representatives of culture pedagogy express themselves as if they believe that language and culture are inseparable here, this can be due to their unwittingly adopting the psychological point of view.

If, as a first-language user, one reads a text in one's own first-language about certain subjects in relation to the first-language context, one may have an experience of inseparability between language and discursive, thematic content and project this feeling out onto the idea of language at the systematic level. Something similar can occur if, as a bilingual speaker, e.g. Danish/German, one reads texts in each of one's languages and for each language experiences such an inseparability.

But this can happen only because at the same time one is subject to a first-language bias and therefore only considers each of the languages in its capacity as first-language. If, as a Danish speaker, one reads a text about Denmark but in a language that is a foreign language to one, e.g.

French, there is not necessarily a basis for such an experience (i.e. an experience of a unity between French language and French 'content'). On the other hand, it is perfectly possible to imagine an experience of unity arising between French language and French *languaculture* if the reading creates a French atmosphere (semantic-pragmatic dimension, identity dimension) via the experiences and connotations one has oneself.

Cultural References and Representations in Language Teaching

Since the process of nationalisation in the last decades of the 19th century, foreign-language teaching has to a great extent focused on texts and themes about the target-language countries – and probably still does so around the world. This has encouraged a simplified conception of a close connection between language and culture. Nevertheless, there have also been several tendencies that have led to a spread of the material in language teaching, which means that in fact a development has been under way for many years that implicitly pulls the rug out from under this conception.

An important development tendency has been for foreign-language teaching (and to a lesser extent second-language teaching) to have moved in an intercultural, culture-comparative direction and thereby to have included texts and themes that related to the students' own society. This has, for example, paved the way for people talking and writing about Denmark (in English) in English teaching, etc. That means that, to a greater extent, use is now made of external (in relation to English) cultural references and representations.

A second tendency has been the increased contact on the part of language teaching with non-target-language countries (study trips, e-mail, etc.), where teachers and students get to work with cultural phenomena that can be partially different from those they know from the target-language countries or the students' own country and ones they have to reflect on via the use of the target-language as an international language of communication. Here there is in the same way a need to make use of external references and representations.

A third tendency has been an increasing interest in raising cross-cultural or more general subjects in language teaching, such as human rights and the environment (Risager, 1989) as well as a certain interest in including literature that has been translated into the target-language from other languages.

A fourth tendency has been towards using foreign and second-languages as teaching languages in relation to other subject areas, partly in short-term interdisciplinary cooperation, partly in real foreign-language educational programmes (content-based language instruction). For immigrants and refugees this is the typical situation: most of the teaching takes place in their second-language.

So there are signs of a radical spread on the content side[4] in foreign languages – a spread which I feel is positive in the sense that it can demonstrate the broad subject-related usefulness of the target-language: it can be used for much more than internal cultural references and representations. This spread I have partially illustrated by means of the example with *Tour de France*. Here there is a great diversity of content-related aspects and points of view, many cultural references to French and European conditions in connection with cycling, geography, etc., and several different cultural representations to do with Danish and Dutch cycling traditions, etc.

This tendency for the content side to spread applies specifically to foreign-language teaching. The question is, though, how much it influences first-language teaching (e.g. Danish in Denmark for the Danish-speaking majority) and second-language teaching (e.g. Danish in Denmark for linguistic minorities). The national education systems traditionally have a national education on their agenda that tries to convey knowledge about the country, people and history within a more or less clearly national paradigm – and via either the first-language or the second-language. The idea of the inseparability of language and culture (in the sense of cultural content) is probably kept alive more in first- and second-language subjects than in foreign-language subjects.

Does 'Language' Have a Cultural Content?

It must firstly be said, as in the case of macro-contexts (Chapter 10), that it is linguistic/languacultural/discursive *practice* that can have a thematic (cultural) content, and that the individual's linguistic/languacultural/discursive resources enable him or her to verbalise particular cultural contents. 'Language', on the other hand, is a discursive construction and as such cannot have any thematic content. A language, e.g. the Danish language, (naturally) does not deal with a defined amount of thematic content.

As mentioned in Chapter 8, one can for practical reasons choose to make an overview of the common amount of the languacultural resources (or potentials) one can imagine in a linguistic community. One can, for example, choose to draw up a comprehensive (maximalistic) description of the languaculture in the form of a huge encyclopedia, one which would also be able to explain a series of common cultural references (cf. many of the entries in *Longman's Dictionary of English Language and Culture*,

(Summers, 1992)). The resources used to create these references are, as mentioned, a part of the languaculture.

One could imagine the enormous task of collecting all (written) texts that exist in Danish, either originally in Danish or translated from other languages, and of investigating whether one can characterise their total thematic content. And one could imagine the other enormous task of collecting all the (written) texts that have to do with things Danish, no matter in what language they have been written. Will it be relevant to try to demarcate the common amount of these two collections, i.e. the texts that both have been written in/translated into Danish and have to do with things Danish? My own opinion is that there may well be interesting issues hidden here to do with Danish *languaculture*, first and foremost as regards the role Danish languaculture has played in internal cultural references and representations. But it would be absurd to claim that the Danish language is inseparable from a particular thematic universe. The idea of unity between a particular 'language' and its 'cultural content' at the textual macro-level is a construction that makes no sense.

Conclusion

When one has *the sociological point of view* as one's point of departure and looks at linguistic/languacultural/discursive practice, one must distinguish between the textual micro-level and the textual macro-level. As far as the micro-level is concerned, one can on the one hand conclude that there is a clear connection between language and culture here, insofar as the lexicalisations that have been created in the course of time make it possible in some cases to make precise internal cultural references to elements in the first-language contexts of the language, references that are more precise than if one used other languages. On the other hand, one can also conclude that language and culture here can indeed be separated insofar as one can make cultural references to the given context with the aid of other languages, only not always as precisely and quickly. As far as the macro-level is concerned, one can conclude that there is no necessary connection insofar as any subject can be expressed with the aid of any language, via normal translation and/or via other forms of communication or explanation.

When one has *the psychological point of view* as one's point of departure and looks at linguistic/languacultural/discursive resources, one must conclude that there is inseparability between language and culture here: the ontogenetic psychological and social process of development is a process of construction in which new linguistic and cultural experiences are added on and integrated with old ones.

When one has *the system-oriented point of view* as one's point of departure and looks at language as a system, one must conclude that the potential that makes internal cultural references and representations possible is a part of the languaculture in general, especially the semantic-pragmatic dimension. But to claim a unity between 'language' and 'culture', in which culture is understood as a thematically defined, discursive content, makes no sense.

As stated in the conclusion to Chapter 9, there are three stages in the analysis of the relationship between language and culture, whereby three different interfaces are illustrated between language and culture:

- between language and languaculture (Chapter 8);
- between language/languaculture and discourse (Chapter 9);
- between language/languaculture/discourse and the rest of culture (Chapters 10 and 11).

In the previous two chapters we have, then, been dealing with the third stage in the analysis of the relationship between language and culture and have looked in two 'directions': partly towards the cultural context (Chapter 10) and partly towards the cultural content (Chapter 11).

So we have looked at the relationship between language and culture from the linguistic point of view – and that is also why the concepts of context and content are at all relevant. But there is also a need for a more overall society-orientated analysis, whereby we transform the macro-contexts into socially organised cultural processes (flows). This I will come to in the next chapter.

Notes

1. Here an opposite question can also be formulated: if, for example, one is dealing with cultural and social conditions in Germany, is there any necessity in that case to be involved with the German language? This question, which has to be raised in all ethnographical work, will not, however, be discussed in the present context, in which language is the point of departure. But I would point out that Turkish, for example, can be an excellent way in to understanding German society, just as Arabic can be an excellent way in to understanding French society.
2. Byram has since abandoned the more unambiguous assertion of the identity between language and culture (language-and-culture), cf. Byram (1997).
3. So the discipline of translation has a relational approach to linguistic and cultural differences, similar to parts of linguistic anthropology, e.g. Agar.
4. When in English teaching one reads (also relatively modernised editions of) Shakespeare, this already implies a certain dissociation between present-day English and the older contexts to which Shakespeare was referring.

Chapter 12

Linguistic, Discursive and Cultural Flows

Introduction

This chapter is intended to provide a picture of how linguistic, discursive and cultural flows move along various paths, forming local configurations where they integrate with each other, e.g. in language teaching. I pick up the thread from Chapter 5, where I introduced Hannerz's theory of cultural flows and cultural complexity. What he calls cultural flows I have divided into linguistic, discursive and other cultural flows. To put it another way: while Hannerz makes use of a particularly broad and inclusive concept of culture that is designed to comprise all meaning, I have for analytical reasons limited the concept of culture to an 'exclusive' concept that comprises only the cultural processes that are neither linguistic (in the differential sense) nor discursive. As stressed in Chapter 1, this is an analytical choice that must not be taken to mean that I am of the opinion that language and discourse are not cultural phenomena.

Among Hannerz's central concepts are the four frameworks of cultural flow (cf. Chapter 5):

- the life forms;
- the market;
- the state;
- the social movements.

These four frameworks are used in the following, where I give a brief outline of the linguistic, discursive and cultural flows in the world and the relationship between them.

Finally, I return yet again to the teaching vignette *Tour de France*. This time I analyse it as a local integration process that collects and transforms certain linguistic, discursive and cultural flows in a special way, made up of the life forms, market, state and social movements.

Linguistic Flows

As became apparent in Chapter 7, linguistic flows are highly complex, as language is perhaps the most complex system of signs that exists. I have distinguished between flows of first-language/early second-language and of foreign language/late second-language, and between linguistic flows as resource flows (acquisition/learning or migration), as text flows and as lexical flows. And I have emphasised that linguistic and languacultural flows are not one and the same thing. In addition, there is the actual multiplicity of languages in the world (as first-languages – and then there are also the interlanguages).

Abram de Swaan stands for a theory of the linguistic world-system, a theory that is an analogy to Wallerstein's world-system theory (de Swaan, 1993). He bases this on a structuralist conception of language in which the various languages in the world are ranked in relation to each other via such factors as the number of users, the communication radius and the societal, political importance. Like other world-system theorists, he builds on the centre-periphery mode of thought, focusing on the global language hierarchy with English as the 'supercentral' language, under which there are 10–12 large 'supranational' languages, many of which have, apart from their national function, a mediating function as a lingua franca (he mentions Mandarin Chinese, Hindi, Spanish, Arabic, Bengali, Portuguese, Russian, Japanese, German, Malaysian and French). Below these are a number of national languages and beneath them a number of (subnational) regional languages. The endangered and moribund languages come last and are also part of his field of interest, although his research concentrates more on the central languages than the peripheral ones.

De Swaan does not think in terms of linguistic flows, and he does not have as differentiated a conception of linguistic flows as I express. I would prefer a more integrative and dynamic approach that stresses linguistic flows and local mixes in a broader perspective that takes in society and culture – a perspective which in principle attempts to unite the micro-level and the macro-level (in a concept that one could call the global linguistic ecumene). One can include Hannerz's theory of the four frameworks in this perspective and investigate how each of them organises the linguistic flows in a different way.

The life forms organise the many first-languages of everyday life – both those with and those without written languages. It is the life forms that form the framework for the continuation of the first-languages in families and other small-scale communities. They can also form the framework for a language shift where parents, for example, do not pass on their own first-language to their children and for various reasons prefer another language. The life forms also organise the eventual use of other languages – as second / foreign languages – in everyday life, in the workplace, at school, etc. Within the life-form framework there is an ongoing informal language policy concerning the choice of language in various situations and domains.

The market is to an ever-increasing extent a transnational framework for the spreading of English (as first, second and foreign language) throughout the world. But it is also a framework for the use of other widespread languages, with the aim of reaching particular groups of consumers. The market conveys, for example, text flows including lexical flows via the diffusion of words and expressions that are linked to particular goods and activities. Within the market framework an informal language policy also takes place, and it can generally be characterised as profit- and lifestyle-orientated, where English in particular is used as a symbol of modernity and Western identity.

The state has a major formal language-political influence on linguistic flows. It can decide the use of particular languages within its territory; it can decide which languages are to be taught in the public education system, and it can to a certain extent exclude certain languages (a form of 'unfree flow'). The state has a major influence on the language policy of language teaching, and how one deals with the interlanguages, the languacultures and linguistic identities in general. The state language policy is – in relation to that of the other frameworks – geopolitically determined and more or less traditionalist.

The social movements – political, religious, artistic, etc. – need to spread their message broadly, so they typically form a framework for the use of more widespread languages with a large potential communication radius, e.g. English, Arabic or Spanish. The informal language policy of the NGOs is therefore generally geared to both national and transnational communication.

English occupies a particular position today in the global linguistic ecumene (as it also does in de Swaan's linguistic world-system). The reason for this is first and foremost linked to the history of British colonisation, but also to the subsequent support for the use and dissemination of the English language in the post-colonial societies and elsewhere. This is described, for example, by Alastair Pennycook in his book *The Cultural Politics of English as an International Language* (1994). He refers to – and criticises – the general (dominant) discourse that the English language is culturally neutral as an international means of communication. He claims that the spread of the English language cannot be separated from power

structures and inequalities at the global level. At the same time, he underlines that English is used for various purposes in widely different local
cultural and political contexts around the world. This double situation he
calls 'the worldliness of English' and, with the aid of teaching examples,
he demonstrates that the situation makes it possible for people around the
world to organise English teaching in such a way that it is orientated
towards critical pedagogical goals, e.g. the strengthening of learners'
awareness of the forms and origins of post-colonial suppression.
However, a question arises here concerning the relationship between
English and certain discourses, which I will deal with in the next section.

Discursive Flows

A discourse is based on content and perspective. It may be a question of
major systems of ideas, such as religions or political ideologies, or ideas
communicated by social movements such as environmental movements,
feminist movements, peace movements, etc. Or it may be a question of
professional discourses such as the pedagogical discourse, or possibly
everyday discourses about daily doings, rituals and festivities, etc.
Furthermore, it may be a question of the processes that Fairclough refers
to as 'the marketization of discourse' and 'the technologization of
discourse', where certain forms and genres of discourse dominate and
spread out over others (Fairclough, 1992). Fairclough, as mentioned, has
begun to use the concept of 'the global order of discourse', which is an
indication of an emerging conflicting order of discourse at a global level
(Fairclough, 1997). This concept is more explicitly politically and ideologically orientated than Hannerz's concept of the global ecumene, although
less system-orientated than the world-system theory.

As I have defined the concept of discourse, discourses are primarily
borne by verbal language, though they can be accompanied by signs from
other sign systems (parts of 'the rest of culture'): yin/yang, the cross, the
crescent, logos and trademarks, etc.).

Migration means something for discursive flows: people migrate and
take their discursive resources with them. But migration means less for
discursive flows than for linguistic ones, because linguistic resources are
far more structured than discursive ones. The individual has knowledge
(receptive and possibly productive) of only a small and finite number of
languages (if we ignore the large number of loan words from various
languages). It takes a relatively long time to acquire a language. On the
other hand, the number of discourses an individual has knowledge of or is
familiar with is under all circumstances very large and in principle

infinite, as one cannot make clear distinctions between discourses (which are always analytically constructed). When a person migrates, it does not always have the same profound consequences for discursive flow as it does for linguistic flow. Therefore, it is to a greater extent text flows that are important in a description of discursive flows. And text flows that extend over large distances are conveyed first and foremost by transnational media, the mass media and the Internet – and often, at some point or other in the production process, they are in a written form.

If we look at the four frameworks for the social organisation of discursive flows, we can say that *the life forms* form the framework for everyday discourses in small-scale communities, but also for more less-formulated counter-discourses. *The market* conveys discourses over long distances, channelled either through the (private) mass media or through the commodity market (books, films, etc.). *The state* is a framework for the political struggle for power, which leads to a number of explicit political discourses being circulated, and it also brings discourses into circulation within its own cultural apparati, including national discourses in the education system. The state can also, via censure, prevent discourses from spreading. *The social movements* organise resistance discourses as well as innovative and utopian discourses, which they try to spread orally from person to person and via text flows of other types.

As mentioned, discourses spread across linguistic communities, so an important feature of discursive flows is the transformations they undergo when translated and subject to other looser forms of adjustment: adaptation, retelling, etc.

In connection with these interlingual discursive flows, English is probably the language that is now the most common 'relay language' at a global level. It is the language into which most texts are translated and at the same time the language from which most texts are translated. It is perhaps also the language in which most texts are written (by non-first-language speakers), and the language in which most texts are read, so to speak (once more by non-first-language speakers). This gives English a key position in discursive flows: the English languaculture – in all its variability – exerts a powerful influence on discourses in the world. This applies to all dimensions of the languaculture: the semantic and pragmatic dimension, the poetic dimension and the identity dimension. I must stress once again here that a language is never culturally neutral in the sense languaculturally neutral: languaculture of some origin or other is always assigned to it.

Does this mean that one is to imagine an inseparability between the English language and certain discourses? On the basis of my discussion in

Chapter 9, my answer is in the negative. The English language can be separated from discourses that it bears at any point in time. Every discourse in English can be translated to another language, only under certain languacultural conditions that the translator must consider (as well as the expected previous knowledge and attitudes of the addressees). To link English to any discourse is an act that has political implications, but it is not determined by either the discourse or the English language. In his above-mentioned book Pennycook says something similar, but, when all is said and done, he finally retains a form of inseparability between language and particular discourses:

> The relationship between 'English' and global discourses of capitalism, democracy, education, development, and so on, is neither a coincidental conjunction – English just happens to be the language in which these discourses are expressed – nor a structural determinism – the nature of English determines what discourses are spoken, or the nature of discourses determines what language they are spoken in. Rather, there is a reciprocal relationship that is both historical and contemporary. Colonial discourses and discourses of contemporary world relations have both facilitated and been facilitated by the spread and construction of English. English and a range of local and international discourses have been constituted by and are constitutive of each other, both through the history of their connections and their present conjunctions. Particular global and local discourses create the conditions of possibility for engaging in the social practice of using 'English', they produce and constrain what can be said in English. At the same time, English creates the conditions of possibility for taking up a position in these discourses. Clearly, then, language can never be removed from its social, political and discursive contexts … (Pennycook, 1994: 33)

Pennycook is of course right in saying that, very broadly speaking, one can demonstrate a parallel development between the wide dissemination of English and Western forms of culture in British- and American-dominated parts of the world. But the large generalisation in this assertion is clear when one thinks of the colossal variation in the social networks within which English is spoken around the world as a first, second and foreign language for innumerable subjects and with innumerable perspectives. Moreover, he completely ignores different languages: discourses about capitalism, democracy, education and development exist just as much in many other languages, e.g. Danish.

It is symptomatic that Pennycook in the last sentence quoted slips into talking about 'language'. This enables the reader to undertake a generic reading, whereby the statement becomes completely correct: one can never remove linguistic practice (any practice) from its context (any context). But what Pennycook wishes to say is presumably that one can never remove *English* from its discursive context. This, however, would be an example of confusing language seen as a system with language seen as practice, for a 'language' (system level) cannot have a concrete historical context – only linguistic practice is able to do this. I also believe that Pennycook is guilty here of something he otherwise argues so excellently against in the rest of his book: the general tendency of linguistics and language pedagogy to essentialise 'language'. What he implicitly bases himself on in the quotation is *'the identity dimension of the English language at the system level*: 'the English language' as a symbol of modernity and Western lifestyle – democracy, education and development – or perhaps imperialism, suppression and decadence. And when one realises that he is talking about the English language at system level, his statement is correct: these various linguistic identities that are ascribed to the English language on the basis of various understandings of history naturally have important social, cultural and political implications, for instance in English teaching around the world. But there is nothing that can actually 'constrain what can be said in English' (the practice level).

This should not overshadow Pennycook's important points regarding historical linkages between the English language and colonialist discourses in connection with English teaching in post-colonial societies such as Hong Kong and Australia, where he has worked. As he writes in a later book, *English and the Discourses of Colonialism* (Pennycook, 1998), English teaching has contributed to colonialist discourses being perceived as 'adhering to English' (in the contexts involved, it should be added). But here the concept of languaculture and its various dimensions would be suitable as an analytical instrument: Pennycook is actually talking about the identity dimension (discourses and ideologies about the English language in certain contexts), not about the semantic and pragmatic potential of the English language – and not at all about the varied use of English around the world.

Cultural Flows

The parts of culture that are non-linguistic and non-discursive (the rest of culture) are of course (also) myriad and complex – and impossible to outline briefly here. I would refer to Hannerz's (also relatively general) picture in Hannerz (1992a and 1996), where the focus is on cultural complexity and transnational connections. Here I will make do with single comments that are relevant for an analysis of language teaching.

One area is material everyday culture: clothing, food and drink, the use of space and time, non-verbalised (i.e. implicit, silent) customs, traditions of upbringing and learning strategies, etc. In cultural flows of this type migration is an important factor, just as in language: we are in many cases dealing with unconscious patterns of behaviour that are not so easy to change and which are linked to the identity of the individual. Just as linguistic flows are borne by the individual (idiolectal), cultural (and discursive) flows are too; at one and the same time they are socially influenced and unique. They are mainly organised by the life form framework: reproduction and production of everyday life via practical interaction in small-scale communities.

Another area is visual representations of every kind: computer art, photography, painting, cartoons and living images of various kinds: TV entertainment, feature films, sports coverage, etc. Flows of this kind do not circulate so much via migration as via the national and transnational media. They are often linked to musical forms (and naturally also often to discourses – in particular languages), and they are particularly organised by the market and determined by its profit and lifestyle orientation.

As Hannerz points out, both types of flow move from the centre to the periphery, and vice versa. In connection with such forms of culture as music, fashion, gastronomy and dancing, it is clear that the flows move both ways, mediated by the structures of the culture industry, the media and the world market. In connection with languages, we can also speak of a two-way process: on the one hand, a spread from the centre to the periphery of a small number of major languages, spearheaded by English; and, on the other hand, a linguistic flow that moves from the centre to the periphery in connection with migration for reasons of labour or exodus, which increases linguistic complexity in the countries of immigration. Discursive flows in the global ecumene are naturally also highly complex, but can perhaps be said to be more one-sidedly influenced by Western, neo-liberal, 'marketised' (Fairclough) discourses. There are also alternative discourses to this, e.g. post-colonial critique or that of the social movements, but they find it difficult to spread because of the control of the flow of information by the media sector. Here, however, the Internet offers certain possibilities.[1]

Tour de France: A Local Integration Process

Hannerz views the education system as a central part of the state's cultural apparatus. 'There is hardly a more central complex within it than education, in the sense of institutionally specialized transmission of knowledge and development of cultural competence' (Hannerz, 1992a: 83). What role does a part of this system, language teaching, play in relation to linguistic, discursive and cultural flows in the world?

The teaching sequence must not be thought of as a closed box inside which one learns 'German' and where the subjects are merely a pretext for learning the language (developing communicative competence). It should be seen as a social practice among many others, as an element of certain more comprehensive dynamics and processes: 'something' comes into the learning space; 'something' happens in the sequence, and 'something' comes out of it again. If one includes the analytical tool of the four frameworks for linguistic, discursive and cultural flows, one can link what is going on within the learning space to what is going on outside.

The life forms find expression in the way the teacher and the students function during the short while they are together: how they interact linguistically in ways specific to the school as an institution; what languages they choose to use with each other both in the actual teaching situation and outside it. What subjects and points of view interest them separately as individuals that also have a life outside the school. How they position themselves spatially and socially in relation to each other and how they use their bodies, dress, etc. In the life form framework, everyday life at the school is connected to everyday life outside it, with a greater or lesser degree of continuity.

The market mainly enters the teaching sequence in the form of the German newspapers and magazines that are used, i.e. the 'German perspective' of German public opinion is introduced in a journalistic form into the Danish German lesson. The students are thereby presented with certain journalistic genres: reports, (reported) interviews, etc. The cultural representations contained in the material, in both text and images, help to provide the students with mirrors for their own lifestyles, perspectives, identities and images of the world. The walls of the German classroom are also decorated with posters and postcards from the Austrian Alps, produced by the tourist industry in Austria and also mediated via the market. The market framework communicates a more or less worldwide circuit of production, distribution and consumption of goods, and the class has been connected to this circuit via the teacher's purchase and use of the German printed matter in the teaching.

The state is present in many ways in the teaching: the Danish state has laid down what objective status German is to have among the foreign languages on offer in the educational context involved. It has shaped the teacher's education and the teaching itself via executive orders, guidelines and examination requirements, etc. It has been responsible for the building and the other material resources (also mediated by the market). As part of the state bureaucratic hierarchy, the German class is subject to both open control and the allocation of resources.

The social movements have provided impulses for the actual interaction in the class, e.g. ideas and norms about gender equality. This subject is also dealt with discursively in some of the material the teacher has brought along. She has, for example, found a brochure about the special *'Women's Tour de France'* and discusses the question of a gender hierarchy in the world of sport.

It is mainly the teacher who has the formal responsibility for choosing input for the teaching, although the students can also be included here. This thematises the asymmetry that is typical of most teaching situations. Hannerz proposes that a distinction be made between six dimensions of symmetry/asymmetry in (linguistic, discursive and) cultural flows: the degree of common ground in the baseline, input mode, input quantity, scale, material resource linkage and power linkage (Hannerz, 1992a: 55ff.).

The degree of common ground in the baseline has to do with the experiences and competencies under which the linguistic, discursive and cultural flow takes place: if there is a high degree of common experience among the individuals concerned as well as a common awareness of them ('I know that you know that I know', etc.), there is a high degree of symmetry and flow will probably be relatively easy. If they have relatively different experiences, we are dealing with some degree or other of asymmetry, which will influence flow and maybe create misunderstandings and conflicts. In the *Tour de France* sequence there is a clear asymmetry between the teacher and the students at least in the sense that the teacher is the 'expert' in the German language, while the learners are 'novices'. Moreover, the situation is characterised by general diversity rather than uniformity: linguistic, ethnic and social diversity. This means that there is quite a big difference in the languacultural and discursive resources of those involved – and therefore every chance of both misunderstandings and new points of view.

Input mode has to do with the sign system or the code that is being used. The German sequence, like other language teaching, is dominated by a (verbal) linguistic mode, but a number of other sign systems are also included: photos, drawings, maps and charts, drama and song – fairly varied input that has been introduced mainly by the teacher for pedagogical reasons. But it could just as well have been introduced by the students.

Input quantity has to do with the path taken by the main part of the content of the flow. In the language class in question, it is (as usual) the teacher who is responsible for most of the oral communication; she narrates, gives directions, praises and criticises. She is also the one who has bought the German magazines. The students read and discuss and engage in role-play activities; some of them write fictitious extracts from 'a cyclist's diary', and some try to rewrite the song about 'The ten small cyclists' and to sing it.

Scale has to do with the difference between one-to-one communication and one-to-many communication, i.e. with the extent to which there is a leap in scale in connection with the communication. Whereas face-to-face communication often takes place at the same scale level, Hannerz characterises mass communication as a 'leap from micro to macro levels in cultural process' (Hannerz, 1992a: 59). In the *Tour de France* class there is naturally often a leap in scale level from the teacher (the one) to the students (the many). We are very much dealing with a communication process in which the teacher tries to pass on knowledge, norms and behaviour to a whole class of students.

Material resource linkage has to do with the fact that cultural flow is made possible and limited by who it is that has access to what material resources. It can have to do with who it is that has access to communication technologies, or can afford to buy particular things. In the German class there is, among other things, considerable variation in how much students have travelled abroad, e.g. to France or German-speaking countries.

Power linkage has to do with the fact that cultural flow is influenced by who it is that can back up their messages with a use of power[2], both at the micro-level in interpersonal communication and at the macro-level. In the context of language teaching, it is obvious that the teacher has most access to power in the form of her role not only as teacher but also as everyday assessor and examiner.

These dimensions of symmetry and asymmetry in linguistic, discursive and cultural flow make it possible to examine the morphology of the flows in the social networks of the class involved: where do the flows operate relatively freely; where do they meet resistance, where are they clearly altered – and why? What role do linguistic and cultural identities and norms play in this process?[3]

Conclusion

The flow metaphor (the reifying tendency of which I have drawn attention to, cf. Chapter 5) makes it possible to consider 'language' and 'culture' as practice phenomena that spread out along various paths by virtue of human interaction in social networks, at the micro-level, and thereby at various higher levels (meso- and macro-levels). This chapter has indicated the complexity of an image in which linguistic, discursive and cultural flows intersect and mix locally in a great variety of ways.

In this image, a language-teaching sequence can be seen as a special local integration of flows that come from many places. This method is naturally not limited to language-teaching situations, where the special focus is of course on the linguistic aspect. In my opinion, every situation ought initially to be viewed from this dynamic and holistic perspective.

Notes

1. The Indian anthropologist Arjun Appadurai has framed a theory which, like that of Hannerz, is based on an idea of cultural flows (Appadurai, 1990, 1996). Appadurai believes that developments in the modern world can be understood via a distinction between the following five 'dimensions of global cultural flow': ethnoscapes, technoscapes, finanscapes, mediascapes and ideoscapes. Modern developments are characterised by disjuncture between the five landscapes, so that they flow and develop along different paths to an increasing extent. All the time, new global and local configurations are formed where the various landscapes mix with each other (conjunctures). Appadurai's theory is not as useful in the present project as Hannerz's, as Appadurai does not address the micro-level or connect the micro-level and the macro-level. But his concepts of disjuncture and conjuncture can also be used in my perspective, in which language and culture are described as phenomena that separate and regroup in new configurations.
2. Hannerz has been inspired by Foucault in his concept of power, describing power as omnipresent: 'a ubiquitous aspect of all human interaction' (Hannerz, 1992a: 60).
3. This process-orientated approach I have developed in Risager, 1999, which contains a discussion of the importance of looking at the textbook as a part of a social and cultural practice, i.e. of looking at it partly as an example of a cultural representation and partly as a result of a production process (the author as ethnographer?) and as input for a collective reception process in the class.

Chapter 13

The Language-Culture Nexus

Introduction

I have now given an account of the many dimensions of the relationship between language and culture, and have stressed that language and culture are actually separable from each other in certain respects. In this chapter I intend to look at how the relationship between language and culture can be described in the communicative event, where all the elements are linked. It is important to stress that the link between language and culture is created in every new communicative event[1], but also important to be aware of whether one is studying only 'convergent' language-culture nexuses and forgetting the 'divergent' ones. I also give an account of a division between experienced and imagined communities, and finally I propose that the core of the 'connection' between language and culture is the meaning and reference potential of language in relation to physical, social and cultural reality.

The Communicative Event

The basic unit of the link between language and culture is a particular interpretation of the communicative event – a concept that is central in linguistic anthropology, especially within the ethnography of communication. Saville-Troike defines a communicative event as follows:

> The *communicative event* is the basic unit for descriptive purposes. A single event is defined by a unified set of components throughout, beginning with the same general purpose of communication, the same general topic, and involving the same participants, generally using the same language variety, maintaining the same tone or key and the same rules for interaction, in the same setting. (Saville-Troike, 1989: 27, italics in the original)

This definition seeks to ensure an analytical demarcation of the object of study, focusing on the inner stability of the event: same general purpose, same general topic, etc. It has not been formulated in order to analyse the relationship between language and culture, so I intend to supplement it with the necessary perspective for my own purpose.

Firstly, I would say that the concept of communication is really some-what unclear here. It is both too narrow and too broad. On the one hand, there is a reference to verbal-language (oral) communication, i.e. a rela-tively narrow understanding of communication. On the other hand, it is also possible to read the definition as meaning that communicative events comprise all kinds of (human) communication, i.e. a broader semiotic concept of communication that could form a broader framework for ethno-graphic studies. In the following, however, I will retain the term 'commu-nicative event', but make more precise what I mean by it: a social/cultural event in which (verbal) language is used (including paralanguage and kinesics) that is characterised by a relative stability as regards aim and subject-matter. This places linguistic practice as a central part of something that is more comprehensive, and which also includes languacultural, discursive and other cultural practice. Furthermore, I will widen the focus of the above definition from oral interaction to include written production and reception (all forms of text, literary and non-literary).

The Language-Culture Nexus: A Local Integration

As can be seen from my presentation up till now, I believe that one must view the communicative event in a larger context. One must understand it theoretically as a linkage of various flows coming from various places. Compared to this, the picture of the communicative event offered by the ethnography of communication is microscopic and static. The concept of *language-culture nexus* emphasises a number of features of the communica-tive event:

- it is a local integration of linguistic, languacultural, discursive and other cultural flows in more or less differing social networks;
- in written language it is normally divided into a production and a reception phase that can be more or less staggered in time and/or place;
- it takes place in a complex micro- and macro-context (or in several, in the case of written language);
- it is characterised by a discursive content of a more or less cohesive nature, possibly including cultural references and representations, internal or external;
- it can be multilingual, i.e. characterised by diverse forms of code-switching;
- it has a place in each of the entire life-contexts of the participants (subs. producers and receivers) and is interpreted by each of them in the light of this life context.

Local integration is a dialogical process in which the participants co-construct, negotiate or struggle for meanings and identities. There is always a power dimension in the communicative event.

The Language-Culture Nexus: Convergent or Divergent?

In the language-culture nexus, language and culture can blend in a great variety of ways – and this mix can be described as relatively convergent or relatively divergent.

A fairly convergent language-culture nexus could be the following: a conversation at Rønne Tourist Office (Rønne is the main town on the small Danish island of Bornholm); those engaged in conversation were born in Rønne and speak modern Rønne dialect with Rønne languaculture; and the discourse has to do with summer tourism in Rønne. Another example could be the one I mentioned in Chapter 2 in a comment on the *Tour de France* example: a teaching sequence in Danish as a second language that takes place in Denmark; the teacher has Danish as her first language; the students have various linguistic backgrounds; but only Danish is spoken and the work is on an article from a Danish newspaper, written by a journalist with Danish as his first language, on a subject that can be said to be typically Danish, e.g. the considerable production of pigmeat. Here we have a large concentration of national categories, all of which have to do with the same theme: 'Danishness'.

A fairly divergent language-culture nexus could be the following: a telephone conversation between an office employee at Berlin Zoo and an employee at Aalborg Zoo (Aalborg is a city in Northern Jutland in Denmark). The person talking in Berlin speaks German with a tinge of Hungarian languaculture because this person is a Hungarian immigrant. The person talking in Aalborg speaks German with some Aalborg languaculture. They discuss a project involving an exchange of lions. Another example could be that I write an e-mail to a colleague in Sydney about the evaluation of a PhD thesis on sociolinguistics. The mail is in English and is influenced by my Danish languaculture. My colleague has French as his first language, and this also affects his use of English.

There is an important theoretical-methodological point here: if one investigates *only* convergent situations, one can easily come to the conclusion that there is, generally speaking, a close connection between language and culture. And one will perhaps generalise this assertion to talk about the unity between language and culture ('the marriage between language and culture'), possibly linked to an idea of national or ethnic identity. But if one turns one's gaze to divergent situations, such a conclusion is less likely. Linguistics has allowed itself to a far too large extent to make do with looking at convergent situations, and this is probably an important reason for the continuing dominance of first-language bias in large sections of linguistics.

I would like to mention a single example of this from linguistic anthropology: in 1987, Joel Scherzer wrote an exciting article about what he understands by the language-culture nexus. He says, among other things:

> It is discourse that that creates, recreates, focuses, modifies, and transmits both culture and language and their intersection, and it is especially in verbally artistic and playful discourse, such as poetry, magic, verbal dueling, and political rhetoric, that the resources provided by grammar, as well as cultural meanings and symbols, are activated to their fullest potential and the essence of language-culture relationships becomes salient. (Scherzer, 1987: 295)

He provides a number of examples of discourses (in the linguistic sense) taken from the Kunas in Panama, and they illustrate very well a close connection between language and culture in the discourse. But these are examples of what I call a convergent language-culture nexus. The article deals with first-language speakers, and the discourses take place in a first language context. But what discourses would we hear/see if it was a question of a Kuna Indian speaking his first-language in New York, or an Indian anthropologist trying to take part in the Kunas' political discourses in Panama?

The link between language and culture is created in each new communicative event and can change drastically simply because one of the participants, for example, gets a telephone call from a friend elsewhere in the world. But this is the practice point of view, the sociological angle. If we look at the participants' individual life contexts – the psychological angle – they do not create new configurations at will. In the example with the two negotiators in the zoos, there may very well be complex and conflicting life histories, but the Hungarian immigrant in Berlin cannot suddenly speak a German influenced by Aalborg languaculture, and the man in the office in Aalborg Zoo cannot suddenly speak a German influenced by Hungarian languaculture. In the course of their conversation, however, they can of course influence each other's language use, either briefly or perhaps for a longer period of time within certain areas.

Objective and Subjective Dimensions of the Language-Culture Nexus

In the description of the language-culture nexus I have emphasised the *empirical complexity*, both 'internally' in the communicative event, and 'externally' in the relation to the context. This means that I have an 'objective' approach as my point of departure here. I distinguish between two different epistemological levels in the analysis of the language-culture nexus[2]: on the one hand, an analytical approach that is relatively objectively oriented; and on the other hand, an analytical approach that is relatively subjectively oriented. Both are 'constructions', but the former seeks to describe and analyse the empirical complexity of the linguistic and cultural *practice*, while the latter seeks to describe the language users' own *experiences and ideas*, including their categorisations, identifications and narratives concerning the relationship between language and culture. These two levels interact in the single communicative event, since the personal experiences and ideas of the participants will probably influence the way they actually use the language.

In the more objective sense, the language-culture nexus is a practice that is created in the interaction (or in the production and reception of text), and that is maintained or altered in the linguistic, languacultural and discursive practice of the social networks. But this interconnection can be split up at any time as the communicative event changes character: those involved can switch to another discourse; someone can enter into the conversation who speaks the language as a foreign language; one can depart and continue the conversations via the Internet; one can travel to another country and continue the conversation there, etc.

In the more subjective sense, the language-culture nexus can be discursively constructed around, for example, ideas of 'us' and 'them', 'our language' and 'our culture', etc., and ideas can develop of causal or organic links between language and culture – possibly linked to the national idea, as in the National Romantic mode of thought.

Language-Culture Nexuses at Higher Levels

The concept of language-culture nexus is primarily linked to the micro-level, to the single communicative event, but for analytical purposes one can attempt to define language-culture nexuses at higher levels. The analysis of the *Tour de France* is an example of a language-culture nexus at a higher level than the single communicative event. We are dealing here with the relationship between language and culture during a lengthy teaching sequence, in a class that constitutes a community, centred on certain activities that have a common overall aim.

In this connection it is important to distinguish between experienced (or 'lived') and imagined communities. A small family unit (nuclear family, or something similar) forms the framework of an experienced community, and there linguistic/languacultural practice develops in a dialectic with discursive and other cultural practice. Other small-scale communities could be a kindergarten, a school staff, a school class, a small firm, a hospital ward, a transnational team of researchers, a multinational royal family, etc. In such cases it is possible empirically to investigate language-culture nexuses both at the micro-level and at a slightly higher level. How does linguistic/languacultural practice in speech and writing take place in this (monolingual or multilingual) experienced community? What themes and perspectives are verbalised by discursive practice? How is cultural (non-verbal) practice included: buildings and objects, sounds and music, the use of the body, etc.? And how is this totality organised socially?

The small-scale experienced communities correspond to what Hannerz refers to as 'micro-cultures': the lowest level of cultural community (in principle, right down to two persons), where one can find 'shared meanings directly tied to specific, likewise shared, experiences of people, settings, and events' (Hannerz, 1992a: 77). It should be noted that Hannerz, in his elementary unit, refers here to the inner locus ('shared meanings', 'experiences'), whereas I in the language-culture nexus refer to the outer locus (the language-culture nexus is created in linguistic practice). One could say that Hannerz's discourse reveals here its roots in cognitively oriented cultural anthropology (just as, for example, Agar). In such a cognitive context it also makes sense to use the metaphorical expression' tied to': about an inner, mental connection.

There is a continuous transition from the experienced communities to imagined communities (Anderson, 1991 (1983)), of which the 'members' are so many that they do not have a chance of knowing each other, and therefore do not have the possibility of acting together in personal interaction either. An imagined community is based only to a limited extent on an actual common network – or maybe not at all. It is precisely a community that is only imagined first and foremost. Imagined communities can vary in extent and do not have to be territorialised: they could be a nation, a municipality, a generation, a trade union, a transnational school network, the transnational Esperanto movement, etc.

When one focuses on (experienced and imagined) communities, one has, however, to be aware of dealing with a focusing that is an extension of a long structuralist tradition in both linguistics and anthropology: the interest in defining and describing linguistic communities through the study of their common and homogeneous linguistic system (langue/

competence), and the completely parallel interest in defining and describing cultural communities through the study of their common and homogeneous cultural system ('a culture'). As Pratt (1987) writes, this 'linguistics of community' has to be thrown into relief by, and in many cases replaced by, a 'linguistics of contact' that focuses on how linguistic practice takes place across social differentiations and how language is used in more or less conflict-ridden encounters between dominating and dominated groups, and between groups with different identities, etc.

This perspective should, in my opinion, also be assumed when one examines the relationship between language and culture: even though one can define an experienced community in, for example, a school class, based on certain activities that result in certain ways of using language and of verbalising certain subjects from certain angles (a 'micro-culture'), there is always some degree of difference as well as latent or open conflict between various interpretations and motives. And this will presumably be traceable in breaks and clashes in linguistic and discursive practice (cf. Chouliaraki, 1998; Dendrinos, 1992). That one nevertheless can call the class a community is because there is an extensive common understanding of the rules of the game and of the various perspectives of the situation on the part of those involved.

The Core of the Language-Culture Nexus: Reference to Reality

In the language-culture nexus, then, language and culture are linked in a particular configuration. Can one on the basis of this analysis arrive at an understanding of what the core is regarding the 'connection' between language and culture? I believe that the core in this connection is the meaning and reference potential of language. It is via its meaning and reference potential that language 'goes beyond itself' and links up with (the rest of) physical, social and cultural reality.[3] Here, however, it is once more useful to distinguish between language in a generic and a differential sense.

When we talk about human language in the generic sense, it is characteristic of language that it enables people to refer to the outside world in a very broad sense: both past, present and future, and both everyday reality and imagined worlds. When we talk about a particular language, I have described in Chapter 11 how the languacultural accumulation through time has made precise, swift references possible to first-language contexts, via borrowings from other languages and via lexicalisations. Thereby, a relatively high degree of semantic and pragmatic congruence[4] has developed between linguistic practice in a particular language and the first-language contexts. So *in general* it will be easier to make internal references than external references.

I can, for example, be on a visit to China and refer (in Danish, which is my first language) to *julenisser* (Christmas pixies) in my cardboard box in the basement back home. This will be a realisation of a semantic congruence between the lexical possibilities of the Danish language and the recollection I and the person I am talking to have of the physical objects in my basement in Roskilde, Denmark. I will have utilised the meaning and reference potential of the Danish language, embodied in my own languacultural resources. This, it should be noted, is something I can do even though I do not find myself in a first-language context in Denmark.

Here I would refer back to Chapter 1, where I mentioned Kramsch's introductory summary of the relationship between language and culture in three points (Kramsch, 1998a):

- language expresses cultural reality;
- language embodies cultural reality;
- language symbolises cultural reality.

It is in the first point: 'language expresses cultural reality' that Kramsch talks about what I would call the meaning and reference potential of the individual language. So I believe that point 1 is the most important and most wide-ranging in the relationship between language and culture.[5]

Points 2 and 3 are important in emphasising that language in itself is culture. But here we are dealing with *languaculture*: point 2 roughly corresponds to what I call the semantic-pragmatic dimension of languaculture, and point 3 to what I call the identity dimension of languaculture. In other words, points 2 and 3 are not examples of *going beyond* language, but merely point to properties of language itself.

Conclusion

We have now looked at the concept of language-culture nexus: its multidimensional content and the epistemological layers in the analysis of it. I have stressed the importance of fully realising whether one is investigating convergent or divergent language-culture nexuses, and mentioned that the language-culture nexus can be analysed both at the elementary level (in a single communicative event) and at higher levels, in various forms of experienced communities. I have also dealt with what is really meant by the statement that language and culture 'cohere', pointing out that the core of this interconnection is the meaning and reference potential of the language involved, or – to use terms from practice – the utilisation by the language users of their languacultural resources to refer to their outside world as precisely as is considered relevant.

Notes

1. Cf. Gregersen's view of the dynamic sign and its place in a sociolinguistics that is both expression- and content-orientated (Gregersen, 1991: 231ff.).
2. Cf. the two corresponding levels in connection with the concept of context, Chapter 10.
3. When I write 'the rest of physical reality', it is so as to emphasise that language also has a physical side: soundwaves, ink on paper, etc.
4. Here I am using Fishman's concept of congruence in a slightly extended sense. Fishman has used it in order to conceptualise the relationship between a social situation/a domain and the language use that is typically linked to it (Fishman, 1971).
5. So as not to completely forget the physical world, I would, however, prefer the expression physical, social and cultural reality rather than 'cultural reality' – though I recognise the fact that physical reality is always perceived and understood via discourse (in, e.g. Fairclough's sense).

Chapter 14

Language and Culture: A Multidimensional Relationship

Language and Culture: Separability and Inseparability

The analysis of the relationship between language and culture has consisted of a deconstruction of the concept of language and – analogously though less developed – that of culture.

The foundation for this has been a division of the concept of language into three loci: linguistic practice, linguistic resources and the discursive construction of the 'linguistic system' as a unified, cohesive system. It is these first two loci that are the natural ones (characteristic of the human species), between which the linguistic process mainly develops. The third locus has been historically created, but also plays an important role in the conception language users have of their own linguistic practice and their linguistic identity.

Subsequently, I have worked my way through a number of stages in the analysis of the relationship between language and culture. These stages are to be understood as a number of shifts of perspective, during which I shift from language to looking at languaculture, from languaculture to discourse, and from discourse to the rest of culture. The operation can be summed up as in Fig. 14.1:

The left-hand column I have also called the sociological point of view. It deals with practice, and here I have argued that language and culture at all three stages, with a few reservations, can be separated from each other.

Firstly, language and languaculture are partially separable since a person acquiring/learning a language assigns to the new language languacultural elements from his/her own first language and possibly other earlier acquired/learned languages.

Secondly, language/languaculture and discourse are separable, because discourse, conceived as a content-based phenomenon, spreads across languages, although undergoing some transformations during the translation process.

Thirdly, language/languaculture/discourse is separable from the cultural context as people can migrate from one cultural context to another. Moreover, language/languaculture/discourse is separable from

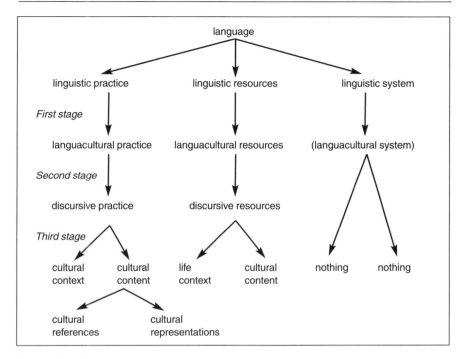

Figure 14.1 From language to culture

its thematic cultural content, including a content that relates to a first-language context. This applies both at the textual micro-level (internal cultural references) and at the textual macro-level (internal cultural representations).

The central column I have also called the psychological point of view. It has to do with the individual (or an aggregation of individuals that function as a corporate actor), and here I have argued that linguistic, languacultural, discursive and other cultural resources are inseparable in the life history of the single individual. This applies to both the monolingual and the multilingual individual. We are dealing with a lifelong process of development that constantly builds further on earlier material. This does not necessarily mean that the development has been experienced as harmonious or continuous.

The right-hand column I have also called the system-oriented point of view. It has to do with the idea of the linguistic system, and here I have argued that one can choose to describe language as a system – and if necessary add a description of a (general) languacultural system to it.

But there is no 'discursive system' that corresponds to the linguistic system, and the linguistic system cannot of itself have a concrete cultural context or a special discursive, thematic content. Only linguistic practice can have that.

When one links the three points of view, one gets an explanation as to why the idea of the inseparability of language and culture is so tenacious: the idea is actually correct, but only from the psychological point of view, not from the sociological. Language and culture are thus both inseparable and separable at one and the same time. Language has considerable elasticity as a tool in all types of context and in connection with all kinds of content. So I have sometimes called language a Velcro fastener: language can easily change context and thematic content, but once it has been introduced into a new place and/or is used for a new content, it quickly integrates and 'latches on'.

The idea of the inseparability of language and culture at the system level is probably due to two different but interacting tendencies: on the one hand, the single individual has a tendency to project his or her own subjective feeling of the connection between his or her own personal language, culture and identity onto the community, e.g. the nation, and thus imagine that there is a connection at the system level for which there is, however, no empirical basis. On the other hand, this psychological tendency has been used politically in connection with the building-up of nations and nationalism, in which an image of a single nation, or a single folk, is construed, characterised by a common national culture expressed via a common national language.

Language and culture 'hang together' in the single multidimensional language-culture nexus. It is also possible, on a reasonably defensible empirical basis, to talk about generalised language-culture nexuses in small-scale experienced communities such as a school class. But, at levels above that, we are dealing with more or less insubstantial constructions: London language and culture? Southern England language and culture? The expression 'English language and culture' is at an even higher level of abstraction, but sounds more common. This, however, must be because we are so used to banal nationalism in the modern world, and because national identities are so prominent, not least in Europe.

Implications for Language and Culture Pedagogy

In the following I will first outline a number of implications for language and culture pedagogy[1], and then point to some further perspectives for linguistics in general.

The first implication for language and culture pedagogy is that the empirical field is not 'the language area' in a geographical sense but the worldwide network of the target language. Where and in what situations do people speak, read and write the target language? How is the target language used on the Internet by ordinary people and interest groups? What role does the language have in transnational migration of all sorts? What role does it have in transnational companies, markets and media? In international politics? In all these situations, it is important to consider that the target language carries languaculture with it. It has specific semantic-pragmatic, poetic and identity potentials – both possibilities and limitations; and this specificity – these differences from other languages – should be an important preoccupation for foreign and second-language studies.

The second implication is that the analytical object is not only (texts in) the target language as first language, but also as second and foreign language. The target language is learned and spoken by many kinds of people and for many different reasons. So an awareness of the complex functions of the target language opens up for studies of multilingualism and multiculturality in all places where the target language is spoken. How is the target language – French, for instance – used by Arabic immigrants in France? How is it used by Chinese immigrants in Canada? Questions like this raise issues concerning the relations between language and identity: the use and construction of linguistic identities and the role of language in the construction of cultural identities, national or ethnic, etc. They also raise issues about the role of languages in the power structures of society and the world. They may focus attention on various forms of linguistic and cultural encounters and conflicts, and on processes of translation and interpretation, both linguistic and cultural. They may lead to insights into the great languacultural variability of the language in question.

The third implication is that the study of a specific language is not confined to specific discourses or specific thematic areas. Discourses, topics and genres may spread from language to language by various kinds of translation or transformation, and so a language community is never a closed discourse community, though certain discourses may be preferred in certain local and social contexts at certain points of time. Thus it is not necessarily the case that foreign- and second-language studies should always focus on the (native) literature of target-language countries. The link between the study of language and the study of literature is not 'natural', but a historical construction once important in the nation-building processes. When this link is maintained today, it has to be specially motivated, for foreign- and second-language studies may focus just as well on social studies, cultural studies, media studies, business studies, art studies, etc., etc.

The fourth implication is that it is necessary to construct foreign- and second-language studies that are characterised by an integrative view of both language, text, discourse and (the rest of) culture and society. For instance, the target language should be seen as a social and cultural phenomenon, and literature and other texts in the target language should be seen as linguistic phenomena. Although texts are usually studied as cultural products carrying some kind of global content or meaning (representing cultural reality in some way or other), they are always also instances of linguistic practice in a specific language.

To sum up, one can say that language and culture pedagogy must adopt a much more differentiated attitude to the question of the complex relationship between language and culture, and if it is to understand itself as a field of research and practice, it must take just as great an interest in transnational as in national issues.[2]

Further Perspectives

To analyse the relationship between language and culture as I have done is, under all circumstances, a theoretical construction – as I pointed out in Chapter 1. One of the most important aims I have had in distinguishing between language, languaculture, discourse and culture is to counteract the tendency to reductionism in this area. In my opinion, it is unfortunate to deal with the complex relationship between language and culture by creating certain concepts that reduce culture to discourse, or culture to language, or discourse to language. The concept of discourse, in particular, is used at present to colonise both the concepts of language and culture – resulting in considerable vagueness and ambiguity.

When linguists, e.g. language and culture pedagogues, talk about culture in relation to language, I often get the feeling that what they actually mean corresponds to the concept of languaculture. They use the concept of culture in a tacitly shortened way – and such an understanding allows the category of culture to be determined by that of language. This I see as being one of the most fundamental problems of the linguistic way of dealing with the concept of culture.

It should by now have become obvious how important it is to distinguish between the three points of view: the sociological, the psychological and the system-oriented, and also how important it is that all three are included if one wishes to gain as full a picture as possible of the relationship between language and culture. If this work is to be pursued further, it presupposes a meeting – and preferably a dialogue – between disciplines that at present are far removed from each other in terms of theory and method: sociolinguistics / anthropological linguistics, cognitive linguistics and system linguistics (in both its formal and functional variants).

A study of the relationship between language and culture must also get beyond the traditional first-language bias. In my opinion, it is high time for scientific and public attention to be devoted to a greater extent to language used as a second language and as a foreign language, the development of interlanguages, and the multilingual individual in a multilingual society. Present-day internationalised and globalised societies cannot benefit from neglecting the resources that multilingual people have, which could be used to much greater effect in society and in their own lives.

When discourses, genres and topics flow across linguistic communities or linguistic networks, it is also high time for greater attention to be paid to the problematics of translation from both the public and the academic side – and here I am thinking not only about research into translation strategies and translation critique, but also about research into the political, sociological and cultural aspects of translation, including the choice to translate or not to translate particular texts. As I write in Chapter 9, there is a need to link translation studies to critical discourse analysis, so that one can come to investigate how, for example, certain discourses are transformed on their journey from one linguistic community to another. This is of interest not least when one takes the media situation of the world into consideration.

Last, but not least, I hope that by means of this book I can inspire others to carry out interdisciplinary linguistic studies that make use of other academic disciplines. This is not always possible, because of institutional barriers and economic restrictions. But work on an integrative view of language presupposes interdisciplinary openness, and that presupposes that there is an educational and research environment that invites the various subjects and disciplines to show an interest in each other and possibly to meet in interdisciplinary educational and research projects.[3] Studies of an integrative view of language can really flourish only in a cooperation with other disciplines that deal with society, culture and the human psyche.

Notes

1. The following section is based on part of Risager (2004a).
2. In Risager (2003) I have written in much more detail about the implications as part of an analysis of the discourse of culture pedagogy concerning language, culture and nation, and a discussion of the possibilities of a transition from a national to a transnational paradigm in teaching language and culture.
3. Many of the ideas expressed in this book have been developed into a Master's programme at my university in Roskilde, Denmark. The programme (which started in 2000) is called 'Cultural Encounters', and focuses on studies of identity, ethnicity, nationality, multilingualism and multiculturalism, discourse studies, post-colonial studies and studies of cultural and linguistic globalisation. Its central aim is to study the relationships between culture and language in complex societies.

References

Agar, Michael (1994) *Language Shock. Understanding the Culture of Conversation.* New York: William Morrow.

Agar, Michael (1997) The biculture in bilingual. In N. Coupland and A. Jaworski (eds) *Sociolinguistics.* New York: St. Martin's Press, pp. 464–471.

Anderson, Benedict (1991) *Imagined Communities* (2nd edn). London: Verso (1983).

Appadurai, Arjun (1990) Disjuncture and difference in the global cultural economy. *Public Culture* 2 (2) pp. 1–24.

Appadurai, Arjun (1996) *Modernity at Large. Cultural Dimensions of Globalization.* Minneapolis, etc.: University of Minnesota Press.

Ardener, Edwin (1989 (1971)) Social anthropology and language. In Edwin Ardener *The Voice of Prophecy and Other essays* (ed. by Malcolm Chapman) Oxford and New York: Blackwell, pp. 1–44.

Bakhtin, Mikhail M. (1981) *The Dialogic Imagination.* Austin, TX: University of Texas Press.

Bakker, Peter (1997) *A Language of Our Own. The Genesis of Michif, the Mixed Cree-French Language of the Canadian Métis.* Oxford, etc: Oxford University Press.

Barth, Fredrik (1969) *Ethnic Groups and Boundaries.* Oslo: Universitetsforlaget.

Barthes, Roland (1970 (1957)) *Mytologier.* København: Gyldendal.

Bassnett, Susan (2002) *Translation Studies* (3rd edn) London and New York: Routledge.

Bauman, Zygmunt (1998) *Globalization. The Human Consequences.* Cambridge, UK: Polity Press.

Bauman, Zygmunt (1999 (1973)) *Culture as Praxis.* London and Boston: Routledge & Kegan Paul.

Beck, Ulrich (2000) *What is Globalization?* Cambridge, UK: Polity Press. (German edition 1997).

Benedict, Ruth (1946 (1934)) *Patterns of Culture.* New York: Penguin.

Berger, Peter and Luckmann, Thomas (1991 (1966)) *The Social Construction of Reality. A Treatise in the Sociology of Knowledge.* Harmondsworth: Penguin.

Berlin, Brent and Paul Kay (1969) *Basic Color Terms.* Berkeley, CA: University of California Press.

Berman, Ruth A. and Slobin, Dan Isaac (1994) *Relating Events in Narrative. A Crosslinguistic Developmental Study.* Hillsdale, NJ: Lawrence Erlbaum Ass. Publishers.

Berns, Margie (1990) *Contexts of Competence. Social and Cultural Considerations in Communicative Language Teaching.* New York and London: Plenum Press.

Billig, Michael (1995) *Banal Nationalism.* London: Sage Publications.

Blum-Kulka, Shoshana, House, Juliane and Kasper, Gabriele (eds) (1989) *Cross-cultural Pragmatics.* Norwood, NJ: Ablex.

Boas, Franz (Year not indicated (1911)) *Introduction to the Handbook of American Indian Languages.* Washington, DC: Georgetown University Press.

Böhme, Hartmut (1996) Vom Cultus zur Kultur(wissenschaft). Zur historischen Semantik des Kulturbegriffs. In Renate Glaser und Matthias Luserke (Hrsg.) *Literaturwissenschaft – Kulturwissenschaft. Positionen, Themen, Perspektiven.* Opladen: Westdeutscher Verlag, pp. 48–68.

Börsch, Sabine (1982) *Fremdsprachenstudium – Frauenstudium?* Tübingen: Stauffenberg Verlag.

Börsch, Sabine (ed.) (1987) *Die Rolle der Psychologie in der Sprachlehrforschung.* Tübingen: Gunter Narr Verlag.

Bourdieu, Pierre (1977 (1972)) *Outline of a Theory of Practice.* Cambridge: Cambridge University Press.

Bourne, Jill (1988) 'Natural acquisition' and a 'masked pedagogy'. *Applied Linguistics* 9 (1) pp. 83–99.

Brown, Roger W. and Lenneberg, E.H. (1954) A study in language and cognition. *Journal of American Social Psychology* 49, pp. 454–462.

Bruno, G. (1977 (1891)) *Le Tour de la France par deux Enfants.* Paris: Librairie Classique Eugène Belin.

Brøgger, Fredrik Chr. (1992) *Culture, Language, Text: Culture Studies Within the Study of English as a Foreign Language.* Oslo: Scandinavian University Press.

Byram, Michael (1989) *Cultural Studies in Foreign Language Education.* Clevedon: Multilingual Matters.

Byram, Michael, Morgan, Carol and colleagues (1994) *Teaching-and-Learning Language-and-Culture.* Clevedon: Multilingual Matters.

Byram, Michael (1997) *Teaching and Assessing Intercultural Communicative Competence.* Clevedon: Multilingual Matters.

Byram, Michael and Risager, Karen (1999) *Language Teachers, Politics and Cultures.* Clevedon: Multilingual Matters.

Calvet, Louis-Jean (1987) *La guerre des langues et les politiques linguistiques.* Paris: Payot.

Cameron, Deborah (1995) *Verbal Hygiene.* London and New York: Routledge.

Cenoz, Jasone and Jessner, Ulrike (eds) (2000) *English in Europe. The Acquisition of a Third Language.* Clevedon: Multilingual Matters.

de Certeau, Michel, Julia, Dominique and Revel, Jacques (1975) *Une politique de la langue. La Révolution Française et les patois: L'enquête de l'Abbé Grégoire.* Paris: Gallimard.

Chouliaraki, Lilie (1998) Regulation in 'progessivist' pedagogic discourse: Individualized teacher-pupil talk. *Discourse and Society* 9 (1) pp. 5–32.

Chouliaraki, Lilie and Fairclough, Norman (1999) *Discourse in Late Modernity. Rethinking Critical Discourse Analysis.* Edinburgh: Edinburgh University Press.

Cicero, *Tusculanae Disputationes*, Vol. II, chap. V, §13.

Comenius, J.A. (1649) *Ianua lingvarum reserata.* Amsterdam: Apud Ludovicum Elzevirium.

Common European Framework of Reference for Languages: Learning, Teaching, Assessment (2001) Council of Europe. Cambridge, etc.: Cambridge University Press.

Cook, Guy (2000) *Language Play, Language Learning.* Oxford, etc.: Oxford University Press.

Cooper, Robert L. (1982) A framework for the study of language spread. In Robert L. Cooper (ed.) *Language Spread. Studies in Diffusion and Social Change.* Bloomington, IN: Indiana University Press, pp. 5–36.

Cooper, Robert L. and Spolski, Bernard (eds) (1991) *The Influence of Language on Culture and Thought. Essays in Honour of Joshua A. Fishman's Sixty-Fifth Birthday.* Berlin: Mouton de Gruyter.

Cowie, A.P. and Evison, A (1992) *Concise English-Chinese Dictionary.*

Crozet, Chantal and Liddicoat, Anthony J. (2000) Teaching culture as an integrated part of language: implications for the aims, approaches and pedagogies of language teaching. In Anthony J. Liddicoat and Chantal Crozet (eds) *Teaching Languages, Teaching Cultures.* Applied Linguistics Association of Australia, Melbourne, Vic.: Language Australia, pp. 1–18.

Cummins, Jim (2000) *Language, Power, and Pedagogy. Bilingual Children in the Crossfire.* Clevedon: Multilingual Matters.

Daneš, František (1988) Sprachkultur. In Ulrich Ammon, Norbert Dittmar and Klaus J. Mattheier (eds) *Sociolinguistics, Soziolinguistik.* Berlin and New York: Walter de Gruyter, pp. 1697–1703.

Dann, Otto (1996) *Nation und Nationalismus in Deutschland 1770–1990.* München: Verlag C.H. Beck (1993).

Darnell, Regna (1969) *The Development of American Anthropology 1879–1920: From the Bureau of American Ethnology to Franz Boas.* University of Pennsylvania.

Davies, Alan (2004) The native speaker in applied linguistics. In Alan Davies and Catherine Elder (eds) *The Handbook of Applied Linguistics.* Malden, MA, etc.: Blackwell, pp. 431–50.

Dendrinos, Bessie (1992) *The EFL Textbook and Ideology.* Athens: NC: Grivas Publications.

Dijk, Teun van (1997) The study of discourse. In Teun van Dijk (ed.) *Discourse as Structure and Process.* London, etc.: Sage Publications, pp. 1–34.

Doyé, Peter (1996) Foreign-language teaching and education for intercultural and international understanding. In Evaluation and Research in Education 10 (2 and 3) pp. 104–12. Special issue of Education for European Citizenship. Guest editor: Michael Byram.

Duranti, Alessandro (1997) *Linguistic Anthropology.* Cambridge, UK: Cambridge University Press.

Eggins, Suzanne and Martin, J.R. (1997) Genres and registers in discourse. In: Teun van Dijk (ed.) *Discourse as Structure and Process.* London, etc.: Sage Publications, pp. 230–56.

Elias, Norbert (1969 (1939)) *Über den Prozess der Zivilisation.* Frankfurt a. M.: Suhrkamp.

Fairclough, Norman (1989) *Language and Power.* London and New York: Longman.

Fairclough, Norman (1992) *Discourse and Social Change.* Cambridge: Polity Press.

Fairclough, Norman (1997) Discourse across disciplines: Discourse analysis in researching social change. *AILA Review* 12, pp. 3–17.

Fink, Hans (1988) Et hyperkomplekst begreb. Kultur, kulturbegreb og kulturrelativisme I. In Hans Hauge og Henrik Horstbøll (red.) *Kulturbegrebets kulturhistorie.* Aarhus: Aarhus Universitetsforlag, pp. 9–23.

Fishman, Joshua A. (1960) A systematization of the Whorfian hypothesis. In *Behavioral Science* 5, pp. 323–39.

Fishman, Joshua A. (1971) The sociology of language: An interdisciplinary social science approach to language in society. In Fishman, Joshua A. (ed.) *Advances in the Sociology of Language I.* The Hague and Paris: Mouton, pp. 217–404.

Fishman, Joshua A. (1972) Domains and the relationship between micro- and macrosociolinguistics. In John J. Gumperz and Dell Hymes (eds) *Directions in Sociolinguistics. The Ethnography of Communication.* New York: Holt, Rinehart and Winston, pp. 435–453.

Fishman, Joshua A. (1982) Whorfianism of the third kind: Ethnolinguistic diversity as a worldwide societal asset. *Language in Society* 11, pp. 1–14.

Fishman, Joshua A. (1991) *Reversing Language Shift. Theoretical and Empirical Foundations of Assistance to Threatened Languages.* Clevedon: Multilingual Matters.

Fishman, Joshua A. (1996) Language and culture. In Adam Kuper and Jessica Kuper (eds) *The Social Science Encyclopedia* (2nd edn). London and New York: Routledge, p. 452.

Fishman, Joshua A. *et al.* (1985) *The Rise and Fall of the Ethnic Revival: Perspectives on Language and Ethnicity.* Berlin *et al.*: Mouton Publishers.

Foley, William A. (1997) *Anthropological Linguistics. An Introduction.* Oxford, UK, Blackwell.

Freadman, Anne (2001) The culture peddlers. *Postcolonial Studies* 4 (3), pp. 275–95.

Friedman, Jonathan (1994) *Cultural Identity and Global Process.* London *et al.*: Sage Publications.

Friedrich, Paul (1986) *The Language Parallax. Linguistic Relativism and Poetic Indeterminacy.* Austin, TX: University of Texas Press.

Friedrich, Paul (1989) Language, ideology, and political economy. *American Anthropologist* 91, pp. 295–312.

Færch, Claus, Haastrup, Kirsten and Phillipson, Robert (1984) *Learner Language and Language Learning.* København: Gyldendal.

Galisson, Robert (1991) *De la langue à la culture par les mots.* Paris: CLE International.

Galisson, Robert (1994) D'hier à demain, l'interculturel à l'école. Actes du colloque international: enseignement des langues et intercompréhension européenne (17–18 déc. 1993), Athènes: 91–104.

Gee, James Paul (1996) *Social Linguistics and Literacy: Ideology in Discourses.* London: Taylor & Francis.

Geertz, Clifford (1973) Thick description: Toward an interpretive theory of culture. in: Cl. Geertz: *The Interpretation of Cultures. Selected Essays by Clifford Geertz.* New York: Basic Books, pp. 3–30.

Geertz, Clifford (1983) *Local Knowledge.* New York: Basic Books.

Geertz, Clifford (1988) *Works and Lives. The Anthropologist as Author.* Cambridge, UK: Polity Press.

Giles, Howard (1994) Accommodation in communication. In R. Asher (ed.) *Encyclopedia of Language and Linguistics.* Oxford: Pergamon Press, pp. 12–15.

Goebl, Hans *et al.* (eds) (1996) *Kontaktlinguistik, Contact Linguistics, Linguistique de contact.* Vol. 1–2. Berlin and New York: Walter de Gruyter.

Goodenough, Ward H. (1964 (1957)) Cultural anthropology and linguistics. In Dell Hymes (ed.) *Language in Culture and Society.* New York: Harper and Row Publishers, pp. 36–39.

Goodwin, Charles and Duranti, Alessandro (1992) Rethinking context: An introduction. In Alessandro Duranti and Charles Goodwin (eds) *Rethinking Context. Language as an Interactive Phenomenon.* Cambridge: Cambridge University Press, pp. 1–42.

Graddol, David (1997) *The Future of English?* London: British Council.

Gregersen, Frans (1991) *Sociolingvistikkens (u)mulighed.* Tiderne Skifter.

Grosjean, François (1982) *Life with Two Languages. An Introduction to Bilingualism.* Cambridge, MA: Harvard University Press.

Gudykunst, William B. (1998) *Bridging Differences. Effective Intergroup Communication* (3rd edn) Thousand Oaks, etc.: Sage Publications.

Gumperz, John J. (ed.) (1982) *Language and Social Identity.* Cambridge: Cambridge University Press.

Gumperz, John J. (1992) Contextualization and understanding. In Goodwin, Charles and Alessandro Duranti (eds) *Rethinking Context. Language as an Interactive Phenomenon.* Cambridge: Cambridge University Press, pp. 229–52.

Gumperz, John J. and Levinson, Stephen C. (eds) (1996) *Rethinking Linguistic Relativity.* Cambridge: Cambridge University Press.

Haberland, Hartmut (1989) Whose English, nobody's business. *Journal of Pragmatics* 13, pp. 927–938.

Haberland, Hartmut (1993) Probleme der 'kleinen' Sprachen in der EG: Beispiel Dänisch. in: Heteroglossia, Quaderni dell'Istituto di Lingue Straniere. Università degli studi di Macerata 5, pp. 79–128.

Hall, Stuart (1992) The question of cultural identity. In Stuart Hall, David Held and Tony McGregor (eds) *Modernity and Its Futures.* Cambridge, UK: Polity Press, pp. 273–316.

Hall, Stuart (1996) Cultural studies: Two paradigms. In John Storey (ed.) *What Is Cultural Studies?* London and New York: Arnold, pp. 31–48.

Hall, Stuart (1997) Introduction to: Hall, Stuart (ed.) *Representation. Cultural Representations and Signifying Practices.* London, etc.: Sage Publications, pp. 1–11.

Halliday, M.A.K. (1978) *Language as Social Semiotic. The Social Interpretation of Language and Meaning.* London: Edward Arnold.

Halliday, M.A.K. and Hasan, Ruqaiya (1989) *Language, Context, and Text: Aspects of Language in a Social-Semiotic Perspective.* Oxford: Oxford University Press.

Hannerz, Ulf (1980) *Exploring the City.* New York: Columbia University Press.

Hannerz, Ulf (1990) Cosmopolitans and locals in world culture. *Theory, Culture and Society* 7 (2–3), pp. 237–251.

Hannerz, Ulf (1992a) *Cultural Complexity. Studies in the Social Organization of Meaning.* New York: Columbia University Press.

Hannerz, Ulf (1992b) The global ecumene as a network of networks. In Adam Kuper (ed.) *Conceptualizing Society.* London and New York: Routledge, pp. 34–56.

Hannerz, Ulf (1996) *Transnational Connections. Culture, People, Places.* London and New York: Routledge.

Hansen, Erik and Jørn Lund (1994) *Kulturens Gesandter. Fremmedordene i dansk.* København: Munksgaard.

Harder, Peter (1996) Linguistic structure in a functional grammar. In: Elisabeth Engberg-Pedersen *et al.* (eds) *Content, Expression and Structure. Studies in Danish Functional Grammar.* Amsterdam/Philadelphia: John Benjamins Publishing Company, pp. 423–452.

Harris, Roy (1981) *The Language Myth.* London: Duckworth.

Harris, Roy (1998) *Introduction to Integrational Linguistics.* Oxford: Elsevier Science Ltd, Pergamon.

Harvey, David (1990) *The Condition of Postmodernity*. Cambridge MA and Oxford UK: Blackwell.

Hastrup, Kirsten (1989) Kultur som analytisk begreb. in: Kirsten Hastrup og Kirsten Ramløv (red.) *Kulturanalyse. Fortolkningens forløb i antropologien*, pp. 11–21.

Herder, Johann Gottfried (1952 (1782–91)) Ideen zur Philosophie der Geschichte der Menschheit. in: J.G. Herder, *Zur Philosophie der Geschichte. Eine Auswahl in zwei Bänden*. Berlin: Aufbau-Verlag.

Hinkel, Eli (ed.) (1999) *Culture in Second Language Teaching and Learning*. Cambridge, UK: Cambridge University Press.

Hjort, Peter (1852) *Den danske Børneven. En Læsebog for Borger- og Almue-Skoler*. København: Gyldendal. (6. oplag)

Hobsbawm, E.J. (1990) *Nations and Nationalism Since 1780. Programme, Myth, Reality*. Cambridge: Cambridge University Press (1990).

Holmen, Anne and Karen Risager (2003) Language and culture teaching. Foreign languages and Danish as a second language.*International Journal of the Sociology of Language* 159: The Sociolinguistics of Danish, pp. 93–108.

Houis, Maurice (1968) Langage et culture. In Jean Poirier (dir.) *Ethnologie générale*. Paris: Gallimard, pp. 1393–1431.

Humboldt, Wilhelm von (1906 (1924–26)) Grundzüge des allgemeinen Sprachtypus. In *Wilhelm von Humboldts Gesammelte Schriften, Band V*. Berlin: B. Behr's Verlag, pp. 364–473.

Humboldt, Wilhelm von (1907 (1836)) Ueber die Verschiedenheit des menschlichen Sprachbaues und ihren Einfluss auf die geistige Entwicklung des Menschengeschlechts. In *Wilhelm von Humboldts Gesammelte Schriften, Band VII*. Berlin: B. Behr's Verlag, pp. 1–344.

Hymes, Dell (1974) *Foundations in Sociolinguistics. An Ethnographic Approach*. London: Tavistock Publications.

Høiris, Ole (1988) Kulturbegrebet i antropologien. In Hans Hauge og Henrik Horstbøll (red.) *Kulturbegrebets kulturhistorie*. Aarhus: Aarhus Universitetsforlag, pp. 95–119.

Jakobson, Roman (1960) Closing Statement: Linguistics and Poetics. In Thomas Sebeok (ed.) *Style in Language*. Cambridge, MA: MIT Press, pp. 350–377.

Jakobson, Roman (1987 (1959)) On linguistic aspects of translation. In R. Jakobson, *Language in Literature* (ed. by Krystyna Pomorska and Stephen Rudy). Cambridge, MA: The Bellknap Press of Harvard University Press, pp. 428–435.

Jameson, Fredric (1984) Postmodernism, or the cultural logic of late capitalism. *New Left Review* 146, pp. 53–92.

Jäger, Siegfried (1993) *Kritische Diskursanalyse. Eine Einführung*. Duisburg: Duisburger Institut für Sprach- und Sozialforschung (DISS).

Kachru, B.B. (1986) *The Alchemy of English. The Spread, Functions and Models of Non-native Englishes*. Oxford: Pergamon Press.

Kay, Paul and Kempton, Willett (1984) What is the Sapir–Whorf hypothesis? *American Anthropologist* 86 (1), pp. 65–79.

Keesing, Roger M. (1974) Theories of culture. *Annual Review of Anthropology* 3, pp. 73–97.

Keesing, Roger M. (1994) Theories of culture revisited. In Robet Borofsky (ed.) *Assessing Cultural Anthropology*. New York etc.: McGraw-Hill, pp. 301–311.

Kindaichi Kyozuke (1959 (1954)) Jikai. Tokyo: Sanseido. (tredje udg.)

Knorr-Cetina, Karin D. (1981) The micro-sociological challenge of macro-sociology: Towards a reconstruction of social theory and methodology. In K. Knorr-Cetina and Cicourel, A.V. (eds) *Advances in Social Theory and Methodology. Towards an Integration of Micro- and Macro-sociologies*. Boston, MA etc.: Routledge and Kegan Paul, pp. 1–47.

Kramer, Jürgen (1997) *British Cultural Studies*. München: Wilhelm Fink Verlag.

Kramsch, Claire (1989) New directions in the teaching of language and culture. In: NFLC Occasional Papers, Washington, DC (National Foreign Language Center at the Johns Hopkins University, pp. 1–13.

Kramsch, Claire (1993) *Context and Culture in Language Teaching*. Oxford: Oxford University Press.

Kramsch, Claire (1996) Wem gehört die deutsche Sprache? In *Die Unterrichtspraxis/ Teaching German (Deutsche Sprache und Kultur in den Amerikas)* 1, pp. 1–11.

Kramsch, Claire (1998a) *Language and Culture*. Oxford: Oxford University Press.

Kramsch, Claire (1998b) The privilege of the intercultural speaker. In Michael Byram and Michael Fleming (eds) *Language Learning in Intercultural Perspective. Approaches Through Drama and Ethnography*. Cambridge, UK: Cambridge University Press, pp. 16–31.

Kramsch, Claire (2002a) Language and Culture Re-visited. Plenary delivered at the AILA congress in Singapore, December 2002 (personal communication).

Kramsch, Claire (2002b) Introduction: How can we tell the dancer from the dance? In Claire Kramsch (ed.) *Language Acquisition and Language Socialization: Ecological Perspectives*. London: Continuum, pp. 1–30.

Kramsch, Claire (2004) Language, thought, and culture. In Alan Davies and Catherine Elder (eds) *The Handbook of Applied Linguistics*. Malden, MA, etc.: Blackwell, pp. 235–261.

Kramsch, Claire, forthcoming. The multilingual subject. In I. de Florio Hansen and A. Hu (eds) *Mehrsprachigkeit und multikulturelle Identität*. Tübingen: Stauffenberg Verlag.

Krashen, S. and Terrell, T. (1983) *The Natural Approach: Language Acquisition in the Classroom*. Hayward, CA.: Alemany Press.

Kroeber, A.L. (1945) The ancient 'oikumene' as an historic culture aggregate. *Journal of the Royal Anthropological Institute* 75, pp. 9–20.

Kroeber, A.L. and Kluckhohn, Clyde (1952) *Culture – A Critical Review of Concepts and Definitions*. New York: Vintage Books.

Kuper, Adam (1992) *Conceptualizing Society*. London etc.: Routledge.

Lado, Robert (1957) *Linguistics Across Cultures: Applied Linguistics for Language Teachers*. Ann Arbor: University of Michigan Press.

Lantolf, James P. (1999) Second culture acquisition. Cognitive considerations. In Eli Hinkel (ed.) *Culture in Second Language Teaching and Learning*. Cambridge, UK: Cambridge University Press, pp. 28–46.

Leach, Edmund (1964) Anthropological aspects of language: Animal categories and verbal abuse. In Eric H. Lenneberg (ed.) *New Directions in the Study of Language*. Cambridge, MA: The MIT Press, pp. 23–63.

Le Page, R. and Tabouret-Keller, A. (1985) *Acts of Identity: Creole-based Approaches to Language and Ethnicity*. Cambridge: Cambridge University Press.

Lévi-Strauss, Claude (1958) *Anthropologie Structurale*. Paris: Plon.

Lévi-Strauss (1966) *Introduction à M. Mauss, Sociologie et Anthropologie*. Paris: Presses Universitaires de France, pp. IX-LII

Lier, Leo van (1996) *Interaction in the Language Curriculum. Awareness, Autonomy, and Authenticity*. London and New York: Longman.

Lucy, John A. (1992a) *Language Diversity and Thought. A Reformulation of the Linguistic Relativity Hypothesis*. Cambridge, UK: Cambridge University Press.

Lucy, John A. (1992b) *Grammatical Categories and Cognition. A Case Study of the Linguistic Relativity Hypothesis*. Cambridge, UK: Cambridge University Press.

Lucy, John A. (2000) Introductory comments. In Susanne Niemeier and René Dirven (eds) *Evidence for Linguistic Relativity*. Amsterdam: John Benjamins, pp. ix-xxi.

Lund, Karen (1997) Lærer alle dansk på samme måde? En længdeundersøgelse af voksnes tilegnelse af dansk som andetsprog. Special-pædagogisk Forlag.

Lund, Karen (1999) Sprog, tilegnelse og kommunikativ undervisning. In Anne Holmen og Karen Lund (red.) *Studier i dansk som andetsprog*. København: Akademisk Forlag, pp. 11–69.

Lund, Karen and Karen Risager (2001) Dansk i midten. *Sprogforum* 19, pp. 4–8.

Lyons, John (1995) *Linguistic Semantics. An Introduction*. Cambridge: Cambridge University Press.

Mailhac, Jean-Pierre (1996) The formulation of translation strategies for cultural references. In Charlotte Hoffman (ed.) *Language, Culture and Communication in Contemporary Europe*. Clevedon: Multilingual Matters, pp. 132–151.

Malinowski, Bronislaw (1923) The problem of meaning in primitive languages. In C. Ogden and I. Richards (eds) *The Meaning of Meaning*. New York: Harcourt Brace and World, pp. 296–336.

Marcus, George E. and Fischer, M.J. (1986) *Anthropology as Cultural Critique: An Experimental Moment in the Human Sciences*. Chicago: Chicago University Press.

Márkus, György (1993) Culture – The making and the make-up of a concept. An essay in historical semantics. *Dialectical Anthropology* 18 (1), pp. 3–29.

Martin-Jones, Marilyn (1995) Code-switching in the classroom: Two decades of research. In: Lesley Milroy and Pieter Muysken (eds) *One Speaker, Two Languages. Cross-disciplinary Perspectives on Code-switching*. Cambridge, UK: Cambridge University Press, pp. 344–355.

Maurais, Jacques (2003) Towards a new global linguistic order? In Jacques Maurais and Michael A. Morris (eds) *Languages in a Globalising World*. Cambridge, UK: Cambridge University Press, pp. 13–36.

Mey, Jacob L. (1985) *Whose Language? A Study in Linguistic Pragmatics*. (Pragmatics and Beyond Companion Series 3). Amsterdam/Philadelphia: John Benjamins Publishing Company.

Miller, Robert L. (1968) *The Linguistic Relativity Principle and Humboldtian Ethnolinguistics*. The Hague: Mouton.

Milroy, James (1992) *Linguistic Variation and Change*. Oxford: Blackwells.

Milroy, James and Milroy, Lesley (1985) *Authority in Language. Investigating Language Prescription and Standardization*. London and New York: Routledge.

Modiano, Marco (2000) Euro-English: Educational standards in a cross-cultural context. *The European English Messenger* Vol. IX (1), pp. 33–37.

Mühlhäusler, Peter (1986) Pidgin and Creole Linguistics. Oxford: Blackwell.

Murphy, Elizabeth (1988) The cultural dimension in foreign language teaching: four models. *Language, Culture and Curriculum*, 1 (2), pp. 147–62.

Myers-Scotton, Carol (1997) Code-switching. In Florian Coulmas (ed.) *The Handbook of Sociolinguistics*. Oxford, etc.: Blackwell, pp. 217–237.

Møller, Janus m.fl. (red.) (1998) *Tosproget udvikling.* Københavnerstudier i tosprogethed, Køgeserien 4.

Nelson, Andrew Nathaniel (1975 (1962)). *The Modern Reader's Japanese-English Character Dictionary.* (2nd revised edn).

Newmark, Peter (1988) *A Textbook of Translation.* New York etc.: Prentice Hall.

Niemeier, Susanne and Dirven, René (eds) (2000) *Evidence for Linguistic Relativity.* Amsterdam: John Benjamins.

Nieweler, Andreas (2001) Sprachübergreifend unterrichten. Französischunterricht im Rahmen einer Mehrsprachigkeitsdidaktik. In: Der fremdsprachliche Unterricht, Französisch 1, pp. 4–13.

Norton, Bonny (2000) *Identity and Language Learning. Gender, Ethnicity and Educational Change.* Harlow, England etc.: Pearson Education.

Ochs, Elinor (1988) *Culture and Language Development. Language Acquisition and Language Socialisation in a Samoan Village.* Cambridge: Cambridge University Press.

Oksaar, Els (1985) Sprachkultur und mündliche Kommunikation. *Der Deutschunterricht* 37, 1, pp. 6–20.

Oksaar, Els (1988) *Kulturemtheorie. Ein Beitrag zur Sprachverwendungsforschung.* Hamburg: Joachim Jungius-Gesellschaft der Wissenschaften.

Oomen-Welke, Ingelore (2000) Umgang mit Vielsprachigkeit im Deutschunterricht – Sprachen wahrnehmen und sichtbar machen. *Deutsch Lernen* 2, pp. 143–163.

Ortner, Sherry B. (1984) Theory in anthropology since the Sixties. In: *Comparative Studies in Society and History* 26, pp. 126–66.

Palmer, Gary B. (1996) *Toward a Theory of Cultural Linguistics.* Austin, TX: University of Texas Press.

Pavlenko, Aneta (1999) New approaches to concepts in bilingual memory. *Bilingualism: Language and Cognition* 2 (3), pp. 209–230.

Pavlenko, Aneta (in press), Bilingualism and thought. In A. de Groot and J. Kroll (eds) *Handbook of Bilingualism: Psycholinguistic Approaches.* Oxford: Oxford University Press.

Pennycook, Alastair (1994) *The Cultural Politics of English as an International Language.* London and New York: Longman.

Pennycook, Alastair (1998) *English and the Discourses of Colonialism.* London and New York: Routledge.

Phillipson, Robert (1992) *Linguistic Imperialism.* Oxford: Oxford University Press.

Pike, Kenneth L. (1967 (1954)) *Language in Relation to a Unified Theory of the Structure of Human Behavior.* The Hague and Paris: Mouton et Co.

Platt, Elizabeth and Salah Troudi (1997) Mary and her teachers: A Grebo-speaking child's place in the mainstream classroom. *The Modern Language Journal* 81, pp. 28–49.

Potter, Jonathan and Wetherell, Margaret (1987) *Discourse and Social Psychology.* London: Sage.

Poyatos, Fernando (1993) *Paralanguage. A Linguistic and Interdisciplinary Approach to Interactive Speech and Sound.* Amsterdam/Philadelphia: John Benjamins Publishing Company.

Pratt, Mary Louise (1987) Linguistic utopias. In Nigel Fabb *et al.* (eds) *The Linguistics of Writing.* Manchester: Manchester University Press, pp. 48–66.

Preisler, Bent (1999) *Danskerne og det engelske sprog*. København: Roskilde Universitetsforlag.

Quasthoff, U.M. (1994) Context. In: R.E. Asher (ed.) *The Encyclopedia of Language and Linguistics*. Oxford: Pergamon Press, pp. 730–737.

Rampton, Ben (1999) Deutsch in inner London and the animation of an instructed foreign language. *Journal of Sociolinguistics* 3/4, pp. 480–504.

Ringbom, Håkan (1987) *The Role of First Language in Foreign Language Learning*. Clevedon: Multilingual Matters.

Risager, Karen (1989) World studies and foreign language teaching: A perspective from Denmark. *World Studies Journal* 7, 2, pp. 28–31.

Risager, Karen (1993) Buy some petit souvenir aus Dänemark! Viden og bevidsthed om sprogmødet. In K. Risager, A. Holmen and A. Trosborg (eds) *Sproglig mangfoldighed – om sproglig viden og bevidsthed*. Association Danoise de Linguistique Appliquée, Roskilde University, pp. 30–42.

Risager, Karen (1999) Critique of textbook criticism. In Dorthe Albrechtsen *et al.* (eds) *Perspectives on Foreign and Second Language Pedagogy*. Odense: Odense University Press, pp. 53–62.

Risager, Karen (2000) Bedeutet Sprachverbreitung immer auch Kulturverbreitung? In Ulrich Ammon (Hrsg.) *Sprachförderung. Schlüssel auswärtiger Kulturpolitik*. Frankfurt a. M. osv.: Peter Lang, pp. 9–18.

Risager, Karen (2003) *Det nationale dilemma i sprog- og kulturpædagogikken. Et studie i forholdet mellem sprog og kultur*. Copenhagen: Akademisk Forlag.

Risager, Karen (2004a) A social and cultural view of language. In Hans Lauge Hansen (ed.) *Disciplines and Interdisciplinarity*. Copenhagen: Museum Tusculanum Press, pp. 21–34.

Risager, Karen (2004b) Dansk som verdenssprog. Sprog og sprogkultur. In: Christine B. Dabelsteen and Juni Söderberg Arnfast (eds) *Taler de dansk? Aktuel forskning i dansk som andetsprog*. Københavnerstudier i tosprogethed 37, pp. 153–169.

Risager, Karen (forthcoming), Sproglige eksklusionshierarkier. De hundrede sprogs betydning. In *Anthology* edited by Lise Paulsen Galal, University of Copenhagen.

Roberts, Celia *et al.* (2001) *Language Learners as Ethnographers*. Clevedon: Multilingual Matters.

Robertson, Roland (1992) *Globalization. Social Theory and Global Culture*. London etc.: Sage Publications.

Romaine, Suzanne (1995) *Bilinguilism* (2nd edn). Oxford: Blackwell.

Sapir, Edward (1921) *Language. An Introduction to the Study of Speech*. Harvest Books.

Saville-Troike, Muriel (1989) (2nd edn). *The Ethnography of Communication. An Introduction*. Oxford, UK: Blackwell.

Scherzer, Joel (1987) A discourse-centered approach to language and culture. *American Anthropologist* 89 (2), pp. 295–309.

Schieffelin, Bambi B, Woolard, Kathryn A. and Kroskrity Paul V. (eds) (1998) *Language Ideologies. Practice and Theory*. New York and Oxford: Oxford University Press.

Schiffrin, Deborah (1994) *Approaches to Discourse*. Oxford, etc.: Blackwell.

Scollon, Ron and Scollon, Suzanne Wong (1995) *Intercultural Communication. A Discourse Approach*. Oxford: Blackwell.

Scotton, Carol Myers and Okeju, John (1973) Neighbors and lexical borrowings. *Language* 49 (4), pp. 871–889.

Seidlhofer, Barbara (2001) Brave new English? *The European English Messenger* X, 1, pp. 42–48.

Simmel, Georg (1968 (1908)) Exkurs über den Fremden. In *Georg Simmel, Gesammelte Werke II: Soziologie*. Berlin: Duncker & Humblot, pp. 509–512.

Skutnabb-Kangas, Tove (2000) *Linguistic Genocide in Education or Worldwide Diversity?* Mahwah, NJ: Lawrence Erlbaum.

Smith, Anthony D. (1986) *The Ethnic Origins of Nations*. London: Blackwell.

Snell-Hornby, Mary (1988) *Translation Studies. An Integrated Approach*. Amsterdam, Philadelphia: John Benjamins.

Spencer, Jonathan (1996) Symbolic anthropology. In Alan Barnard and Jonathan Spencer (eds) *Encyclopedia of Social and Cultural Anthropology*. London and New York: Routledge, pp. 535–539.

Sperber, D. and Wilson, D. (1986) *Relevance: Communication and Cognition*. Oxford: Blackwell.

Stocking, George W. (1966) Franz Boas and the culture concept. *American Anthropologist* 68, pp. 867–882.

Street, Brian V. (1993) Culture is a verb: Anthropological aspects of language and cultural process. In D. Graddol, L. Thomson and M. Byram (eds) *Language and Culture*. Clevedon: BAAL and Multilingual Matters, pp. 23–43.

Stubbs, Michael (1997) Language and the mediation of experience: Linguistic representation and cognitive orientation. In Florian Coulmas (ed.) *The Handbook of Sociolinguistics*. Oxford: Routledge, pp. 358–373.

Summers, Della (ed.) (1992) *Longman's Dictionary of English Language and Culture*. Harlow, Essex: Longman.

Svensson, Ingrid (1998) Tour'en på tysk. *Sprogforum* 10, pp. 32–34.

Swaan, Abram de (1993) The emergent world language system. *International Political Science Review* 14 (3) pp. 219–226.

Søderberg, Anne-Marie (1999) Do national cultures always make a difference? In Torben Vestergaard (ed.) *Language, Culture and Identity*. Aalborg: Aalborg University Press, pp. 137–171.

Tannen, Deborah (1982) The oral/literate continuum in discourse. In Deborah Tannen (ed.) *Spoken and Written Language. Exploring Orality and Literacy*. Norwood, NJ: Ablex Publishing Corporation, pp. 1–16.

Thomason, Sarah G. (2001) *Language Contact. An Introduction*. Edinburgh: Edinburgh University Press.

Tomlin, Russell S. *et al.* (1997) Discourse Semantics. In Teun van Dijk (red.) *Discourse as Structure and Process*. London, etc.: Sage Publications, pp. 63–111.

Tylor, Edward B. (1903 (1865)) *Primitive Culture. Researches into the Development of Mythology, Philosophy, Religion, Language, Art, and Custom*. London: John Murray, Albemarle Street.

Venuti, Lawrence (1992) *Rethinking Translation. Discourse, Subjectivity, Ideology*. London and New York: Routledge.

Wallace, Anthony F.C. (1961) *Culture and Personality*. New York: Random House.

Wallerstein, Immanuel (1974) *The Modern World System*. New York: Academic Press.

Wallerstein, Immanuel (1990) Culture as the ideological battleground of the modern world system. *Theory, Culture and Society* 7, pp. 31–55.

Wehler, H.U. (1987) *Deutsche Gesellschaftsgeschichte 1700–1815*. München: C. H. Beck.

Weinreich, Uriel (1953) *Languages in Contact*. Den Haag: Mouton.

Weinrich, Harald (1985) *Wege der Sprachkultur*. Stuttgart: Deutsche Verlags-Anstalt.

Weisgerber, Leo (1953–54) *Vom Weltbild der deutschen Sprache I–II*. Düsseldorf: Pädagogischer Verlag Schwann.

Weisgerber, Leo (1962) *Grundzüge der Inhaltsbezogene Grammatik*. Düsseldorf: Pädagogischer Verlag Schwann.

Whitaker, Mark P. (1996) Relativism. In Alan Barnard and Jonathan Spencer (eds) *Encyclopedia of Social and Cultural Anthropology*. London and New York: Routledge, pp. 478–482.

Widdowson, H.G. (1994) The ownership of English. *TESOL Quarterly* 28 (2), pp. 377–388.

Wierlacher, Alois (1993) *Kulturthema Fremdheit. Leitbegriffe und Problemfelder kulturwissenschaftlicher Fremdheitsforschung*. München: iudicium verlag.

Wierzbicka, Anne (1997) *Understanding Cultures Through Their Key Words*. New York: Oxford University Press.

Willett, J. (1995) Becoming first graders in an L2: An ethnographic study of L2 socialisation. *TESOL Quarterly* 29, pp. 473–503.

Williams, Raymond (1977) *Marxism and Literature*. Oxford: Oxford University Press.

Williams, Raymond (1988 (1st ed 1976)) *Keywords. A Vocabulary of Culture and Society*. London: Fontana Press.

Zarate, Geneviève (1993) *Représentations de l'étranger et didactique des langues*. Paris: Didier.